Green Cuisine

Vegetarian Dining Around Seattle & Puget Sound

Wood Pond Press
Seattle, Wash.
West Hartford, Conn.

by
Cameron Woodworth

Prices, hours and menu offerings at restaurants often change seasonally and with business conditions. Readers may want to call ahead to avoid disappointment. The details in this book were correct at presstime and are subject, of course, to change. They are offered as a relative guide to what to expect.

The author has personally researched the places recommended in this book. There is no charge for inclusion.

Readers' reactions and suggestions are welcomed.

First Printing, June 1993.

Cover photo by Earl Belofsky: Food and beverages at the Gravity Bar restaurant in downtown Seattle.

Cover design by Robert V. Smith.

Maps by Barry Hochstrasser.

ISBN No. 0-934260-73-7

Printed on recycled paper. ♾

Published in the United States of America.

First Edition.

Wood Pond Press, based in West Hartford, Conn., also publishes seven travel and dining guidebooks for the New England and the Mid-Atlantic regions. Its books are available through retail stores and trade distributors.

Wood Pond Press
365 Ridgewood Road
West Hartford, CT 06107
(203) 521-0389

Wood Pond Press/West
P.O. Box 15966
Seattle, WA 98115-0966
(206) 781-5763

Contents

Acknowledgments

This guide was possible because of the contributions, tips and advice of dozens, if not hundreds, of people.

My biggest thanks go to my mother and father, Nancy Webster and Richard Woodworth, as they are known across the covers of the East Coast travel guidebooks that they write and publish as owners of Wood Pond Press. Without their example, expertise and encouragement, it would have been much more difficult to complete this book. Thanks also to my brother, Jay, who helped coordinate two different computer systems 3,000 miles apart.

I'm also especially thankful to Mike Potter and Lisa MacKay, wonderful dining companions, friends and advisers.

Much-needed guidance and feedback on various aspects of the book were provided by EarthSave Seattle's board of directors and membership and by my colleagues at the Federal Way City Herald.

Craig Winters offered his expertise on the region's health-food stores as well as knowledge of the history of vegetarian dining in Seattle.

Earl Belofsky took photographs for the front cover and of the author. Laurrien Gilman, owner of the two Gravity Bar restaurants in Seattle, graciously created the food and drinks pictured on the cover. Graphics artist Bob Smith took the elements and made the cover design work. Barry Hochstrasser produced maps of the Seattle area and the Puget Sound region.

I also appreciate the assistance of Jen and Chris Ringo, Daniella Chace, David Huelsbeck, Paul Travis, Carol Hunting, Larry Kaplowitz, Eileen Stark, Eryn Huntington and Mike Haldeman, Jay Glick, Bob Nordlie, Sheila Hoffman, Susan Scott, Todd Fedorenko, Mike Putnam and Kathleen Noonan.

Thanks also to the countless restaurant owners and health-food store employees who suffered incessant questions about their places and other vegetarian resources in their locales.

And a special thank you to Monica Smith, a vegan friend who, while bicycling around the world while I wrote, provided inspiration through her letters containing great insights into the roles that vegetarian foods play in the cuisines of other countries.

About the Author

Cam Woodworth, the son of Connecticut travel-book writers and publishers, caught the travel and dining bug at an early age. Upon graduating from the University of Pennsylvania in 1989, he became a journalist. He worked in Connecticut before moving to the Seattle area, where he became a reporter for the Federal Way City Herald. A vegetarian since EarthDay 20 in 1990, he is an outdoors enthusiast, enjoying long mountain hikes, bike rides, skiing, volleyball games and finding the best places in the Pacific Northwest to watch sunsets. Between excursions to scout out this area's vegetarian restaurants and resources, he serves on the board of EarthSave Seattle and edits that organization's newsletter.

Introduction

Where does a newly arrived vegetarian in town go to find a nutritious bite to eat? As a newcomer to the Seattle area, I faced this problem with every meal out. The challenges I experienced in ferreting out restaurants that serve vegetarian fare in the midst of a milieu of fast food and barbecued chicken -- and the discoveries of the literally hundreds of appealing substitutes so close at hand -- evolved into this guidebook. *Green Cuisine* will tell you exactly where you can find good meatless fare wherever you are in the region.

The opportunities for vegetarian dining have not always been so plentiful. It was not so long ago when only a few restaurants offered meatless cuisine, generally in hippie settings on the fringe of society. Nowadays, vegetarianism is going mainstream. More than 12 million Americans -- one-twentieth of the population and growing and predominantly young -- consider themselves vegetarians.

Perhaps nowhere in this country is that proportion higher than in Seattle, and no other American city (with the possible exception of San Francisco) now has more vegetarian dining options per capita. Seattle always has been on the cutting edge, whether in visionary city planning or strong environmental programs. It's no surprise, then, that the Emerald City is so advanced when it comes to eating that's healthful for the body and for the planet.

Seattle's progressiveness has affected other cities throughout the region. There are great vegetarian discoveries to be made in Port Angeles and Olympia, Issaquah and Bellingham, and in most places in between.

It seems ironic now that such a fortuitous combination of trend and location became so appealing to me. As a child in Connecticut, my eating habits were the bane of my parents' existence. For years, I refused to eat vegetables or fruits, my diet consisting primarily of hamburgers, ham sandwiches and pop-tarts. During our many travels, I was the one who delayed my family by having to special-order hamburgers at McDonald's -- without onions, pickles or any of the accoutrements that were the prepackaged norm. I added pizzas to my diet in high school, and it was not until I was in college that I discovered the joys of salad bars. The rest, as they say, is history. From a person who previously would not touch a vegetable I evolved into a full-fledged vegetarian who would not eat meat (and a vegan, to boot). Seattle became my mecca.

My reasons were both internal and external. For years, I couldn't figure out why I so frequently felt tired and sluggish. An athlete, I figured I should have much more zest for life. As I eliminated meat, sugar and ultimately dairy products from my diet and replaced them with plant-based foods and fresh juices, I gained energy and vitality that I had never felt before. Caring a great deal about the environment and animals, I also wanted to find a manner of eating that would be less taxing on the earth's resources, and one that wouldn't require animals to be slaughtered.

The health benefits of a low-fat, low-cholesterol diet are well-documented. In the 1980s, we learned that people who reduce their meat consumption are less likely to fall victim to cancer, heart disease or strokes. We also learned that eating more fruits, vegetables and grains and fewer junk foods gave us a higher quality of life.

In the 1990s, we're learning more about the connection between what we eat and the health of the planet. Fruits, vegetables, grains and legumes are easier on our natural resources such as South American rain forests and water supply than are beef, pesticides, chemical fertilizers and the like. Clearly, there are many fine reasons for people to become vegetarian.

Healthful dining need not be boring dining. Popular dogma has it that low-fat, low-cholesterol food is brown and bland. In truth, many of the world's most exotic cuisines offer much to the vegetarian. Thai, Malaysian, Middle Eastern, Indian and Mexican restaurants provide a variety of exciting tastes. There is plenty of imaginative American and Canadian vegetarian fare, too, as evidenced by the selections available at more than 100 such eateries in the Puget Sound area.

This guide contains frequent references to ovo-lacto vegetarians, who eat eggs and dairy products, and vegans, who do not. The book also will be useful to those who simply have reduced their meat consumption and are looking for eating establishments with a healthful focus.

Whether you're shopping on Seattle's Capitol Hill and you want a nutritious lunch, or you're vacationing on Whidbey Island and want a delicious dinner, *Green Cuisine* will provide you with the details to make a sound decision.

The restaurant business is a fast-changing one, with old favorites closing and new prospects opening. If you know of a place that should be included in future editions or if you have comments on any of the eateries listed here, please write to me at the address at the front of the book.

And now, here's to lots of good eating.

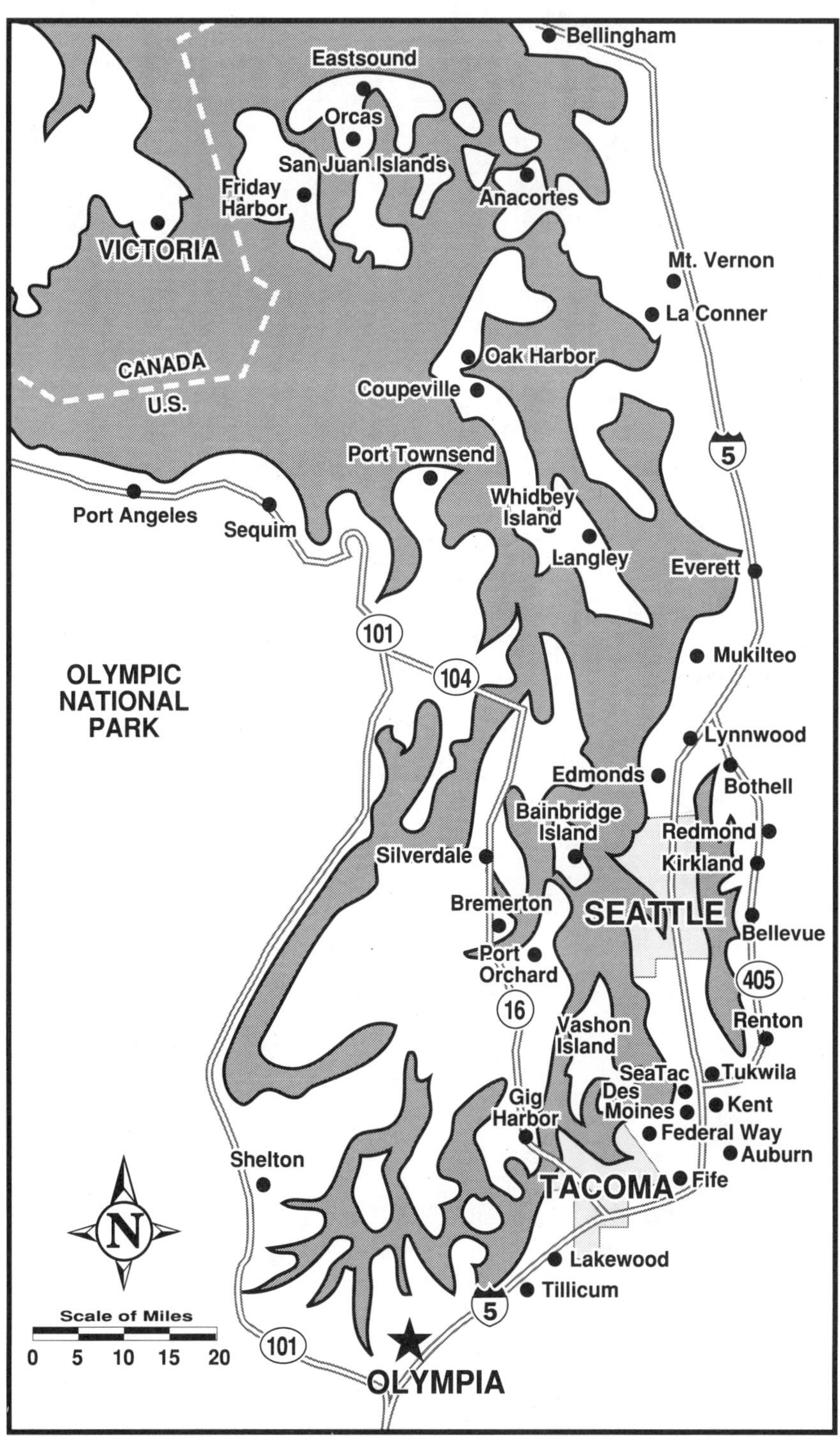
Bellingham
Eastsound
Orcas
San Juan Islands
Friday
Harbor
Anacortes
VICTORIA
Mt. Vernon
La Conner
Oak Harbor
Coupeville
CANADA
U.S.
5
Port Townsend
Port Angeles
Sequim
Whidbey
Island
Langley
Everett
101
Mukilteo
104
OLYMPIC
NATIONAL
PARK
Lynnwood
Edmonds
Bothell
Bainbridge
Island
Redmond
Silverdale
Kirkland
Bremerton
SEATTLE
Bellevue
Port
Orchard
405
16
Vashon
Island
Renton
SeaTac
Tukwila
Des
Moines
Kent
Gig
Harbor
Federal Way
Auburn
Shelton
TACOMA
Fife
N
Lakewood
Tillicum
5
Scale of Miles
0 5 10 15 20
101
OLYMPIA

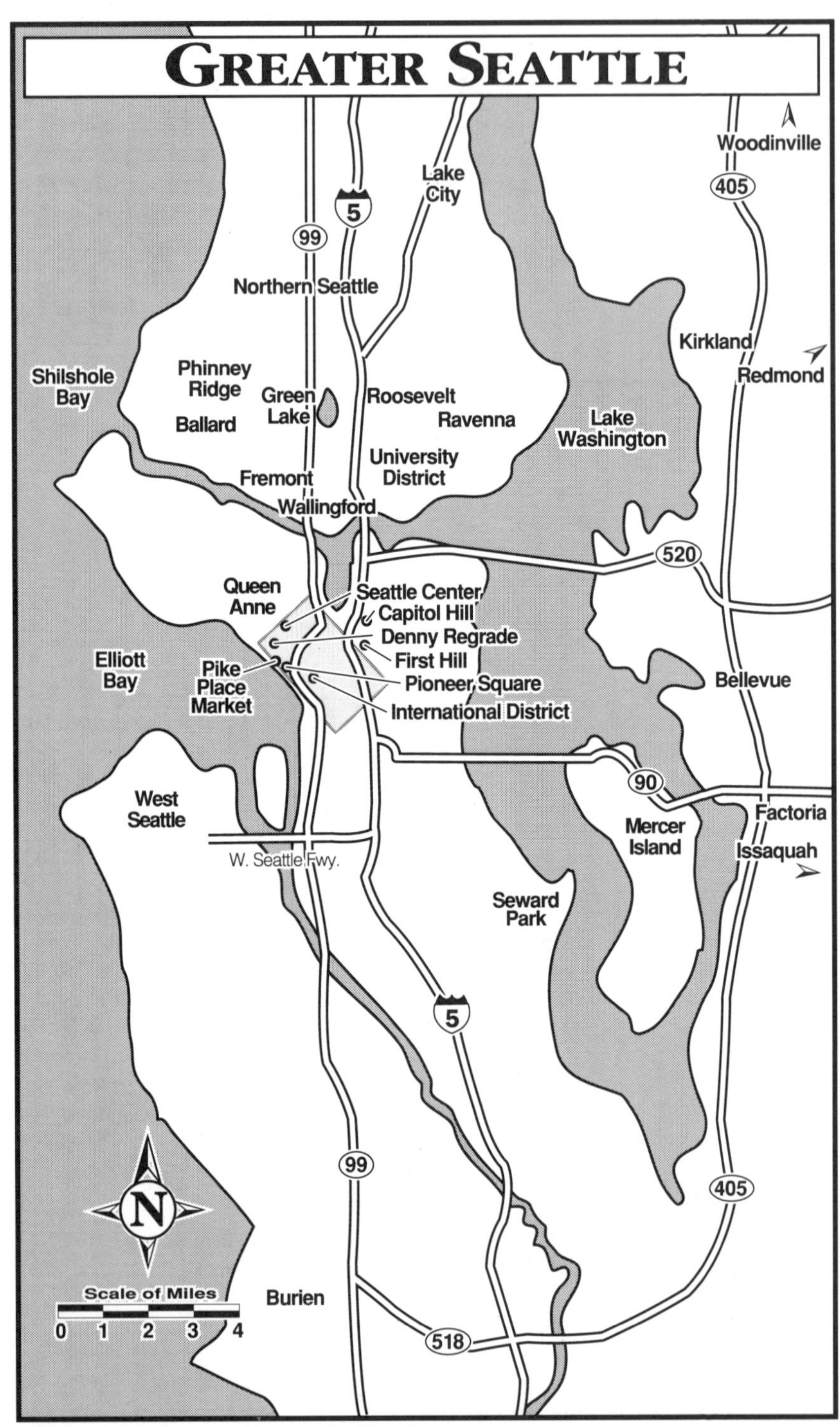

GREATER SEATTLE
Woodinville
405
Lake City
5
99
Northern Seattle
Kirkland
Redmond
Shilshole Bay
Phinney Ridge
Ballard
Green Lake
Roosevelt
Ravenna
Lake Washington
University District
Fremont
Wallingford
520
Queen Anne
Seattle Center
Capitol Hill
Denny Regrade
Elliott Bay
First Hill
Pike Place Market
Pioneer Square
Bellevue
International District
90
West Seattle
Factoria
Mercer Island
Issaquah
W. Seattle Fwy.
Seward Park
5
99
405
N
Scale of Miles
0 1 2 3 4
Burien
518

Seattle Central Business District

You won't find much in the way of exceptional vegetarian food downtown where the suits are — even less so on weeknights or weekends, when the district largely closes down. But there are a handful of treasures here, if you know where to look. The 3-D Veggie Fruit and Juice Bar on 3rd Avenue is a recent addition; besides juices, it specializes in inexpensive Philippine and vegetarian meals. Be sure to visit the Columbia Center shops at the base of Seattle's tallest building at 4th and Cherry. With several health-oriented food booths, this is the closest thing the central business district has to a vegetarian cornucopia. But if you're a tourist and you're downtown, you might as well take the short (and free) bus ride or walk to Pike Place Market, where your eating choices are much more interesting.

3-D Health Express Veggie and Fruit Juice Bar

706 3rd Avenue
621-0779

Breakfast, lunch.
7-3 M-F.
Several vegetarian choices.
No credit cards.

3-D Health Express, which opened in 1993, fills the space once occupied by the New Delhi Deli. Pacita Familar, who grew up in the Philippines, runs the little deli with a juice bar and booths and a counter by the window looking onto busy 3rd Avenue. She specializes in Philippine and vegetarian dishes.

Breakfasts are standard, with egg dishes like the mushroom-tomato-pepper omelet, fresh-baked banana bread and muffins. The lunch menu on the blackboard behind the deli counter offers more interesting choices (most entrées are $3.80). Pacita says her most sought-after dish is steamed vegetables topped with peanut-butter sauce. Also a hit is the vegetarian lasagna. Other options might be stuffed green peppers, cheese enchilada or Thai noodle salad. A vegan black-bean chili is available daily ($1.20); the other soup of the day sometimes is vegetarian (but at our visit it was split pea with pieces of ham).

Nagoya Bento

601 Union Street
622-7752
701 5th Avenue
233-9461

Lunch, dinner.
9-5 M-F.
Several vegan choices.
No credit cards.

For good Japanese vegetarian food that you can feel confident is really vegetarian, come to one of Nagoya Bento's two locations. The one in Columbia

Center (701 5th Avenue) is larger, but it and the one on the ground floor of Two Union Square (near the corner of 6th and Union) serve mostly the same fare.

This is good food to go (everything comes inside black plastic containers, and there are no seats at either of the two eateries). Both Nagoya Bentos display a large vegetarian selection. The tofu vegetable bento ($3.99) makes a wonderful lunch: four large strips of tofu are topped with a fine soy and sesame sauce and, along with lightly sautéed and seasoned vegetables, cover a large mound of white rice. You can also order cucumber sushi rolls for $2.75, miso soup (at Columbia Center) for 75 cents, fried bean curd (six pieces for $3.60), vegetable mix rice bento ($3.25), or yakisoba, the common Japanese fried noodles and vegetables soup ($3.99).

Cafe Zum Zum

946 Third Avenue
622-7391

Lunch, early dinner.
11-5 M-F.
Several vegan choices.
Credit cards accepted.

Cafe Zum Zum is a tiny but classy place that serves Pakistani and East Indian fast food. The cafe is bright and has a high ceiling and large windows to the street, making it a pleasant spot to sit and watch life go by.

Vegans should be pleased here: the owner says the vegetarian dishes are made with vegetable oil rather than butter. But if you get the tortilla, be sure to specify "no butter." Most dishes are $4 or $5. Every day there's a vegetarian special, which might be a spicy eggplant dish served with rice and a tortilla. Other options are a vegetarian curry and a potato-chickpea curry. An open sandwich made with lettuce and any one of three vegetarian dishes is called "vegetarian donne." Vegetable samosas are $2.49, and the vegetarian red lentil soup, $1.50.

Columbia Center Food Courtyard

701 5th Avenue

The ground-floor indoor courtyard at Columbia Center is a delightful place for a fast meal. Plenty of patio tables are strewn across two levels and are surrounded by an assortment of fast-food eateries (many of which focus on healthful foods). A cool water fountain cascades down a central building column. Most of the people who eat here are business folks from the 76-story Columbia Center or nearby buildings. Open M-F.

Macheezmo Mouse (382-1730) provides excellent and healthful fast-food Mexican cuisine. This one is much smaller than the full-size Macheezmo Mouses on Capitol Hill and in the University District. The menu is slightly smaller, too, but you can get a veggie burrito with cheese, a veggie taco salad with cheese or a vegetarian enchilada pie with cheese and sour cream, each for $4. The vegetarian power salad ($4) contains no animal fat. What it does have are greens, brown rice, black beans, steamed broccoli, marinated veggies and salsa. On the side is a non-fat mustard dressing.

Rasa Malaysia (682-6688), one of a chain of small Southeast Asian restaurants in Seattle, dispenses nutritious Asian food, including noodles with peanut sauce, ma pah tofu and vegetarian curry ($3 each), potstickers and steamed vegetables ($2.50 each). The vegetarian combo gives a little bit of everything for $4.

Juicers (233-2797) offers a variety of fresh fruit and vegetable drinks. Carrot juice is $2.15 for a small, $2.75 for a large. Others ($2.75 or $3.25) include beet, cabbage, celery, cucumber, green pepper, spinach, tomato, apple, grapefruit, lemon, orange, pear, pineapple and banana. Create your own blend for an extra 25 cents. You may add ginger, garlic, bee pollen, spirulina or parsley for 25 cents to a dollar. A shot of wheatgrass juice is $1.

Fresh Ideas (340-0810) offers salads and light sandwiches. See description below.

At **Nagoya Bento,** you'll find healthful Japanese fast food. See Page 1 for description.

Tarantula Jack's Championship Chili Parlor (386-5559) serves a $3.89 vegan chili (cheese is optional). It comes with rice.

Other Choices

The food court at Seattle's most upscale mall, Westlake Center, at Pine Street and Fourth Avenue, includes a couple of places where you can order vegetarian food. **Stockpot Soups** always offers a vegetarian soup of the day with Tuscany dipping bread ($2.99/$3.59). **The Ultimate Enchilada** accompanies its assortment of burritos, enchiladas and tacos with lard-free beans. **Mediterranean Avenue** serves tabbouleh, hummus, rice pilaf, house eggplant and baba ghanoush appetizers (each $2.49). It also offers a falafel sandwich for $2.89 and eggplant stuffed with veggies and topped with feta cheese and yogurt for $3.89. The soup of the day is always vegetarian.

Metropolitan Frozen Desserts and Juice Bar (1301 5th Avenue, 623-0480) is in the underground passageway at Rainier Square. Among the choices at the very informal cafe are a selection of fruit and vegetable juices ($1.70 for 10 ounces, $2.60 for 16) and a garden burger made with dairy and eggs. Open 7-6 M-F, 10-5:30 Sat. No credit cards.

Gyros Place (916 3rd Avenue, 340-9032) is a tiny Greek restaurant that provides several meatless dishes in the $4 to $5 range, such as a vegetarian pita garden sandwich, with lettuce, tomato, green peppers and feta cheese, served with potatoes and tzatziki sauce; spanakopita, the Greek spinach and cheese pie; a falafel sandwich, served with potatoes, and horiatiki salad, with tomato, cucumber, onion, green pepper, Greek olives and feta cheese. Open 10:30-3:30 M-F, 11-3:30 Sat. No credit cards.

Fresh Ideas is a chain of downtown sandwich and salad shops. They generally aren't the first choice of vegetarians, but they work in a pinch. You can get a vegetarian sandwich ($4.15) with avocado, cheese and English cucumber, an egg salad sandwich ($3.50), the daily vegetable salad (price varies) or a fresh fruit salad ($2.25 /$3.25). Open 11-2:30 M-F.

Fresh Ideas can be found at these locations:
1191 2nd Avenue, 622-8607.
Seafirst Plaza, 800 5th Avenue, 622-7879.
1329 1st Avenue, 621-0536.
Columbia Center, 701 5th Avenue, 340-0810.
Century Square, 1501 4th Avenue, 343-0435.
Key Tower, 1000 2nd Avenue, 386-7301.

Rama on Post (83 Spring Street, 340-9047) is a fairly pricey Thai restaurant with a bar close to the waterfront. Rama serves vegetarian spring rolls for $4.50. Entrées include steamed vegetables and tofu topped with Rama Mama peanut sauce; broccoli with black-bean sauce; tofu, green beans and other vegetables sautéed in Thai spices, and phad Thai, all in the $7.50 range. Open 11-10 M-Th, 11-11 F, 1-11 Sat. Credit cards accepted.

Two restaurants in the Four Seasons Olympic Hotel (411 University Street) offer stylish vegetarian meals, along with plenty of choices for carnivores, at hefty prices.

At **The Garden Court** (621-7889) you'll find bok choy and sesame noodle salad with vegetarian spring rolls for $7.50; a salad of Greek feta, cucumber, tomato and sweet onion with oregano oil is $8. A vegan nutburger with fennel cole slaw is $7.50. Open for lunch 11-3 M-Sat, dinner 5-11 every day. Credit cards accepted.

The Georgian Room (621-7889) presents a vegan vegetable and tofu curry with basmati rice ($12 and reported to be quite good), grilled Japanese eggplant with pizza bread ($8.50), ricotta ravioli with tomato bean stew ($7.75) and a mixed vegetable salad with oil and yogurt herb dressing ($8). Open for lunch 11:30-2 M-F, dinner 5:30-9:30 M-Sat. Credit cards accepted.

Another pricey place with an interesting vegetarian selection among more mainstream Pacific Northwest entrees is the **Dahlia Lounge** (1904 Fourth Avenue, 682-4142). Choices include housemade gnocchi ($5.50 half, $10.95 whole), made with wild mushrooms, roasted tomato sauce and gorgonzola cream. What sounds really good is the cashew-chile tofu with stir-fried Asian greens and rice cakes ($10.95). You also can get salads and appetizers such as eggplant-garlic dip with grilled pita and green apples ($4.95). Open for lunch 11:30-2:30 M-F, dinner 5:30-10 M-Th, 5:30-11 F-Sat. Credit cards accepted.

The **Gourmet Salad House** (621 3rd Avenue) has a large salad bar for $3.99 a pound. The place serves tofu dishes occasionally. Open 7-5 M-F. No credit cards.

La Salsa Express (613 3rd Avenue, 622-7154) is a tiny stand with a couple of counter seats. It advances some lardless vegetarian Mexican fare, including burritos ($2.95), soft tacos and tostadas ($2.55 each), crisp tacos (99 cents) and enchiladas ($2.99). Open 11-5 M-Th, 10:30-5:30 F. No credit cards.

Pike Place Market and Vicinity

Pike Place Market, at the end of Pike Street in downtown Seattle, is one of the Emerald City's favorite destinations for tourists and natives. And for good reason: the hundreds of arts and crafts kiosks, produce stands, shops and restaurants that make up the market and adjoining buildings are endlessly entertaining.

Founded in 1907, Pike Place Market is open from 8:30 to 5 seven days a week. Food merchants, who get much of their food from Washington state's outstanding farms, arrive at dawn or earlier, setting up colorful fruit and vegetable stands with produce ranging from the traditional (tomatoes, peas and strawberries) to the unusual (taro root, cactus leaves and exotic mushroom and chile pepper varieties). Some of the best food bargains in Seattle can be found here.

The crowded market teems with exciting urban life. Musicians -- playing the blues, new age, classical music or folk rock -- peddle for change. Shop here for pottery, touristy T-shirts, beautiful nature photography or clothing imports from Afghanistan and Central America.

A maze of alleyways and several different buildings, the market demands strong navigational skills. Pick up a free copy of the Pike Place Market News at any of several locations throughout the market for an excellent map. The heart of the market is the Main Arcade, which includes several levels of shops and restaurants. The street level — which extends to the North Arcade — is full of produce, seafood, and arts and crafts stands. The South Arcade, with upscale boutiques, is a more recent addition to the market. Across Pike Place are several more buildings full of shops and restaurants, including the Sanitary Market, the Post Alley Market and the Soames Dunn Building. All are worth exploring.

Like all of Pike Place Market's activities, produce and crafts, the vegetarian scene at the market and nearby is diverse, colorful and rich. Several vegetarian restaurants can be found in the area; many more restaurants and delis offer a good number of meatless options. A couple of Seattle's best are here: Gravity Bar, with its dozens of juices and beautifully prepared lunches and dinners, and Sisters, a delightful German deli with a focus on healthful foods.

Gravity Bar

113 Virginia Street
448-8826

Lunch, dinner, weekend brunch.
11-9 M-Th, 11-11 F, 10-11 Sat, 10-8 Sun.
Mostly vegetarian, many vegan choices.
Juice bar.
Credit cards accepted.

Gravity Bar, a block up the hill from the north end of the market, is one of the premier vegetarian establishments in Seattle, and certainly one of the most fun. (A second Gravity Bar is located on Capitol Hill.) The trendy restaurant serves food for the 21st century in a setting to match. The decor is a curious blend of science-fiction movie set, with black conical tables and funky chairs, and Third World jungle scene, with bamboo poles separating the main dining floor into two sections. It's a great place to watch people, as the restaurant attracts a diverse clientele, from yuppies in Birkenstocks to hippies in bandanas and tie-dyed shirts. But what's best about Gravity Bar is its food and juices: they sparkle with flavor.

Gravity Bar is the creation of Laurrien Gilman, an artist and chef. She and a partner opened the first Gravity Bar in 1986 just down the street toward Pike Place Market. But that space was tiny and, in 1992, Laurrien moved to the new, larger location.

She has made the preparation of food into an art form. The dishes at Gravity Bar are some of the most beautiful in Seattle. A trademark here are the colorful purple cabbage and fruit garnishes that come with many dishes.

Sit at the juice bar and watch bartenders make wonderful fruit and vegetable juice concoctions. You can choose from 67 kinds of juices, like beet carrot cleanse, moon juice (melon and lime), liver flush (grapefruit, lemon, garlic, olive oil and cayenne) and Ginger Rogers (carrot, apple and ginger). Or try a heated juice, like big bang (grapefruit, orange, lemon and cayenne). Add wheatgrass, spirulina, amino acids or electrolytes for optimal health benefits. Drinks cost from $2 to $4.75.

Lunch time brings a variety of salads, soups, roll-up sandwiches and toast plates in the $3 to $5 range. The Gravity Bar salad contains mixed greens, sprouts, tomatoes, avocado and other vegetables served with lemon tahini or dijon vinaigrette. The kimono is made of greens, colorful vegetables and hiziki seaweed, served with an oil-free Japanese dressing and garnished with sesame and pumpkin seeds. Some fans think the most delectable item on the Gravity Bar menu is the spicy noodle salad — buckwheat soba noodles, hiziki seaweed and vegetables dressed in toasted sesame oil and hot peppers, and garnished with avocado and tomato slices.

Soups ($2.50 to $5) include miso, made of spirulina, miso, salsa and tahini, and Holy Mary — sopa azteca blended with brown rice, fresh garlic and extra salsa. The tempeh burger, served with pickles, lettuce, tomato and barbecue sauce on a whole wheat herb and onion bun, is excellent, as is the rice and black bean roll-up.

The dinner menu offers more salads, appetizers like hummus and baba ghanoush with raw vegetables and toasted whole wheat pita bread, and outstanding entrées ($6.95 to $8.95). The Thai green curry is a fine medley of carrots, green beans, red peppers and bamboo shoots in a spicy coconut curry sauce. Bohemian wild rice includes brown rice with shiitake mushrooms, herbs, vegetables and tofu. Lemon leek udon is lemon leek and mushroom sauce served over whole wheat udon noodles.

Brunch is offered from 10 to 2 Saturday and Sunday. The changing choices might include tropical fruit salad, buckwheat sunflower toast with natural fruit conserves, whole wheat buttermilk pancakes with wheat germ, butter or soy margarine and pure maple syrup, and tofu with sun-dried tomatoes and garden vegetables over brown rice. Or try granola and fresh fruit, currants, pumpkin seeds and ginger or the fresh baked specialty muffins and scones of the day.

Most of the food is vegetarian, but Gravity Bar does serve a tuna dish and a caesar salad with anchovies.

Sisters

1530 Post Alley
623-6723

Lunch, dinner.
8-6 M-Sat, 11-5 Sun.
Several vegetarian and vegan choices.
No credit cards.

A meal in this cheery deli, painted in loud yellow with a large window opening onto a busy alley, will brighten even the dampest Seattle day. Founded by three twentysomething sisters — Nirala, Aruna and Miriam Jacobi — from Frankfurt, Germany, Sisters does not fit the image of a German deli full of bratwurst and Bavarian meats. Instead, it serves healthful soups, salads and sandwiches, many of which are vegetarian or vegan. Sisters is tucked away in the Post Alley, just east of the Main Market. Sit inside at one of the few counter seats looking onto the busy pedestrian alley, or outside in nice weather.

Four of seven sandwiches on the menu are vegetarian; one is vegan. Each costs $4.75 and is served on foccacia bread. The sandwiches are toasted and therefore taste more flavorful. Try the wonderful nasruddin: hummus, baked eggplant, tomato, olives and herbs. The gesundheit is made of sun-dried tomato, cream cheese, avocado sprouts, tomato and herbs. Or you might prefer the zorba, with feta cheese, baked eggplant, tomato and extra virgin olive oil.

Usually, one or two of the delicious daily soup choices are vegetarian. They might include a spicy but slightly watery Indian potato/cauliflower tofu soup, tomato provencal with almond cream, or a chilled cucumber-yogurt soup. Sisters recently offered a white-bean cassoulet soup and Jamaican squash soup on the same day. A cup is $1.95; a bowl, $2.75. The changing salads might include couscous with curried vegetables, sprouted lentil and mushrooms, German potato and tabbouleh.

Sabra Mediterranean Sandwich Shop

1916 Pike Place
441-4544

Lunch, dinner.
Summer: 9-7 M-Sat, winter: 10-4 M-Sat.
Strictly vegetarian, mostly vegan.
No credit cards.

The only all-vegetarian Mediterranean restaurant in Seattle, Sabra faces a tiny, ivy-laced courtyard at the back of the Soames Dunn Building, just east of the North Arcade. There are just a few seats in this informal restaurant, which serves up terrific falafel and hummus. Or if sunny skies prevail, sit outside.

Sabra offers a number of excellent pita sandwiches ($2.75 to $3.75), all covered with a delicious tahini sauce and topped with cucumbers and tomatoes. The falafel sandwich is made of the chickpea patty that's a staple of Middle

Eastern and Mediterranean cuisine. Baba ghanoush, an eggplant dish, also makes a fine sandwich. Yaakov's delight combines baked eggplant, tahini and tomatoes. Moti's special blends baked eggplant with parsley, avocado, scallions and tomatoes.

Platters include baba ghanoush, hummus and falafel for $4.50. Tabbouleh ($3 or $4.50) is a refreshing bulghur salad with tomatoes and parsley. Soups include split pea and Greek lentil ($1.20 small, $2.40 large).

Sound View Cafe

1501 Pike Place #501
623-5700

Breakfast, lunch.
7-5 M-F, 7-5:30 Sat, 9-3:30 Sun.
Several vegetarian and vegan choices.
No credit cards.

Pike Place Market-goers have long enjoyed eating at this casual breakfast-style restaurant with a natural foods focus. Not all the food here is vegetarian, but a healthy amount is. People come here for good food, a relaxed atmosphere and some of the most spectacular views of Elliott Bay and the Olympic Mountains from any Seattle restaurant. Huge windows along the west wall offer glimpses of Washington state ferries and other marine life.

Sound View Cafe is somewhat hard to find. At the end of Pike Street, enter the Main Arcade under the famous Public Market sign and walk west down to the end of Flower Row. Turn right and pass through the swinging doors; Sound View Cafe is there on the left.

The restaurant is set up cafeteria-style. First, choose from several interesting vegetarian salads that greet you at the entrance, perhaps greens with Thai dressing, spinach with curried vegetables, tabbouleh, or pasta with garlic and green onion dressing. Most salads cost $2.50 for a small bowl; $5 for a large. At the main counter, order one of the four soups ($1.40 for a cup, $2.15 for a bowl). Usually, a couple include no animal products. Choices range from mushroom goulash to cream of curried vegetables. The eggplant sandwich and the hummus sandwich are $3.55 each.

Big eaters at breakfast might sample an order of tofu scrambler for $3.50; additions of broccoli, mushrooms or other vegetables are 50 cents each. The generous plate comes with four pieces of whole wheat toast and fried potatoes. So large were the portions during one visit that this ravenous eater had to leave food on his plate. The nutty granola, and oatmeal with apple, raisins and nuts, are $1.65 for a small bowl, $2.60 for a large.

Order a pot of herbal tea or a caffeinated drink while you wait for a sandwich or omelet, and read a newspaper, carry on casual conversation or just savor those awesome views. A personal touch: The cashier writes down your first name when she takes your order. When the cook has finished preparing your dish, he walks out and cries, "Good morning, David!" or whomever, to get your attention.

Cafe Counter Intelligence

94 Pike Street, Suite 32
622-6979

Breakfast, lunch.
Variable hours — best to call first.
Mostly vegetarian; some vegan choices.
No credit cards.

Located on the second floor of the Corner Market Building just east of the Main Arcade, Cafe Counter Intelligence is one of the city's 'hipper' vegetarian restaurants. The tiny room is painted in wacky shades of yellow and purple; eclectic art hangs on the walls. The restaurant is popular with artists and writers.

The atmosphere is laid back and the service sometimes slow: pick up a magazine or newspaper from the pile of periodicals near the front door to peruse while you wait for your meal. You can sit at the counter and talk with the food preparers. Or take one of the window seats and watch the market scene across the street.

Cafe Counter Intelligence is mostly vegetarian (it offers one salmon dish for lunch), but heavy on the dairy products. Omelets and other egg dishes are popular here. (Some health-conscious folks might not be thrilled that smoking is permitted.) But vegans have choices, too, including salads and sandwiches.

For breakfast ($3.50 to $6.25), the waffles are excellent, based upon our visit. Made with oat and buckwheat flours and flavored with orange and vanilla, they come with real maple syrup. Yogurt, nuts and homemade preserves can be added. The chili rise — eggs scrambled with basmati rice, vegetables, sweet peppers, beans, white cheddar cheese and salsa -- is served with eight-grain toast. Rice cream is basmati rice steamed in half and half with a taste of cinnamon and honey and topped with red-flame raisins and walnuts.

Lunch choices ($4.25 to $6.25) include the C.I. special — homemade soup with croutons and grated cheese, and fruit or vegetable salad with an Italian baguette. The counter roll, beans, basmati rice and marinated vegetables rolled in a whole wheat tortilla, is served hot with melted cheese and salsa. Leaves and greens includes a variety of vegetables with homemade croutons and grated white cheddar cheese, served with tahini dressing and a baguette. The restaurant offers one or two soups daily, ranging from tomato basmati rice to squash pear. Soup with bread and cheese is $4.25.

If you're not really hungry, you might stop by for some fruit or vegetable juice or herbal tea. Caffeinated drinks also are favored here.

Rasa Malaysia

1514 Pike Place
624-8388

Lunch, early dinner.
9-5:30 daily.
Half vegetarian; several vegan choices.
No credit cards.

Rasa Malaysia is a chain of five tiny Southeast Asian restaurants in Seattle.

All are good places to stop for a quick, cheap and reliably good lunch or dinner. Portions are generous. This one really is more a stand than a restaurant, and there are only a few stools at a couple of counters where people can sit.

You'll find Rasa Malaysia in the Sanitary Building on Pike Place, just across from the Main Arcade. It's located next to a produce stand and other shops. Watch market-goers barter and browse as you eat.

These lunch dishes each cost $3: mee goreng (stir-fried noodles with peanut sauce), sayor lodeh (vegetable curry over steamed white rice), ma poh tofu (steamed tofu in bean sauce) and the gado gado salad (steamed vegetables and tofu with peanut sauce). Vegetarian potstickers are six for $2.50. Fresh fruit quenchers ($1.50 each) include strawberry-banana, ginger-lemon cooler and melon-lime.

The Juice Emporium

Pike Place
623-5383

Juice bar; a couple of vegetarian lunch options.
9-6 every day.
Strictly vegetarian.
No credit cards.

In the Triangle Building just across the street from the Main Arcade, this all-vegetarian juice bar serves a variety of fresh-squeezed fruit and vegetable juices and fruit smoothies. Carrot juice costs $1.75, $2 or $2.50. Fruit smoothies are $2.50 or $3.50. A baked potato with salsa topping costs $2.25; plain is $2.

Other Choices

In the buildings just to the east of the Main Arcade are a number of eateries. One of the better ones for vegetarians, located in the Stewart House building, is **Cucina Fresca** (1904 Pike Place, 448-4758), a small Italian deli with several vegan salads and vegetable preparations (roasted marinated eggplant, sautéed mushrooms). Typical deli prices. Open 9:30-6 M-Sat, 11-5 Sun. No credit cards.

Saigon Restaurant (1916 Pike Place, 448-1089) dishes out a handful of vegetarian choices for under $4: tofu soup, tofu salad, braised tofu in a tomato sauce and rice with sautéed vegetables. Open 11-5 M-Sat. No credit cards.

The Garlic Tree Restaurant (94 Stewart St., one-half block east of the market, 441-5681) serves Chinese stir-fries ($5 to $7), including two vegetarian entrées for lunch and four for dinner. Try the vegetable garden or vegetable tofu. Or have vegetable or tofu chapche (transparent noodles with vegetables) for dinner. Open 11-7:30 M-Th, 11-8:30 F-Sat. No credit cards.

The Kaleenka (1933 First Avenue, 728-1278), a Russian restaurant up the hill a block east of the market, serves three vegetarian dishes for dinner ($9.25 to $11.50). The vegetarian ragu layers a medley of vegetables with cheese in a mushroom sauce. The ragu à la Kaleenka tops mushrooms and sour cream with swiss and parmesan cheese. Vareniky pirogi are Ukrainian dumplings filled with farmer's cheese or peppered potatoes and sour cream.

Ukrainian-style borscht with sour cream and rye bread is $3.85 for dinner. Lunch offers fewer vegetarian selections: a bowl of borscht costs $1.90 or $3.35; green salad is $1.95 or $3.25. Open 11-5 M-Sat, 5-9 M-Th, 5-10 F-Sat. Credit cards accepted.

The **Wild Ginger Asian Restaurant and Satay Bar** (1400 Western Avenue, 623-4450), a block south of the market, offers a couple of delicious vegetarian dishes. This restaurant is posh and popular. For lunch, have the monk's curry ($6.95, or $8.95 for dinner), with eggplant, tofu, potatoes and other vegetables in a Thai curry sauce. If you're strict about your eating choices, steer clear of the tofu vegetarian ($6.95), which is served with an oyster sauce. For lunch or dinner, fresh vegetables grilled at the satay bar ($1.50 per skewer, one kind of vegetable per skewer) are a refreshing choice. Also on the dinner menu is triple-cooked noodles ($7.95) -- Chinese egg noodles that are deep-fried, boiled and then stir-fried, and topped with vegetables from Pike Place Market. Lunch 11:15-3 M-Sat, dinner 5-11 Sun-Th, 5-midnight F-Sat. Satay bar 11:15 a.m.-1 a.m. M-Sat, 5-1 Sun. Credit cards accepted.

The Aegean (1400 First Avenue, 343-5500) serves Greek food in an attractive, mostly white dining room with posters of Greece on the walls and unusual gold lights that hang 15 feet down from the ceiling to just above the tables. The restaurant specializes in such Greek vegetarian appetizers ($4 to $5) as hummus and tzatziki, and more unusual choices like saganaki ($4.95), pan-fried kasseri cheese flamed at your table with brandy and lemon, and melizanosalata, a mixture of eggplant, garlic and herbs. You can also order entrées ($6 to $7) including spanakopita or domates gemistes (tomatoes, peppers, zucchini and eggplant stuffed with nuts, basil, garlic, spices, tomato sauce and mushrooms). Open 11-10 Sun-Th, 11-11 F-Sat. Credit cards accepted.

Crepe de Marie (624-2196), a tiny stand at the south end of the Main Arcade, four stalls west of the newsstand, has a smattering of vegetarian omelets ($3.50 to $5) -- though vegans need not stop here, since there are no animal-free items on the menu. Try crepe vegetarian (tomato, cucumber, pepper, spinach and basil sauce), crepeaux fraises (fresh strawberries and vanilla cream), or crepeaux tomates (tomato, scallions, herbs de provence and basil with a mozzarella sauce). Open 10-5 daily; closed on Sundays except in summer and during Christmas shopping season. No credit cards.

Burrito Express (1429 1st Avenue), at the southeast corner of the Main Arcade, just south of the intersection of Pike Street and 1st Avenue, is a tiny fast-food, take-out booth that serves vegetarian tacos, tostadas and burritos, using no lard or preservatives. Vegetarian items are $3 or less. No seating available. Open 11-5 every day. No credit cards.

At **World Class Chili** (1411 First Avenue, in the South Arcade, 623-3678), try the vegetarian chili. Pay $3.97 for a Texas-size bowl; $6.88 for Alaska-size. Open 11-6 M-Sat. No credit cards.

Pioneer Square

Filled with interesting old buildings, Pioneer Square is one of the few truly historic places in Seattle. A lot of activity takes place here: tourists flock to the Underground Tour, to see some of the early origins of the city; transients hang out in public squares and ask for handouts, and Seattle natives take in the interesting shopping for antiques and other products.

The vegetarian scene here is fair, with only a handful of places that serve quality plant-based meals, but is improving. Some restaurants are adding meatless items as demand warrants. Your best bets are the Indian Taj Restaurant and The Elliott Bay Cafe.

India Taj Restaurant

625 1st Avenue
233-0160

Lunch, lunch buffet, dinner.
11:30-2:30, 5-10 M-Th, 11:30-2:30, 5-2 F, 1-2 Sat, 5-10 Sun.
Many vegetarian choices.
Credit cards accepted.

A huge white model of the Taj Mahal in a glass case greets you as you walk into this restaurant. India Taj serves northern Indian fare. The best deal is the lunch buffet, $5.95 for all you can eat (11 to 2:30 weekdays). It allows you to sample a vegetarian soup, a couple of Indian salads (chickpea, and tomato, cucumber and onion), fruit, the Indian bread naan, basmati rice, a dal and two changing meatless entrées. The menu lists 10 vegetarian specialties ($5.50 to $7), plus assorted breads and appetizers. Some examples: vegetable jalfrazie blends sautéed vegetables with various spices; bhindi masala is okra cooked in onion, tomatoes and spices; aloo ghobi combines sautéed cauliflower and potatoes, and aloo bangan is an eggplant and potato dish. Go for the vegetarian thali dinner ($11.95) when you're really hungry. It includes pappadam (a wafer-thin bread made with lentil flour and fried in butter), pakoras (vegetables mixed with lentil and flour batter and then deep fried), two vegetables, dal, raita, pickles, puri (a deep-fried puffy bread) and pudding.

The Elliott Bay Cafe

101 S. Main St.
682-6664

Breakfast, lunch, dinner.
7-10:30 M-F, 10-10:30 Sat, 11-5 Sun.
Several vegetarian and vegan choices.
No credit cards.

There's nothing like selecting a good book or a magazine and sitting down to a warm meal. The Elliott Bay Cafe, in the basement of the Elliott Bay Book Company, is the perfect place for doing so. You get food for the tummy and nourishment for the mind in a large, spacious dining room full of bookshelves and a newspaper rack. In an adjoining room, authors and poets frequently give readings and talks.

The cafe is set up cafeteria-style, so pick up a tray and choose from salads, soups, bagels, breads and sandwiches. There's always a Thai vegetable salad with a too-bland peanut sauce ($2.50); the other rotating salads might be garden green or pesto pasta. Generally one or two of the soups of the day are vegetarian ($1.55 or $2.50), perhaps vegetarian chili or potato dill. The hummus sandwich is good fare for $3.95. It's served on whole wheat, light rye or sourdough bread with lettuce, tomato and sprouts. There's usually a special entrée, which might be vegetarian lasagna ($4.50, $5.75 with a cup of soup). The quiche of the day costs $3.50.

OK Hotel Cafe and Ballroom

212 Alaskan Way S.
386-9934

Breakfast, lunch, dinner.
7-4 M, 7-midnight Tu-F, 8:30-midnight Sat, 8:30-4 Sun.
Several vegetarian choices.
No credit cards.

The OK Hotel Cafe, in a beautiful historic, typically Pacific Northwest old hotel underneath Highway 99 (the elevated highway by the waterfront), planned to expand its menu in 1993 to include more vegetarian items, due to the demand from customers. It's an interesting place, with an art gallery and art studios upstairs. In the back room, live music is played Tuesday through Saturday nights. Smoking is permitted in the restaurant.

The breakfast menu ($1.75 to $4.50), available until 11 weekdays and 3 on weekends, is best for ovo-lacto vegetarians. You might try the mushroom, onion and jack egg scramble, served with homefries, fruit garnish and choice of rye, whole wheat or sourdough toast or an english muffin. The Tijuana scramble includes cheddar cheese, salsa and sour cream. The breakfast burrito (homefries optional) wraps three eggs, jack or cheddar cheese, sour cream and salsa in a flour tortilla. It's served with fruit garnish and sprouts. Vegans should opt for granola with fruit, or oatmeal.

Choices and prices are the same for lunch and dinner ($4 to $5 for entrées and most appetizers). Appetizers include a hummus plate with pita bread, Greek olives, cucumber, tomato and sprouts; tortilla chips and salsa, and a quesadilla plate of two flour tortillas fried with jack and cheddar cheese and topped with olives, tomato, sprouts, sour cream and salsa. The vegan garden salad can be topped with hummus. Sandwiches are hummus and jack, with cucumber, tomato and sprouts in a pita or sandwich bread; veggie cream cheese, and grilled mushroom jack, made with grilled onion, tomato and sprouts. The soup of the day, which is always vegetarian, is $2 or $2.50 and comes with bread.

Other Choices

The Swan Cafe and Nightclub (608 1st Avenue, 343-5288) yields a number of vegetarian and vegan choices for lunch and dinner. Start with the vegan black-bean soup ($1.95/$2.95), with optional sour cream. About half the time, the soup of the day also is vegetarian. Meatless salads include the Greek ($5.50), with feta, olives, greens, assorted vegetables and dressing, and the house. The "100 percent vegetarian burger" is just that: vegan, and comes with chips. The Swan offers two vegan sandwiches: the seasonal garden salad sandwich, and avocado, tomato and sprouts. Or choose the grilled eggplant parmesan Mediterranean-style sandwich in a pita pocket. (The burger and sandwiches range from $3 to $4.50.) The seasonal vegetables and fettuccine dish ($5.50) can be made with or without parmesan (however, fettuccine is made with eggs). The three-cheese tortellini alfredo is $6.95. The bar menu (available from 8 p.m. until closing) includes the vegetarian burger and assorted appetizers. Full kitchen open from 11 to 8 M-Sat. Credit cards accepted.

Stop at **The Bagel Express** (205 1st Avenue S., 682-7202) for good bagels and vegetarian bagel sandwiches ($2.90 each). You can order the avocado, with cream cheese, tomato and sprouts; the hummus, with cucumber, sprouts and tomato; the cheese, made of swiss, cheddar, sprouts, tomato and mayo, or cream cheese, with tomato, cucumber, red onion and sprouts. Open 7 to 6 M-F, 8-6 Sat. No credit cards.

International District

Vegetarians wanting to eat out will do best to avoid the International District (known as Chinatown until the mid-1980s). You will find tofu dishes here, but they're almost invariably mixed with pork or beef and prepared in chicken broth. Most of the menus don't even contain vegetarian selections. You'll have much more success finding quality meatless Asian food in other neighborhoods scattered throughout the city. However, if you're in the neighborhood, there are a couple of places you can visit.

One International District attraction that vegetarians should note is the wonderful Japanese supermarket, **Uwajimaya** (519 6th Avenue S., 624-6248, open 9-8 every day). Here, you'll find one of Seattle's best assortments of exotic produce and Asian cooking ingredients.

The **Bangkok House** Thai restaurant (606 S. Weller Street, 382-9888) offers seven vegetarian choices ($4.75 to $5.75), including two hot and sour soups, vegetarian phad Thai and stir-fried tofu and vegetables with cashews. Open 11-10 Sun-Th, 11-11 F-Sat. Credit cards accepted.

Just northwest of the International District is a humble but excellent eatery, the **Ranee Thai Restaurant** (121 Prefontaine Place S., 223-9456). Four lunch choices are $3.95 each: phad Thai, tofu curry, spinach and tofu topped with peanut sauce and "Summer Palace," a dish of tofu, green beans and other vegetables sautéed in a hot sauce. Dinner includes those choices (about $4.75 each) as well as vegetables delight with lemon grass, lime leaves and chile paste, tofu with cashews and tom-kha-tofu, a hot and sour soup. Open 11 to 8 M-F, 12-9 Sat. No credit cards.

Next door to Ranee Thai is the **Viet My Restaurant** (129 Prefontaine Place S., 382-9923), which serves five vegetarian entrées in the $4 range. Try the curry tofu, tofu chow mein with mushrooms and vegetables or tofu saté with vegetables and rice noodles. Open 11-3, 5-9 M-F. No credit cards.

Denny Regrade

Denny Regrade is the area between the central business district and the Seattle Center to the north. Here are many modern and old office buildings, apartments and nightclubs, and a few restaurants. The vegetarian fare isn't especially plentiful, but you will find a few good places to eat.

Cyclops

2416 Western Avenue
441-1677

Breakfast, lunch, dinner.
9-11 M-Th, 9-2 a.m. F, 10-2 a.m. Sat, 10-11 Sun.
Many vegetarian and vegan selections.
No credit cards.

If you like the gritty, urban Belltown neighborhood in Denny Regrade, chances are you'll love this eccentric restaurant. The cyclops motif is really played out here: under the neon restaurant sign that hangs over the bright green exterior, a giant cyclops eye peers out at you. Look for a purple one-eyed monster looking out from inside the dessert and pastry case. This is the kind of place for twentysomethings and counterculture types. With its strange art on the walls (an antique bike hanging over a table, Bible quotes about cannibalism and an antler poking out from the center of a wheel), more traditional sorts may feel out of place. Tables and chairs look as if they came from a 1950s diner. The large, dark dining room, with an open kitchen at the back, has as its motto "Good food that's good for you," and most of it is. The menu lists many vegetarian meals (but is oriented more toward ovo-lacto vegetarians than vegans).

The bright green breakfast menu (with choices mostly in the $3.50 to $5.95 range), printed in newsletter style, lists several tasty dishes. The tofu scramble is very good. In most places, this dish is made with mashed tofu, but here large tofu chunks share the plate with red and green peppers, onions, garlic and herbs. The accompanying homefries are deliciously flavored with coriander. Whole wheat toast (with butter on the side) completes the order. Another interesting dish is potato pancakes, flapjacks made of potatoes, red peppers and green onions, topped with homemade applesauce. You also can get french toast, egg-and-pepper scramble with cheddar cheese, homefries and toast or the Cyclops omelet, which consists of feta, spinach, mushrooms and olives.

The lunch menu ($4.50 to $4.95) is comprised of such Middle Eastern standards as baba ghanoush, hummus and an eggplant sandwich made with marinated eggplant, artichoke cream and sun-dried tomatoes, topped with parmesan cheese and baked on bread. The pesto pizza is covered with cilantro pesto, sun-dried tomatoes, mozzarella and onions.

Pasta dishes (most $6.95), available for lunch and dinner, include one covered with a cilantro-walnut pesto and topped with tomato coulis and grated parmesan, and pasta gorgonzola, made with cheese, apples and walnuts in a light cream sauce. That dessert case in which the cyclops lies might contain (depending on the day) carrot cake and hazelnut-apricot tart.

Thai House

2228 2nd Avenue
728-0900

Lunch, dinner.
11-10 M-Th, 11-11 F, 12-11 Sat, 3-10 Sun.
Many vegetarian dishes.
Credit cards accepted.

Thai House serves 16 meatless dishes ($5.25 to $5.95), from tofu-ginger sautéed with vegetables to phud ka-na, broccoli stir-fried with black-bean sauce and tofu. Among others are tom yum tao-hoo, a traditional Thai soup made with tofu, mushrooms and bamboo shoots; kang puk, mixed vegetables in coconut milk, Thai red curry and spices, and emerald salad, with lettuce, cucumber, clear noodles, tomato, egg, tofu, onion and a chile dressing.

Bangkok Hut Thai Restaurant

2126 3rd Avenue
441-4425

Lunch, dinner.
11:30-3 M-Sat, 5-10 daily.
Several vegetarian choices.
Credit cards accepted.

You'll find 14 more or less standard vegetarian dishes ($4.95 to $5.95) here, including hot and sour soup with lemon grass and vegetables, hot and spicy bean cake with bamboo shoots, spicy eggplant with Thai chile sauce, sautéed spinach with black-bean sauce and vegetarian angel, stir-fried tofu in a bed of spinach topped with peanut sauce.

Other Choices

Tump-Nak Thai (419 Denny Way, 441-5024) offers four vegetarian selections. Lunch ($5.50) includes gaeng kael wan (eggplant and tofu in green curry). tropical jungle (red curry, tofu and mixed vegetables), phad Thai and swimming tofu. Dinner prices are $6.95. Open 1-3, 5-10 M-Th, 11-3, 5-11 F, 1-11 Sat, 3-10 Sun. Credit cards accepted.

Casa U-Betcha (2212 1st Avenue, 441-1026) is a bizarrely decorated restaurant with a bar and a funny name. It's a trendy nightspot that serves mostly Mexican food for carnivores, plus a few vegetarian selections. For starters, you can order a vegetarian black-bean soup made with roasted garlic, cumin, carrots, celery and chiles or the cold Spanish vegetable soup, gazpacho (both $4.95 at lunch, $5.95 at dinner). Casa U-Betcha also serves burritos, enchiladas and chimichangas ($7.95 each for lunch, $9.95 for dinner) as well as such cheesy appetizers as nachos and tapas Barcelona, grilled marinated eggplant and a mushroom dish with fire-roasted peppers and white bean-roasted garlic puree ($6.95). Open 11:30-4:30 M-F, 5-11 M-S. Credit cards accepted.

Lower Queen Anne

The several blocks including and surrounding the Seattle Center — legacy of the 1962 World's Fair and now home of Seattle's most recognized landmark, the Space Needle, as well as a science museum and amusement park — offer vegetarians several good eating choices. Most notable is the Bamboo Garden, an all-vegan Chinese restaurant serving meat-like dishes so realistic that they deceive many customers. Other fine eateries include the Bahn Thai (one of the most popular Thai restaurants in town), Cafe Loc for Vietnamese fare, Mother Nature's (a local health-food market and take-out deli that serves a variety of soups and sandwiches) and Ozaki Cafe, which offers an unusually large selection of vegetarian dishes for a Japanese restaurant.

This section includes food booths in the Seattle Center, as well as restaurants along nearby Roy and Mercer streets, Queen Anne Boulevard and other roads.

Bamboo Garden Vegetarian Cuisine

364 Roy Street
282-6616

Lunch, dinner.
11-10 daily.
Strictly vegan.
Credit cards accepted.

How many vegetarians would think of ordering beef in golden sauce, chicken nuggets or sweet and sour pork? They (and plenty of carnivores) do it all the time at Bamboo Garden, undoubtedly Seattle's most unusual vegetarian restaurant. Half the dishes on the menu include meat, chicken or fish. But this isn't the real stuff: the chefs here deftly manipulate soybean products to simulate the taste and texture of animal foods.

The meat analogs fool a lot of people. Some vegetarians bring meat-eating friends or family members to Bamboo Garden, and don't let them know they're eating plant-based food until the end of the meal. In fact, the waiters and waitresses sometimes find they must warn diners before they eat that all the meat items come from soy. Many vegetarians love Bamboo Garden because it gives them a chance to be nostalgic. And the menu here allows people who recently have given up meat to satisfy any leftover cravings. Other vegetarians don't like it; they don't want to have anything to do with meat. But, on balance, Bamboo Garden serves excellent Chinese food that should satisfy most vegetarians and meat-eaters. And for those who don't want fake meat, there are plenty of standard vegetable dishes.

The menu covers 75 choices. For starters, try the crispy fried egg roll (three for $3.25), puffy fried beef roll ($3.50) or golden fried chicken nuggets ($3.60). Soups ($6 to $8) include braised chicken and shark fin, seaweed bean curd and botanic garden.

For your entrée (in the $6 to $9 range), you might choose hot and spicy mushrooms delight or vegetarian sausage and pork in hunan sauce. Servers urge Westerners to steer clear of the Buddha's feast, made with stewed mushrooms and black moss with stuffed bean curd wrap — but many Chinese diners (and some Americans) love the slimy stuff. Also good are lemon chicken, sweet and sour taro fish (made from taro, a relative of the yam) and stir-fried turkey with celery. The fresh enoki mushrooms with broccoli looks like a pasta plate, made with the long and stringy mushrooms. Stewed chicken in curry sauce with potatoes and fresh vegetables, Szechuan eggplant and assorted mushrooms simmered in satay sauce each arrive at the table still sizzling.

Several lunch and dinner combinations offer excellent values and allow you to explore Bamboo Garden's exotic menu. At lunch, an egg roll, fried won ton, beef roll, chicken chow mein and sweet and sour pork cost a total of $4.55. Dinner D ($19.95 for two people, $9.95 for each additional person) includes soup, fried won tons, egg rolls, beef rolls, potstickers, chicken chow mein, sweet and sour pork and chicken broccoli.

The one part of the meal that is not vegan is the fortune cookies, which are made with eggs.

Bahn Thai Restaurant

409 Roy Street
283-0444

Lunch, dinner.
11:30-3 M-F, 4:30-10 M-Th, 4:30-11 F, 4-11 S-S.
Several vegan selections.
Credit cards accepted.

Bahn Thai consistently draws raves from local critics, and has won several Best Thai restaurant awards in the Seattle Weekly annual poll. Vegetarians like the ornate restaurant for its large selection of meatless dishes. Dinner entrées cost $5.50 each. There are tofu with cashew nuts, sautéed with onions and baby corn; Bahn Thai tofu, served on a bed of spinach and topped with peanut sauce; phad pug plik king tofu, sautéed with onions, green beans, tofu and ginger in a curry paste, and "showered green," assorted vegetables topped with peanut sauce. In all, the dinner menu (available all day) includes 10 vegetarian entrées and one soup: tom yum pug ($5.50), made hot and sour with vegetables, lemon grass, tofu, kaffir leaf and chile paste. The lunch menu ($4 to $5, 11:30-3 M-F) includes showered green; hot garden, spicy sautéed vegetables, and phad pug plik king tofu.

Mother Nature's Natural Foods

516 1st Avenue N.
284-4422

Lunch bar.
9:30-6 M-Sat.
Mostly vegetarian, several vegan options.
No credit cards.

A health-food fixture that's been around since the early 1970s, Mother

Nature's used to be known as Queen Anne Vitality. The store, just a short walk from the Seattle Center, is still much the same. In fact, some customers continue to write "Queen Anne Vitality" on their checks, almost a decade after the name change.

Here you'll find a decent stock of health foods, vitamins, books on health and a tiny lunch counter that serves wholesome, fast-food soups, sandwiches and drinks to go. A specialty is the veggie chicken sandwich ($3.75), made with textured vegetable protein slices that look and taste like chicken, topped with real or vegan mayo. The lentil loaf ($3.75), made with egg whites, comes with mustard, sprouts and tomato. You can get a garden burger made with dairy products or a vegan tofu burger served on a whole wheat bun ($4.25). The soup of the day, usually vegan, is $1.35 for 8 ounces, $1.75 for 12 ounces, and $2.15 for 16 ounces. The vegetarian chili, meanwhile, is served every day and costs $1.45, $1.95 and $2.35 for those same sizes. You can also get fruit smoothies here.

Ozaki Cafe

372 Roy Street
283-7872

Lunch, dinner.
11-10 M-Sat, 4-9 Sun.
Several vegan choices.
Credit cards accepted.

The Ozaki Cafe, a small, attractive restaurant a block north of the Seattle Center, serves a good number of vegetarian Japanese dishes. The Ozaki tofu bowl ($4.25 for lunch only) blends mushrooms, carrots, onions, broccoli, bean sprouts and tofu with a ginger sauce. Most choices are available for lunch or dinner (dinner entrées include rice and soup or salad). You can ask for the udon soup ($4.25 for lunch, $5.25 for dinner) without pork or chicken. Then it will consist of bean sprouts, napa cabbage and green onions. You can do the same with the ramen noodle soup ($4/$5.25). As an appetizer, try the vegetable rolls ($4/$5.50). The ginger tofu dish ($4.50/$5.95) is a pleasing choice. Yakisoba ($4.95/$6), a stir-fried buckwheat noodle soup, comes with tofu or vegetables.

The Ozaki Cafe also serves three dishes for $4 at lunch and $5.75 at dinner: rice stick noodles, curry tofu and hot and spicy Japanese tofu. Available at dinner only is the hot and sour tofu soup ($5).

Cafe Loc

407 Broad Street
441-6883

Lunch, early dinner.
11-6 M-F.
Several vegan choices.
No credit cards.

It's hard to beat Cafe Loc's values. The prices in this simple Vietnamese eatery almost directly underneath the Space Needle seem almost as old as the

1962 World's Fair itself: all the vegetarian dishes are under $4. Still, the portions are quite filling. It's an appealing place with pink tablecloths, fake flower arrangements and canisters of silverware on each table. In warm weather, an outdoor patio allows good views of the Seattle Center's amusement rides across the street.

Choose among one meatless appetizer, three soups and eight entrées (all in the $3.25 to $3.75 range). Start with the spring rolls or bean thread, hot and sour or rice noodle soup. The ginger tofu dish includes strands of ginger with button mushrooms, greens and tofu over white rice, for a flavorful meal. Other good choices are curry tofu, cashew vegetables and sweet and sour tofu.

Seattle Center House Food Pavillion

305 Harrison Street

Most of the fast-food booths in the Seattle Center's food pavillion (which also is home of several touristy shops, children's activities and performances) are open the same hours as the pavillion, which change seasonally.

Cafe Loc is owned by the same people who run the full-size Cafe Loc restaurant at the south edge of the Seattle Center. Here you can get egg rolls ($1 each), a cashew vegetable plate served over white rice ($3.85), or vegetarian stir-fried noodles ($3.85).

The Bean Pod offers baked potatoes with various toppings: butter and sour cream ($1.99), broccoli and cheese ($2.49) and cheese, mushrooms and chives ($2.99). The veggie supreme sandwich ($3.99) is a mountain of avocado, cucumber, mushrooms, lettuce, cream cheese and tomato.

Kabab Corner serves hummus and baba ghanoush appetizers ($3.19 each) and a falafel plate for $4.99.

Other Choices

Thai Heaven Restaurant (352 Roy Street, 285-1596), next door to the Bamboo Garden, is a large and elegant restaurant with an extensive selection of vegetarian dishes. Here you can choose from four meatless appetizers, such as Thai spring rolls ($3.95) and yum woon sen ($4.50), a delicious mix of silver noodles, cashews, cucumber and mint leaves seasoned with a zesty lime sauce, and three soups, including tom kah pak ($5.50), a spicy broth with mushrooms and other vegetables, coconut and galango, and 12 vegetarian entrées (in the $5 to $6 range), such as spicy tofu and vegetables, chile pepper rice and vegetarian curry. Open 11-3, 5-10 M-Th, 11-3, 5-11 F, 1-11 Sat, 1-10 Sun. Credit cards accepted.

Try the **Thai House Restaurant** (517 Queen Anne Avenue, 284-3700) for interesting dishes ($4.95 to $5.95) such as tofu phad phed, sautéed tofu with mixed vegetables, basil leaves and chile paste; kang pahk, vegetables cooked in red curry, coconut milk, bamboo shoots and basil, or vegetarian fried rice ($5.50). Open for lunch 11-3 M-F; dinner 5-10 every day. Credit cards accepted.

Tup Tim Thai (118 W. Mercer Street, 281-8833) offers 10 vegetarian dishes (in the $4 to $5 range), including vegetable curry and phad Thai, sautéed vegetables with peanut sauce and hot and sour vegetable soup. Open for lunch 11:30-3 M-F; dinner, 5-10 M-Sat. Credit cards accepted.

Thai Restaurant (101 John Street, 285-9000) is a pleasant Southeast Asian place with a bar, a couple of blocks west of the Seattle Center. Choose from nine vegetarian entrées ($5.50 to $6.50), among them fried rice, bean curd and broccoli, bean curd in chile sauce and phad Thai. Lunch: 11:30-2:30 M-F, 12-2:30 S-S. Dinner: 5-9 Sun-Th, 5-10 F-Sat. Credit cards accepted.

O'Char (500 Elliott Avenue West, 286-1772) offers a variety of Thai vegetarian options. Meatless lunch dishes ($4.50) include steamed spinach topped with spicy peanut sauce, phad Thai and fried rice with egg. For dinner, you can order five spring rolls for $3.95, or one of eight vegetarian entrées for $5.50, such as cucumber, pineapple, tomato, onion and bell pepper in a sweet and sour sauce; ginger vegetables; steamed vegetables with black pepper and garlic, or veggie lover — sautéed vegetables with soy sauce. Open for lunch 11-3 M-F; dinner 5-10 (until 11 F, Sat.). Credit cards accepted.

Orestes Restaurant (14 Roy Street, 282-5514) serves Greek food in a white Greek building that doesn't quite fit in with all the traditional American architecture nearby. Here you'll find a smattering of vegetarian dishes, mostly among the appetizers. For lunch, Orestes serves hummus and melitzano (an eggplant dip), each for $2.50 ($3.45 and $3.65, respectively, for dinner); tzatziki, a yogurt, cucumber and garlic dip, is $2.75. Cheese lovers might enjoy the saganaki ($5.25 for lunch, $6.50 for dinner), sautéed goat cheese with lemon. Briam ($5.95, lunch only) is a vegetarian casserole of carrots, celery, onion, eggplant and zucchini, cooked with olive oil and herbs, and served with spinach pie. Spanakopita ($3.25/$3.75) is a phyllo pastry stuffed with spinach and feta cheese. Open 11:30-10 Sun, Tu-Th, 11:30-11 F-Sat. Credit cards accepted.

La Gaviota (174 Roy Street, 281-7233) serves Mexican and Spanish cuisine. Many of the Mexican dishes are vegetarian, but only a couple of the Spanish ones are: the spicy potatoes tapa ($4.95) and the Spanish omelet ($3.95), made with potatoes, onions and eggs. Beans here are cooked in canola oil. And meat dishes can be modified. Lunch choices (about $4.50) include chalupa with guacamole, a burrito, two enchiladas and chilaquiles. Among dinner items are enchiladas, tostadas, tacos, burritos, chalupas and chimichangas, all made with beans and all under $4. Open 11-9:30 M-Sat. Credit cards accepted.

8/15/93 dinner **Mediterranean Kitchen** (4 W. Roy Street, 285-6713) offers standard Middle Eastern choices for dinner. Appetizers ($3.50-$3.75) include hummus, baba ghanoush, zahrah (deep-fried cauliflower with tahini sauce) and Lebanese labnie (drained yogurt with olive oil, olives and tomatoes). The soup of the day ($5, with bread) is always vegetarian, perhaps yellow split pea, lentil or pinto bean. Three vegetarian entrees are offered ($6-$8.50): the falafel dish, eggplant moussaka and a dinner salad. Open 5-10 M-Th, 5-11 F-Sat, 4-10 Sun. Credit cards accepted.

(Soup was chicken, etc) Large portions - skip appetizers

Eastlake

Eastlake is so-called because the neighborhood — just west of Interstate 5 and Capitol Hill — occupies the east bank of Lake Union. It's a gritty, funky district with cafes, taverns and not much parking.

14 Carrot Cafe

2305 Eastlake Avenue E.
324-1442

Breakfast, lunch.
7-3 M-F, 7-4 S-S.
Some vegetarian choices.
Credit cards accepted.

A Seattle breakfast institution since 1978, the 14 Carrot Cafe was the first of the three Julia restaurants. Julia Miller sold it in 1991 to concentrate her efforts on her thriving Wallingford and Ballard eateries. Terri Proios now owns the place, and has kept the popular menu largely the same, but has made some improvements to the old structure. The clientele is mixed, with high school and college kids vying for tables with middle-aged folks. Music might be R.E.M. or Bach. Two adjoining dining rooms include square and round wooden tables and local artworks. The food is health-oriented (Proios says the most popular food here is sprouts: they show up on everything), but there are plenty of meat dishes and hamburgers. The restaurant plans eventually to expand the hours (no dinner menu is planned; it would be a night-time coffee house) and add live music. Seattle magazine gave the homey place a runner-up award for best breakfast restaurant in town.

The tofu breakfast ($4.25) is a winner: chunks of tofu are sautéed with mushrooms, onions and a dash of ginger-sake-soy sauce, and served with grilled potatoes, toast or an English muffin. Tahitian toast is one of the most sought-after dishes: sourdough bread is filled with sesame-butter, dipped in egg and grilled; it's served with fruit and yogurt (one slice for $4.25, two for $5). Fruit cups, pancakes and omelets also are available.

At lunch, you can get a nutburger with all kinds of toppings. The base is $4.25; salsa, sprouts and onions are free toppings, while others, such as avocado, cost 50 or 75 cents. The banquet salad ($4.25) includes mixed greens, cabbage, carrots, sprouts, sunflower seeds and soy nuts; the banquet plus ($6) adds tomato, green pepper, mushrooms, avocado, almonds, cheddar and swiss cheese. Other dishes are ginger tofu, tofu curry and lasagna.

Other Choices

Than Ying (2241 Eastlake Avenue E., 322-7173) opened in 1992 in the same building that once housed A Small Cafe, a Thai restaurant with a more healthful focus (they even served brown rice) than the newcomer. Still, Than Ying offers a half-dozen soups and entrées (each $5.50), including sautéed vegetables with basil, vegetable curry with coconut milk, and hot and sour tofu soup with vegetables, lemon grass and chile paste. Open 10-10 M-F, 4-10 S-S. Credit cards accepted.

Pro Body Fitness (2501 Eastlake Avenue E., 324-3713), in Eastlake Plaza, a small shopping center, sports a juice bar in addition to supplements, fitness supplies and beds for tanning. The bar carries several drinks, depending on the availability of produce. Some standards are carrot, carrot-apple, carrot-spinach and apple-orange. Other options might be raspberry-apple, apple-grape-blueberry or orange-pineapple. Most drinks are $2 or $2.50. Spirulina or celery are 50 cents extra. Both locals and athletes hang out here. Open 10-7 M-F, 10-5 Sat, 10-3 Sun.

Queen Anne

The options for vegetarian fare atop Queen Anne — a mostly residential neighborhood — are more limited than down the hill to the south in Lower Queen Anne, near the Seattle Center. Queen Anne lost one of Seattle's finest places for wholesome, mostly vegetarian Asian food when Hahn's Southeast Asian Cuisine closed its doors in 1993.

Still, Queen Anne has a couple of winners, most notably Pirosmani, a fancy Georgian/Mediterranean restaurant that replaces Hahn's.

Pirosmani

2220 Queen Anne Avenue N.
285-3360

Dinner.
5-10 Tu-Sat.
Several vegetarian choices.
Credit cards accepted.

Pirosmani's owners claim it is one of only three restaurants in the nation (the others are in New York and Washington, D.C.) to offer food from the former Soviet republic of Georgia. In an old Queen Anne two-story home, it's an elegant and pricey restaurant that blends cuisine from the new country (in the agriculturally abundant southern portion of the onetime superpower) and the Mediterranean, a region whose foods are similar to Georgia's. The restaurant takes its name from the republic's most famous artist, Niko Pirosmani (1862-1918), many of whose paintings hang on the red walls in the two dining rooms that make up Pirosmani. Racks display wines (none actually from Georgia) beside the front entrance.

The menu includes plenty of meat dishes, but some of the restaurant's workers are vegetarians, and they've developed interesting vegetable creations. The menu changes seasonally. Opened in 1993, the restaurant planned to be open for dinner Sunday and for lunch sometime in the future.

Most of the meatless choices on the spring menu come among the appetizers ($3.25 to $7.50). Georgian starters include khachapuri and spinach pkhali (Georgian cheese bread made with a blend of mozzarella and feta, and spinach paté with walnuts, cilantro, garlic and onion), badrijani nigvzit and gadazelili (eggplant folded over a puree of walnuts, cilantro and garlic, and farmer's cheese with mint, served with Georgian flatbread). From the Mediterranean half of the menu, try the mixed greens salad or panzanella (an Italian peasant bread salad with tomato, cucumber, lemon, herbs and extra-virgin olive oil).

Two meatless entrées are featured: from Georgia, ajapsandali ($13), a vegetable stew made with eggplant, tomatoes, peppers, potatoes, cilantro and tarragon, and from Italy, the vegetarian mixed country plate ($14.95), with panzanella, grilled mazithra (a Greek cheese), badrijani nigvzit and caponata (eggplant relish).

Other Choices

The Santa Fe Cafe's Blue Mesa (2205 Queen Anne Avenue N., 282-6644), a companion to the Santa Fe Cafe sitdown restaurants in Ravenna and Phinney Ridge, offers Southwestern takeout fare and gifts. Options include salsas, salads such as wild rice and fiesta corn, and appetizers like artichoke ramekin. Open 11-7 Sat-W, 11-8 Th-F. Credit cards accepted.

Thailand on Queen Anne (1517 Queen Anne Avenue N., 283-3663) dispenses eight vegetarian choices for $5 to $5.50 each, including pad pak kuammit (pan-fried mixed vegetables), Thailand tofu (topped with peanut sauce and spinach) and hot garden (vegetables and tofu in a hot curry sauce). Open 11:30-10 M-F, 3:30-11 Sat, 3:30-10 Sun. Credit cards accepted.

Capitol Hill

One of Seattle's more trendy neighborhoods, Capitol Hill combines impressive mansions, outstanding shopping and dining and a vocal gay community. Capitol Hill has two main shopping streets: Broadway Avenue and, several blocks east, East 15th Street. On Broadway you'll find more restaurants and action. East 15th is more laid back, but claims decent book shops and clothing boutiques.

If you can't find something you like to eat on Capitol Hill, then you don't like food. Almost every kind of cuisine is represented here. The best places include the ultra-hip and almost all-vegetarian Gravity Bar; the Mandarin Restaurant for fantastic vegan Chinese food; the Cause Célèbre Cafe for hearty vegetarian American fare; Bombay Taj, with its excellent Indian lunch buffet, and Macheezmo Mouse for healthful Mexican fast food. Thai restaurants abound.

Gravity Bar

415 Broadway E.
325-7186

Breakfast, lunch, dinner.
8-10 M-Th, 8-11 F-Sat, 9-10 Sun.
Mostly vegetarian; many vegan choices.
Credit cards accepted.

One of two Gravity Bars (the other is downtown, near Pike Place Market), this serves some of Seattle's finest vegetarian food. But a key ingredient for successful dining at this funky establishment is patience. If the food weren't so good and the atmosphere weren't so electrifying, you might write the place off because of its snail's pace when it's overcrowded. (Incidentally, the larger downtown Gravity Bar seems to move more quickly.)

This Gravity Bar, which opened in 1987 just inside the front entrance to the Shops at Broadway, is a bright, modern airy space with large windows that allow patrons to watch all the interesting characters who stroll along Broadway. All the tables resemble upside-down cones and emit light at the top surface. Rock and roll music blares from the speakers. If you sit at the counter (you have to put your legs in a rather strange position, tucked back underneath you), you'll see the large displays of fruits and vegetables ready to be juiced. Gravity Bar serves some 66 variations, hot and cold, plus herbal teas, soy milk and caffeinated drinks. Popular juices include pink flamingo ($3.75), made with apple, lemon, banana, yogurt and strawberries; Saturn return ($4.50), with carrot, celery, apple, ginger and a teaspoon of spirulina, and seven-year spinach ($2.25 for 10 ounces, $3.50 for 16), with carrot, celery and spinach.

Breakfast dishes (most $3 to $6) range from the Gravity porridge and muesli with fresh fruit to sesame rice with tofu and eggs roma (scrambled eggs with feta cheese, sun-dried tomatoes and chopped spinach over rice). Lunch and dinner are much the same as at the downtown Gravity Bar (see Page 5). Favorites include the tempeh burger ($4) and the spicy noodle salad ($5.50), a tasty concoction of buckwheat soba noodles, hiziki seaweed and vegetables, dressed with toasted sesame oil and hot peppers, and garnished with avocado and tomato slices. The savvy menu informs you of what is vegan and what is not. For a good selection of fruit-sweetened baked goods, see the blackboard (which also details daily soup specials).

The Mandarin Restaurant

125 15th Avenue E.
325-1010

Lunch, dinner.
11:30-10:30 M-F, 5-10:30 S-S.
Many vegan selections.
Credit cards accepted.

Come to this Capitol Hill eatery for excellent vegan meals prepared in the traditional "Buddhist monk style" of old China. Here you can order duck or chicken dishes that are so authentic that the fake poultry (actually, a meat analog made of wheat gluten) appears to have skin on it. Some vegetarians balk when they receive these dishes, only to be told by Cathy Jones, the Chinese-American proprietor, "No, no! It's not meat! You can really eat it!" She reports that 60 to 70 percent of the meals she serves are vegetarian. In fact, the meat analogs have been such a hit that the Mandarin Restaurant recently shrunk the meat, poultry and seafood portions of its menu and increased the number of vegetarian entrées. The Mandarin is not as well known as Bamboo Garden, which also serves vegan Chinese food, but you'll do well not to overlook this place.

The decor is pleasant, for the most part. The Mandarin Restaurant combines attractive wooden walls and Chinese paintings and wood carvings with tacky steaming neon teapots on the ceiling. The dining room is spacious and brightly lit. Kids love the multi-tiered fountain in the middle of the restaurant, with its dozens of bright orange goldfish.

You can start your meal with one of five soups ($3.50 to $5): "meatball" fensi, spinach bean curd, hot and sour, egg flower or sizzling rice, so called because the waitress puts the white rice in the vegetable and gluten chunk soup at your table, and it sizzles for a few moments. The vegetarian potstickers ($4.25), served on a bed of lettuce with a dipping bowl of soy sauce, are tasty dumplings filled with water chestnuts, scallions and seasonings. Of course, you can order the usual fried won tons and vegetarian spring rolls ($2.95 per order).

The real prizes are the entrées ($7 to $9). The autumn duck is a personal favorite: stir-fried with vegetables, it comes in a spicy sauce including soy and hoisin (a mixture of soybeans, garlic, chile peppers and spices). Cathy says her most celebrated dish is the emperor's delight, an assortment of faux "meats" and vegetables in a special sauce. Vegetarian mongolian beef and clay pot tofu also are standards. Mu shu vegetables are flour pancakes stuffed with stir-fried eggs and vegetables (they'll do it minus the eggs, if you ask). Far East abalone sounds like an especially interesting dish, based as it is on a kind of shellfish found along the coastlines of California, Mexico and Japan. You can also try vegetarian almond fried chicken.

The Globe Cafe and Bakery

1531 14th Avenue E.
324-8815

Lunch, dinner, weekend brunch.
11-9 M-F, 10-10 S-S.
Almost entirely vegan.
No credit cards.

A hit especially with the young crowd, the Globe Cafe serves sizable proportions of good food for a decent price. The establishment's decor is hardly beautiful — it's located in a gritty, semi-industrial area — but it has a lot of character. Strange old mirrors are on the walls next to many of the booths, and weird lampshades hover above many of the tables. An assortment of colorful globes is scattered about the cafe. The works by local artists change monthly, and poetry readings are offered every other Friday night. You order your food at the counter at the back of the hodgepodge dining room, where diners have an open view of the busy kitchen. The only items that aren't vegan are the pastries on the upper left shelf of the deli counter and the milk and cream used in the caffeinated drinks.

Brunch, served from 10 to 2 weekends, includes much hearty fare ($4 to $6): scrambled tofu and veggies, served with homefries and toast, is a favorite; french toast is made with homemade potato bread, dipped in a cardamom-spiced eggless batter and served with maple syrup. Corn grits and black beans come with salsa and corn tortillas. An assortment of vegan pancakes includes veggiejacks, cooked with grated vegetables and served with apple butter, fruitjacks, gingerjacks made with grated ginger, diced apples and currants, and sunnyjacks, filled with grated lemons and poppyseeds. Among baked goods ($1 or $2) are wheat-free and sugar-free banana bread, cinnamon rolls and scones.

The lunch and dinner menu (in the $4 to $6 range) features organic steamed veggies with brown rice and lemon-tahini dressing, the global salad with bread and choice of dressing, and Indian dal with rice, chutney and a piece of chapati bread. A cup of the daily soup is $1.65; a bowl is $3. A slice of bread is $1 extra. The bean dish of the day comes with salsa, cornbread and steamed greens. The daily sandwich might be falafel, a burrito or a tofu sandwich. Special entrées bear a similar international flavor, and might represent Thai, Mexican or Middle Eastern cuisine, depending on who's cooking among the large staff.

The Cause Célèbre Cafe

524 15th Avenue E.
323-1888

Breakfast, lunch, dinner, Sunday brunch.
8-9 M-F, 9-9 Sat, 9-5 Sun.
About half vegetarian, with many vegan choices.
Credit cards accepted.

Here is an attractive and homey restaurant that serves excellent vegetarian dishes at very reasonable prices (under $5 for dinner entrées). It's at once casual and classy: water arrives at your table in a wine carafe. The tables are wooden with country-style chairs. In nice weather, you can eat out front on a large patio under the trees. Because many vegans visit the Cause Célèbre, the ownership planned to alter its menu in 1993 to indicate clearly which items are vegan or can be made vegan. It would be a welcome step for a restaurant that traditionally has focused more on the needs of ovo-lacto vegetarians than those who eschew animal products altogether.

Sunday brunch is almost entirely a vegetarian affair, though most of the dishes (in the $3 to $5 range) include eggs or cheese. The special omelets are made with three eggs and served with red finn homefries and 12-grain toast. You have a choice of three variations: sautéed onions, green peppers, cheddar cheese and salsa; spinach, feta cheese and garlic, or cheddar cheese, parmesan cheese and homemade marinara sauce. Or you can build your own omelet ($3.99, plus 35 cents for each addition such as broccoli, onion, avocado, garlic or cream cheese). The orange-pecan waffle sounds like a treat, made with whole wheat flour, buttermilk, eggs, pecans and orange rind. Vegans should stick to the scrambled tofu, served with red finn homefries and 12-grain toast, or the scrambled tofu delight, made with tomatoes, mushrooms, olives, broccoli and garlic (be sure to ask for your toast unbuttered).

Lunch and dinner menus here are largely the same, though the prices are slightly higher for dinner (most are about $4 for lunch, $5 for dinner). The spinach nutburger is one of the finest available meatless patties in Seattle. It's made with spinach, walnuts, carrots, rice, falafel and onions, and is served on a seven-grain bun with vegetable garnish and corn tortilla chips. The daily soup is usually vegetarian: a cup is $1.25, a bowl with a roll is $2.25. Soup, salad and a roll are $3.25. Marinated raw vegetables blended lightly with oil and vinegar make up the Persian salad ($1.50 or $2.25); the tabbouleh salad (uncommonly tasty) costs the same. Vegetarian entrées include lasagna, and you can choose two of the following to fill it: onions, spinach, broccoli, mushrooms, olives or bell pepper. The eggplant parmesan is baked in a red sauce and covered with a medley of cheeses. The vegan tofu and vegetable stir-fry is sautéed with garlic and served on a bed of brown rice. Rice and beans (lunch only) is completed with cheese, salsa, tomatoes, onions, olives and sour cream.

Bombay Taj

130 Broadway E.
329-9005

Lunch, dinner.
11:30-3, 5-10 M-Sat, 12-3, 5-10 Sun.
Several vegetarian dishes.
Credit cards accepted.

Vegetarians who like spicy Indian food won't go wrong here. The fare is above average, though the decor is ordinary. If you're new to Indian cuisine, a good way to sample its variety of tastes and spices is to try the all-you-can-eat lunch buffet. For $4.95, you can choose from two vegetarian dishes, plus dal (the traditional lentil soup that accompanies most Indian meals), salad and naan, a leavened Indian bread cooked in the tandoor oven.

You can also choose from the menu (prices are the same for lunch and dinner: $5 to $7). Mixed vegetables cooked with various Indian spices make up Bombay navratan curry. Also a favorite is the eggplant bharta—whole eggplant baked over an open flame, mashed, seasoned with herbs and then sautéed with onions. The saag aloo is a tasty combination of fresh spinach and potatoes cooked with onions, tomato and spices. An unusual Indian dish offered here is the vegetable pastarama, mixed vegetables cooked with ginger and garlic and served with noodles and sauce. Vegetable biryani, a basmati rice dish, is a meal in itself.

No Indian meal is complete without such appetizers as vegetable samosas, deep-fried pastries filled with spiced peas, or breads. Bombay Taj has the standard list of choices, like naan, aloo paratha (whole wheat bread stuffed with spiced potatoes and cooked with butter in the tandoor oven) and paneer kulcha, leavened bread stuffed with cheese and spices.

End your meal with rasmali, a fatty dessert made of fresh cream cheese soaked in sweetened milk with pistachio topping; rasgula, a fresh cream-cheese cake soaked in a sweet syrup, or kheer, lightly sweetened basmati rice cooked with milk, almonds and pistachios.

Macheezmo Mouse Mexican Cafe

211 Broadway E.
325-0072

Lunch, dinner.
11-10 M-Sat, 12-10 Sun.
Several vegetarian, vegan choices.
No credit cards.

Macheezmo Mouse is a fast-food eatery that many health-minded people would like to see in cities and at interstate highway interchanges throughout the country (as of now, you'll have to settle for Macheezmo Mouse's three Seattle and seven Portland locations). Here you can choose from plenty of low-fat vegetarian dishes, with or without cheese. The produce is fresh, the prices fair, the portions large; rice is brown, and cheese is low-fat. Macheezmo Mouse uses no lard, M.S.G., preservatives, colorings or additives. A welcome change from the usual fast-food burger joints, the chain offers several savvy pamphlets to let you know about the fat and calorie content of various menu items, tips on ordering for maximum health benefits, and information for diabetics. One brochure outlines all of the ingredients in each of the restaurant's dishes and sauces.

Most dishes cost $2.65 to $4.75. The veggie burrito comes in either a flour or whole wheat tortilla filled with brown rice, black beans and jack cheese, topped with "Boss" sauce, salsa and mixed greens. (The menu informs you that 10 percent of its 601 calories come from fat.) The veggie taco salad combines greens, brown rice, black beans, jack cheese, chips, guacamole, salsa and dressing. The bean and cheese enchiladas are smothered in a red chili sauce and served with sour cream, Mexican cheese, greens, salsa and cilantro. Vegans will rub their stomachs in satisfaction after eating the veggie plate, a mixture of brown rice, black beans, greens, marinated vegetables, guacamole, salsa, flour tortilla and cilantro.

Foods come lightly spiced here, but you can add more zest at the salsa bar with chunky jalapeno green sauce, sliced jalapeno, salsa or roma tomatoes, onions and cilantro.

Zula East African Restaurant

916 E. John Street
322-0852

Lunch, dinner.
5-11 M-F, 11-11 S-S.
Several vegan selections.
Credit cards accepted.

This old, well-worn Capitol Hill home just off Broadway has quite a history. For a while, a restaurant here served West African barbecued meats. That closed, and a junk store took its place. In 1992, Zula opened, serving excellent Ethiopian food. The decor here is simple and a strange blend of American and Ethiopian influences: several of the wood tables have American newspaper clippings from the 1930s laminated into their surfaces, while exotic and colorful paintings of Ethiopia's landscape hang on the walls of the two dining areas. Large windows look onto John Street.

Best of the seven meatless options is the vegetarian combination. For $6.95, you get to sample small portions of all the others (which, by themselves, range from $2.50 to $4.50), served atop spongy ingera bread that you use to scoop up the food. The combination offers so much food that two could share it. The tastiest dish is birsen-tsebhi, a spicy stew of red lentils. Shiro is mild split peas cooked with turmeric, onions and ginger. Kinche is a light bulghur dish cooked with butter and spices. However, during the Ethiopian fasting season in the several weeks leading up to Easter, the dish is cooked in oil instead of butter. The other vegetarian dishes always are cooked in oil.

The friendly Ethiopian chef confides that his fresh fruit tart ($2.95), made with an almond base shell and filled with custard topping and glazed fruits, is much loved by his customers.

Rasa Malaysia

401 Broadway E.
328-8882

Lunch, dinner.
12-8:30 M-F, 12-6 S-S.
Half vegetarian; several vegan choices.
No credit cards.

Here's another of the five tiny Southeast Asian restaurants that make up the Rasa Malaysia chain. A little stand in the middle of the Shops at Broadway mall, this is a fun place to eat, and there's a lot of action to watch. The food here is not haute cuisine, but the large portions will satisfy your appetite.

These lunch dishes each cost $3: mee goreng (stir-fried noodles with peanut sauce), sayor lodeh (vegetable curry over steamed white rice), ma poh tofu (steamed tofu in bean sauce) and gado gado salad (steamed vegetables and tofu with peanut sauce). Vegetarian potstickers are six for $2.50. Fresh fruit quenchers cost $1.50 each, and include strawberry-banana, ginger-lemon cooler and melon-lime. You can eat your meal at one of the tables in the mall's indoor courtyard.

Thai Garden Restaurant
613 Broadway E.
726-9058

Lunch, dinner.
11:30-10 Sun-Th, 11:30-11 F-Sat.
Several vegetarian choices.
Credit cards accepted.

More elegant than the average Thai restaurant, Thai Garden's dining room harbors white tablecloths and lots of flowers, and expansive windows looking onto the street.

The selection of vegetarian dishes here is large. Good choices among the 13 dishes (in the $5 to $6 range) are ginger tofu; spicy tofu, cooked with chile paste and vegetables; rama vegetables in a peanut sauce; B.B. broccoli with tofu and a black-bean sauce, and see ew jay, stir-fried wide noodles with soy sauce, egg, tofu and broccoli.

Other Choices

La Cocina (432 Broadway E., 323-1675) makes some good lard-free dishes, and even uses vegetarian eco meat, a meatless soy vegetable mix (made by Ecotrition Foods, a Whidbey Island company) that can be substituted for any meat product on the menu. The huge veggie burrito ($6.30) proved quite good during one visit, with the eco meat substituted for the cheese. Served with rice and black beans, the whole wheat tortilla burrito was stuffed with onions, bell peppers, tomatoes, broccoli, zucchini, carrots and mushrooms, and smothered with salsa. Open 11-11 M-Th, 11-12 F, 11:30-12 Sat, 11:30-10 Sun. Credit cards accepted.

For unusually healthful pizzas and other Italian items, try **Testa Rossa** (210 Broadway E., 328-0878), a pleasantly modern second-floor restaurant with a balcony overlooking activity on the lively street below. The pizzas are the stars here, though they're pricey ($11.50 gets a small for one or two people; a large, which serves three or four, costs $15.95. Stuffed, the prices are $16.25 and $21). Vegetarian choices include basil pesto; black beans, poblano chilies, corn, cilantro and a mild salsa; baked eggplant, roasted red peppers and black olives, and spinach-ricotta soufflé with toasted walnuts. Some of the pizzas can be made without cheese. There's also a decent choice of appetizers, salads and pastas (including fettuccine with mushrooms in a soy-honey-garlic sauce for $8.95). For lunch (served until 4:30), sample the all-you-can-eat vegetarian pizza special for $4.95. Add a buck, and you can have all-you-can-eat soup (usually, it's vegan) and salad. Open 11-10 M-W, 11-11 Th, 11-12 F-Sat, 1-10 Sun. Credit cards accepted.

The Surrogate Hostess (746 19th Avenue E., 324-1944) might be the only restaurant in town that could get away with storing tomato paste and other ingredients in shelves in the main dining area. That's part of its informal charm. Add to that the long wooden cafeteria tables that seat 10 or more (and several parties at once), and you've got a cafe that is quintessentially laid-back Seattle. Breakfast includes numerous egg dishes, pancakes, baked goods and so forth. For lunch and dinner, you can order the vegetarian paté, made of mushrooms and walnuts, or the vegetarian quiche ($3.25), which might be spinach, onion and feta. Several salads are offered for $1.75-$3.50; they could be oriental vegetable salad with orange-ginger vinaigrette, pasta primavera with spring vegetables and a creamy parmesan dressing and orchid noodles with sesame soy, chile flakes, bean sprouts, radishes and scallions. Dinners range from $6 to $8, and sometimes include stir-fried tofu, calzones or a pasta with a meatless sauce. Open 6:30-9 M-Sun. No credit cards.

Just around the corner is **The Surrogate Hostess Retail** store (1907 E. Aloha, 328-0908), which offers take-out items from the restaurant plus other foods and kitchenware. Frozen entrées include spanakopita, vegetable lasagna and macaroni and cheese. Open 8-6 M-F, 8-3 S-S.

Karam's Mediterranean Cuisine (340 15th Avenue E., 324-2370), offers vegetarian appetizers ($3.95-$5.75) such as tabbouleh, baba ghanoush, hummus, karamage (homemade cream cheese consisting of goat milk, garlic and peppermint, topped with oregano, sumac, thyme, sesame seeds and olive oil) and tossed salad. The falafel entrée ($9.95) is served with soup or salad. Open 5-10 Tu-Sat. Credit cards accepted.

Ali Baba Restaurant (707 E. Pine Street, 325-2299) provides a lengthy list of Mediterranean appetizers ($2.50 to $3.50) and entrées ($4.50 to $7). For starters, choose from hummus, baba ghanoush, ful mudames, zahra (deep-fried cauliflower), falafel or tabbouleh. An appetizer plate with most of these is $10.99. The vegetarian combination special includes falafel, grape leaves filled with rice and veggies, hummus and soup or salad and bread. Open 11-10 M-F, 12-10 Sat, 5-9 Sun. Credit cards accepted.

Try **The Oven** (213 Broadway E., 328-2951) for good Middle Eastern fast food in a casual diner setting (prices are in the $3 to $6 range). The mosaique yields sautéed carrots, green peppers, onions, broccoli and cauliflower over white rice topped with a garlic and lemon sauce. Or try the falafel plate or hummus. The Greek salad tops mixed vegetables with feta cheese. A nine-inch vegetarian pizza with mushrooms, onions and green peppers is also available. The vegetarian spinach pie, with onions, olive oil and spices, is a good choice. Open 11-10 Sun-Th, 11-11 F-Sat. No credit cards.

Cafe Cielo (611 Broadway E., 324-9084) is an elegant and pricey jazz bistro that serves Mediterranean fare. The best thing going here is the long list of tapas — popular appetizers served in bars and restaurants in Spain — such as grilled mushrooms marinated with herbs ($3.50) and eggplant parmesan ($3.95). The soup of the day is usually made with vegetable stock, and might be ginger and carrot, black bean, butternut squash or roasted garlic. Vegetarian entrées are less plentiful. For lunch, you can get a grilled eggplant sandwich ($5.50), with choice of mixed green salad or french fries, and the soup of the day. Four interesting pizzas cost $8.25 to $9. Dinner includes pappardella (a wide noodle) with wild mushrooms sautéed with mixed herbs, shallots and garlic, tossed in a light mushroom-butter sauce ($11.95, or $5.95 as an appetizer); fettuccine cielo ($11.50/$5.95), in a nut pesto with caramelized onions, prosciutto, fennel and jalapeno, and linguini pesto tossed with walnuts ($10.50/$5.25). Every day, the bistro features live music, including piano and guitar soloists. Open 11-2:30, 5-10:30 M-Th, 11-2:30, 5-12 F, 10-2:30, 5-12 Sat, 10-2:30 Sun. Credit cards accepted.

Torrey's Eggs Cetera (220 Broadway E., 325-3447) doles out lots and lots of egg dishes, and a fine vegan burger. Substitute the eco pattie for any of the regular burger options ($4-$5), such as the California burger with avocado slices. The homey restaurant also has occasional vegetarian soups and specials (check the board as you enter). Open 6:30-9 M-F, 7:30-9 weekends. Credit cards accepted.

Bangkok Thai Cuisine (112 Broadway E., 324-7804) offers two vegetarian appetizers and five entrées (in the $5 range). The garden delight tops sautéed vegetables with peanut sauce; phat phed tofu with vegetables is cooked in a chile sauce. Open 11:30-10 M-Th, 11:30-11 F, 3-11 Sat, 3-10 Sun. Credit cards accepted.

Angel's Thai Cuisine (235 Broadway E., 328-0515) serves eight vegetarian dishes ($4 to $6), including spring rolls, hot summer jay (stir-fried vegetables and tofu in a red curry sauce), vegetables in wine sauce with garlic, and phad Thai. Open 11:30-10 M-Th, 11:30-11 F, 12-11 Sat, 12-10 Sun.

Siam on Broadway (616 Broadway E., 324-0892) is one of the more popular Thai restaurants on Capitol Hill, and has a small vegetarian menu with five entrées. Fried rice ($5.95) includes vegetables, dried tofu, egg and a touch of sesame oil. The phad Thai is $5.75. 11:30-10 M-Th, 11:30-11 F, 5-11 Sat, 5-10 Sun. Credit cards accepted.

It's not the ordinary bar that serves vegetable burgers and tabbouleh. But it's a sign of the strength of the vegetarian scene on Capitol Hill that the **Deluxe Bar and Grill** (625 Broadway E., 324-9697) serves these dishes and more along with the traditional burger plates. The vegan burger costs $6.75. (If you want it to be really vegan, tell them to skip the cheddar cheese they ordinarily put on top.) Among other options in the $5 to $7 range are tabbouleh, a fit-for-life veggie pita with mayonnaise, a garden veggie sandwich with cream cheese and Davee C's ginger honey stir-fry, served with bread sticks. Deluxe baked potatoes start at $4.10. The kitchen is open from 11-1 M-Sat, 11-midnight Sun. Credit cards accepted.

The **Bacchus Restaurant** (806 E. Roy Street, 325-2888), a block west of Broadway, reserves a significant portion of its menu for vegetarian items. Breakfast includes omelets and pancakes. Lunch and dinner bring appetizers ($4-$5) such as hummus, melitzano (eggplant, garlic, olive oil and herbs), skordalia (mashed potatoes, garlic, olive oil and herbs), kolokithaka tiganita (pan-fried zucchini with garlic and white wine served with tzatziki) and saganaki (pan-fried cheese flamed at your table with brandy). Entrées are $5 to $7 for lunch and $6 to $9 for dinner. They include spanakopita, vegetables sautéed in lemon, wine and butter, vegetarian pastichio (mashed potatoes, zucchini and noodles in a tomato sauce topped with a béchamel sauce and parmesan cheese) and vegetarian moussaka, which tops layers of eggplant and beans with parmesan cheese and a béchamel sauce. Check out the beautiful murals that cover all the walls: they were created by Russian artist Vladimir Pavlovich Shkurkin and illustrate a folktale by Pushkin. Open 11-11 M-Th, 11-midnight F, 9-midnight Sat, 9-11 Sun. Credit cards accepted.

The Byzantion (601 Broadway E., 325-7580) serves assorted Greek dishes. Most include meat, but there are a handful of vegetarian choices such as hummus or tzatziki ($3.50 each), feta, olives and peppers ($3.50) and aginares ($5.95), which are pan-fried artichokes. Also available are omelets for lunch ($4 to $5) and pasta dishes for lunch and dinner ($5 to $7). Open 11-11 M-F, 9-11 weekends. Credit cards accepted.

La Salsa (2355 1/2 10th Avenue E., 325-7482), at the north end of Capitol Hill, serves lardless and preservative-free dishes for vegetarians. A vegetarian burrito ($4.80) comes with guacamole and sour cream. The vegetarian tostada with avocado slices costs $3.95. Enchiladas are $3.25, while tacos are $1.95.

The 19th Avenue Bakery and Cafe (615 19th Avenue E., 720-7031), an elegant eatery that serves some vegetarian soups, salads and sandwiches, opened in early 1993. It's a very clean and modern place with green tables and pale yellow walls adorned with artistic black and white photographs. The cafe offers a few outdoor seats, too. The minestrone soup ($2.95/$3.95) is offered daily and is vegan; the other soup of the day sometimes is vegetarian. Rotating salads ($3.95 or $4.95) might include Chinese vermicelli, garlic-pesto-romano tortellini or garbanzo, fennel and caper. The veggie sandwich ($3.95) is made with hummus; the 19th Ave. specialty includes mozzarella, sun-dried tomatoes and pesto on sourdough. Open 6:30-5:30 M-F, 7-5:30 Sat, 8-4 Sun. No credit cards.

First Hill

The area just south of Capitol Hill and west of downtown is home to two Ethiopian restaurants and a Thai eatery.

Kokeb Ethiopian Restaurant

926 12th Avenue
322-0485

Lunch, dinner.
11-2, 5-10 M-F, 5-10 S-S.
Several vegan options.
Credit cards accepted.

The first Ethiopian restaurant to open in Seattle (back in the early '80s), Kokeb boasts that its Ethiopian food is "considered the best in the nation." Lofty words, but the place, near Seattle University, does please the palate. Its large, spacious dining room usually seems uncrowded (although many Ethiopian Americans visit at night). The TV often is blaring over the tiny bar at the back of the room.

You can choose from eight vegetable entrees ($6.95, or $4.95 for a half-portion) as well as 16 vegan and vegetarian side dishes ($2.50 each). If it's your first time trying Ethiopian cuisine, the combination platter, called yatakilt beyayenetu ($7.95 per person), allows you to sample all eight vegetable entrees. No knives and forks are used here: food is served on injera bread, the round and spongy stuff that you tear with your fingers and use to scoop up the vegetarian stews and salads. Entrees include pureed split-pea stew, spicy cabbage, carrots and potatoes, and mildly spicy powdered pea stew.

Among side dishes are homemade Ethiopian cottage cheese, diced tomato salad with onions and hot pepper and hotly spiced yogurt, as well as smaller portions of the main dishes. Desserts aren't quite healthful, but sound interesting (though not uniquely Ethiopian): the kahlua cheesecake ($3) is made with a cream-cheese filling, crushed chocolate cookie crust and topped with a sour-cream blend. Lemon cake also is $3.

Addis Cafe

1224 E. Jefferson
325-7805

Breakfast, lunch, dinner.
6-10 M-Sun.
A few vegan choices.
Credit cards accepted.

Though less well-known than Kokeb, a few blocks to the north, Addis Cafe is a thriving neighborhood restaurant that prepares excellent Ethiopian food. For the less adventurous, the tiny restaurant also offers a separate menu of American dishes (mostly for carnivores).

What's nice about the Addis Cafe is the strong community feeling that seems to exist here. Getahun Birru and his wife, Metti Mulugeta -- who opened in 1992 after moving here from Ethiopia in 1990 -- are outgoing and friendly. They get to know their customers, a mix of both Ethiopian Americans and (to a lesser degree) students from nearby Seattle University. The decor is simple and the building is somewhat run-down. A breakfast counter is a good place to sit and chat with a friend or the staff. Cigarettes from Ethiopia and the U.S. are in a rack on the wall. Under the glass covering each table are flyers announcing upcoming Ethiopian music and theater performances at nearby halls.

At $5.50, the sampler of Ethiopian vegetarian dishes is the best deal. You get three dishes plus a salad (tomatoes and hot jalapeno peppers) atop several pieces of spongy injera bread (you'd better bring at least two stomachs to finish the massive amount of food). The spicy red lentils is the best of the three, but collard greens and a split-pea stew also are delicious.

Breakfast includes American standards such as omelets, egg dishes and breakfast sandwiches (all with eggs, most with meat), as well as a few Ethiopian specials (one fava bean dish is served with French bread).

Other Choices

Ayutthaya Thai Cuisine (727 E. Pike Street, 324-8833) offers nine vegetarian dishes in the $5 to $6 range. Among them are naked bathing rama (peanut chile sauce over spinach) and bean cake panan (vegetables and tofu sauteed with coconut milk and dry curry). Open 11:30-2:30 M-F, 5-9:30 M-Th, 5-10 F and Sat. Credit cards accepted.

The Central Area/Yesler Terrace

The Central Area and Rainier Valley have few options for vegetarians. But both Assimba Ethiopian Cuisine in the Central Area and Vietnam's Pearl in Yesler Terrace are good places to get a tasty and inexpensive meal.

Assimba Ethiopian Cuisine

2920 E. Cherry Street
322-1019

Lunch, dinner.
11-9 M-Sun.
Several vegan choices.
No credit cards.

You often can gauge the quality of an ethnic restaurant by the number of natives who eat there. By that measure, Assimba might just be the best Ethiopian restaurant in town. The tiny, sparsely furnished eatery is almost always filled with Ethiopian Americans, who love to while away the time chatting with friends. The restaurant was opened in 1991 by Messeret Tessema, the head cook, and her husband, Messelu Ferede, an affable man who is there on the weekends when he has time off from his other job. The dining room holds only five tables, each with a plastic white tablecloth with colored stripes. The white walls are covered with colorful Ethiopian artifacts, tapestries and paintings on animal skins. Incense might be burning to scent the air, and Ethiopian music plays in the background.

Prices are inexpensive and the portions huge. All four vegetarian entrées (in the $5 to $6 range) are vegan, cooked in vegetable oil instead of butter. The ye kike wot is a rather spicy stew of boiled lentils in an onion, garlic, ginger and turmeric sauce. The atakilt combination mixes cabbage, potatoes and carrots. The ye timatim fitefit, a salad of tomatoes, onions and green peppers, is topped with a vinegary Ethiopian dressing. The ye shero wot blends ground peas with onions, tomatoes and green chilies. All entrées are served atop injera, the spongy bread that you tear apart and use to scoop up bites of the stews. The best thing to order is the combination plate ($6.45): that gets you sizable servings of the four aforementioned dishes plus one more (a stew of collard greens), with three pieces of injera. There is almost no way one person could eat so much food; two could share the plate comfortably.

Other Choices

Vietnam's Pearl (708 Rainier Avenue S., 726-1581), a contemporary and spacious restaurant, provides seven vegetarian entrées ($4.50-$5.50), including lemon grass mock chicken, fried tofu sauté with tomato sauce and meatless imperial roll with rice noodles. Tofu salad rolls and tofu sour soup also are offered. Open 11-10 M-F, 11-12 S-S. Credit cards accepted.

Madison Valley and Madison Park

Two of Seattle's top vegetarian restaurants are found in Madison Valley, a mostly residential neighborhood nestled between the University of Washington arboretum, the Central District and Capitol Hill. Cafe Flora offers perhaps the most elegant meatless fare in town, while Five Loaves dispenses pure vegan lunches, dinners and breads. Continue northwest along Madison Street to its end at Lake Washington, where you'll find a collection of trendy shops and restaurants, including Cactus, which serves inspired Southwestern fare.

Cafe Flora

2901 E. Madison Street
325-9100

Lunch, dinner, Saturday and Sunday brunch.
11-10 Tu-F, 9-2, 5-10 Sat, 9-2 Sun.
Strictly vegetarian; many vegan choices.
Credit cards accepted.

Seattle herbivores who want sophisticated vegetarian cuisine head straight for Cafe Flora, an immensely popular addition to the vegetarian scene upon its opening in 1991. Nowhere else in the Emerald City will you find such a selection of haute-cuisine meatless dishes. Meals are pricey and the portions sometimes small, but the food is art, and it *is* delicious. Because the fare is so inspiring and on the cutting edge, Cafe Flora appeals to a broad market, including many carnivores. A bright, sunny restaurant with handsome decor, giant windows to the street and a patio for warm-weather outdoor dining, Cafe Flora is most attractive to vegetarians who eat dairy products. Those who eschew all animal products can find some things to eat, and the kitchen staff will alter dishes when possible, but some vegans say they feel somewhat neglected here.

The menu changes weekly with wide variations between the seasons (prices range from $5 to $12). But you can always expect to find items like the grilled nutburger, a flavorful blend of grains, tofu, nuts and fresh herbs on a whole wheat bun (salsa or cheese are extra); spinach fettuccine tossed in olive oil and topped with sautéed eggplant, sweet peppers, julienned spinach and roma tomatoes in a garlic cream sauce; classic pizza, made with roma tomatoes, basil pesto and smoked mozzarella (from a cow or from soybeans) on an herbed crust, and various salads, including the "composed salad of three grains," a pilaf of quinoa, wheat berries, millet, sweet peppers, currants, onion and garlic in an herbed miso dressing, with mixed greens.

The winter menu includes such dishes as the Himalayan appetizer plate, a combination of dal croquettes, yogurt raita and curried garbanzo beans, with a salad of basmati rice, currants and almonds (served with eggplant pickles, coriander leaf chutney and pappadams); Oaxaca tacos, roasted flutes of corn tortillas filled with spicy mashed potatoes, cheddar and mozzarella, garnished with creme fraiche and feta and served with black-bean stew, pico de gallo and sautéed onions, and Italian-style seitan sandwich, grilled patties of seitan and

Italian herbs with marinated sweet peppers and red onion, served with sun-dried tomato mayonnaise on herbed foccacia.

Brunches (most items in the $5 to $9 range) attract large crowds, so it's best to be prepared to wait a little. At our autumn visit, the oversized menu included standards such as French-style omelets with roasted potatoes, muffin and fresh fruit; granola, fruit and muffin ($2.85), and buckwheat blueberry pancakes, served with banana butter and maple syrup. Also offered were the Oaxaca tacos, grilled nutburger and an open-face sandwich of roasted red peppers, pesto and grilled eggplant with a white-bean salad on the side. Southwestern-style zucchini fritters were served with chipotle butter, sautéed onions and green peppers. But some of us left a bit hungry, wondering if it was worth the tab.

A children's menu also is available, with such options (all under $4) as scrambled eggs with cheddar cheese and peanut-butter toast, nutty burger and spaghetti and tomato sauce.

Five Loaves Deli and Bakery

2719 E. Madison Street

726-7989

Breakfast, lunch, dinner.
7-6:30 M-Th, 10-2 Sun. Closed Sat. In summer, open 11-2:30 F.
Strictly vegan.
No credit cards.

It's not as upscale as Cafe Flora just down the street, but Five Loaves elicits great reviews, especially from vegans. This bakery with a vegan buffet is simple and unpretentious; its philosophical underpinnings come from the Seventh Day Adventist Church, which owns and operates it. The Adventists believe that you come closest to God when your mind is clear, and a good diet of low-fat, cholesterol-free foods like those served here is sure to elevate you spiritually. The small but charming dining area has large windows looking onto the street. A rack of health foods for sale divides a series of country tables and chairs. The food preparers are especially friendly and likely will engage you in all sorts of conversation. They're also highly skilled in the art of creating good dairy-free substitutes for ice cream, sour cream and cheese. If possible, come by here early when the bakers are preparing scrumptious breads and muffins. "Five" Loaves understates it: the bakery in fact offers at least 15 kinds of breads, such as whole wheat raisin, apricot-almond, French bread, and oat bran with sunflower seeds. All are made with whole grains and have no added oils, sugars or preservatives. Muffins are wheat-free, made with oat, barley and millet flours, applesauce for moisture, and fruit juice for sweetening.

The daily hot buffet, offered from 11 to 6:30, yields entrées, soups and fresh vegetables (mostly in the $3 to $6 range). Daily specials include enchilada frijoles on Monday, quiche on Tuesday, black beans and rice on Wednesday and lasagna on Thursday.

Or order directly from the menu such dishes as the super burrito, a huge tortilla loaded with beans, lettuce, avocado, tomato, olives and tofu sour cream topped with salsa and cheese made of cashews, or the sunburger, an oat patty served with the usuals on a fresh whole wheat bun, smothered with tahini and cashew cheese. The peanut-butter favorite is freshly ground peanut or almond butter, honey and bananas on date-nut or whole wheat bread. The falafel pita, with tomatoes, olives, lettuce and a hummus-tahini sauce, is made differently than the Middle Eastern variety: here, the usual garbanzo bean patties are made instead of tofu, walnuts and spinach. The daily soup might be corn chowder or cream of broccoli. Five Loaves also offers different kinds of salads by the pound, including tossed, pasta, potato, fruit and others, depending on the day.

Be sure to save room for the mouth-watering dairy- and sugar-free desserts. They include the specialty, a fruit cobbler, plus tapioca pudding made with fresh almond milk and layered with blackberry and strawberry fruit glaze, and "rice cream," a healthy alternative to ice cream made by the Five Loaves folks. It can be topped with blueberry, raspberry or carob sauce.

The Sunday brunch is really something special. One price lets you eat all you can from a medley of muffins, waffles and french toast topped with fruit sauces and rice cream, hash browns, scrambled tofu, fruit, fruit juice and more. Adults pay $7.39, while seniors get a break at $5.77. Children 7 to 11 pay $3.92; children younger than that pay 50 cents for each year.

Other Choices

Cactus Restaurant (4220 E. Madison Street, 324-4140) dispenses foods of Mexico and the Southwest, most of them vegetarian. Critics consistently give this trendy spot high marks. Tapas, the Spanish appetizers, are mostly under $5, and include grilled and marinated eggplant served with a spicy cilantro paste; a salad of roasted eggplant, squash, tomatoes, red peppers, garlic and herbs, and roasted red peppers marinated in wine vinaigrette with capers and olives, topped with goat cheese. The quinoa and cactus salads ($5.95 each) sound great. The former includes the quinoa grain, scallions, serrano chilies and carrots in a lime vinaigrette, on a bed of greens and garnished with avocado and tomatoes. The latter combines grilled cactus, roasted red peppers, jicama and other seasonal vegetables. Two entrées (both under $9) are vegetarian: the enchilada Santa Fe layers jack cheese, onions and red chile peppers in blue corn tortillas, topped with a fried egg, while the Navajo taco piles anasazi beans, cheese, greens, tomatoes, onions, guacamole and sour cream on Indian frybread. Open 11-2:30, 5:30-10 M-Sat, 5-9 Sun. Credit cards accepted.

Seward Park

Blessed with a location beside Lake Washington, Seward Park is a residential area dominated by a waterfront park of the same name. Other than the PCC, it has few vegetarian resources.

Puget Consumers' Co-op (5041 Wilson Avenue S., 723-2720) has a small deli that serves several good vegetarian salads. You can also choose from an assortment of pre-made veggie sandwiches from the refrigerator. Open 8-10 M-Sun.

Wallingford

Home of Bastyr College — the nation's only certified school for naturopaths — as well as a large number of progressive people who live in the area, Wallingford is a vegetarian hot spot. The main drag here, 45th Street, is lined for several blocks with boutiques and restaurants offering many different cuisines.

Health-conscious folks have greatly influenced the restaurants of Wallingford. Beso del Sol, a Mexican haunt, has stopped cooking its beans in animal lard by popular demand. At The Rosebud Cafe, vegetarian specials sell much faster than beef, chicken or fish — prompting management to devise a new menu with more vegetarian options. And so many vegetarians and health-minded people visit Kitaro Japanese Cuisine that the restaurant has added brown rice.

The best bets for vegetarians in Wallingford are the Blue Planet Cafe, a strictly meatless restaurant; the Honey Bear Bakery, a great people place that makes some of the best breads in Seattle, along with a daily selection of vegetarian soups and salads; Kabul Afghanistan Cuisine, with fantastic Asian spices, and Julia's in Wallingford, a favorite spot for Sunday brunch.

Blue Planet Cafe

2208 N. 45th Street
632-0750

Breakfast, lunch, dinner.
3-10 M, 11-10 Tu-Th, 11-11 F, 9-11 Sat, 9-10 Sun.
Strictly vegan.
Juice bar.
Credit cards accepted.

It's said that digestion works best when you're not stressed, a point not missed at the Blue Planet Cafe. At this pure vegetarian establishment, you truly can relax while you eat your meal. Back in the corner, they'll give you a free 10-minute massage during scheduled hours. Half the people who work at the Blue Planet are licensed massage therapists, explains owner John Blacksmith, who opened the restaurant in 1992 to the delight of local vegetarians.

But massage isn't the big attraction here. After some early disappointments, the Blue Planet has worked out most of the kinks and now offers outstanding American and international meatless dishes — made with organic produce, whenever possible. It's all served in an attractive and expansive dining room where you can listen to good rock 'n' roll music and sit at tables or at the juice bar.

Meals here are best begun with a juice to get the digestive system going, and the Blue Planet offers some good choices. Single fruit or vegetable juices are $2.50 for 12 ounces, $3 for 16. Blends are $3 or $3.50. Some of the more interesting choices include sun spot (orange, banana and papaya), Venus (pineapple, apple, pear and ginger), beetlejus (carrot, beet and celery) and the kitchen sink (carrot, celery, beet, spinach, cucumber, cabbage and green pepper). The Blue Planet wins hands down the claim to Seattle's corniest juice name: "Oh, say can you 'C,'" which includes orange, grapefruit, lemon, apple and cranberry. For a buck, you can add ginseng, lecithin, nutritional yeast, bee pollen, spirulina or fresh parsley. A shot of wheatgrass juice costs $1.25.

The breakfast menu is basic. The whole-grain oat waffles are served with soy margarine and real maple syrup ($3.75; $4.75 with fresh fruit topping). The porridge ($3.75) mixes whole oats with almonds and raisins, and is served with soy milk. Fruit-sweetened, organic apple-walnut granola will cost you $3.75; so will muesli, a fruit-sweetened wheat-free cereal with dried fruits, and apple pudding — a blend of apple juice and flax seeds topped with fruit and seasoned with cinnamon and nutmeg. Wash down your meal with herbal or caffeinated tea, soy milk, hot chocolate with soy milk, or cappuccino, latte or mocha. The Blue Planet breakfast special ($5.75) brings your choice of any hot or cold cereal with a 12-ounce orange, apple, grapefruit or pear juice.

The selections for lunch and dinner (same prices apply for both) are more interesting. You have a choice of seven entrée salads, two or three soups, five sandwiches and four entrées, plus specials listed on the blackboard. If you order a salad ($5.25 to $5.95), the dressings are vegan (lemon-tahini, miso-mustard, herb vinaigrette and oriental ginger), and your choice may include seed cheese — a naturally cultured non-dairy product made of sunflower and sesame seeds. One of the more unusual options is the sea-vegetable salad, a blend of Pacific sea palm, Atlantic kelp, vegetables and sesame seeds, all marinated with ume boshi vinegar and ginger. Traditionalists can stick to the spinach salad, the Daily Planet salad — mixed greens with sprouts, tomatoes and assorted vegetables — or the grazer, a selection of steamed or raw vegetables accompanied by a mound of hummus or seed cheese, pita bread and sprouts. The nori rolls are seaweed wrapped around brown rice, avocado and vegetables, served with tamari-ginger sauce, sliced ginger and wasabe, the Japanese version of horseradish.

A good sandwich is the tofu nutburger ($4.95), on a toasted herb onion roll with lettuce, tomato, red onion, sprouts, pickle spears and mustard, with blue corn chips and homemade salsa on the side. The Southwest burger is the same, but with guacamole and sprouts. While these sandwiches are tasty, you may end up using a fork, since, like most tofu burgers, they tend to fall apart. You also can order a black bean and rice or hummus roll-up ($4.95 each).

If you want a hot entrée (most $6.50), try the Thai dinner, which tops steamed vegetables, tofu and brown rice with a homemade Thai peanut sauce; the stir-fry with assorted vegetables, cashews and tofu in a ginger sauce; the Daily Planet dinner of steamed veggies, tofu and brown rice topped with a lemon-tahini sauce, or the pasta and marinara ($8.50), organic garlic and parsley fettuccine topped with a chunky marinara sauce with steamed vegetables and tofu.

Desserts are hedonistic, though free of refined sugars. One of the best health-food desserts in all of Seattle is the infrequently available carob brownie topped with vanilla Rice Dream, a non-dairy ice cream analog. You also can get a slab of carrot cake sweetened with honey and topped with a coconut-tofu frosting. Chocolate decadence is a two-layer non-dairy chocolate cake with a berry filling and chocolate-tofu frosting. "Cold and sweet" is Rice Dream garnished with fresh fruit or dairy-free chocolate chips. Check the blackboard for dessert specials.

Honey Bear Bakery

2106 N. 55th Street
545-7296

Breakfast, lunch, dinner.
6-10 Sun-Th, 6-11 F-Sat.
Strictly vegetarian, with vegan choices.
No credit cards.

The Honey Bear Bakery is somewhat off the beaten path in a residential neighborhood, but lots of folks make a special trip here for terrific atmosphere and some of the best bread in town. The large dining area is cluttered with wooden seats that seem as if they're about to fall apart, but people love to sit and chat, read a book or write in a journal. At times it can be hard to find a seat. Pictures of mountains hang on the walls; an antique stove rests against one wall. A message board in back announces housing situations and alternative medical practices. Live music — mostly folk but sometimes jazz or acoustic rock — is offered from 8 to 11 Friday and Saturday nights. For many, the Honey Bear Bakery, which opened in 1986, feels like home.

The main attraction is the breads (most loaves under $2), made with whole grains and honey or molasses. The seed of life loaf is one of the tastiest. Others are a dark bread with walnuts and orange flavor, molasses-sweetened sourdough and herb and onion.

But the Honey Bear Bakery also offers short menus for breakfast, lunch and dinner. Breakfasts, of course, include plenty of pastries and other bakery items, as well as granola and fruit. For lunch or dinner, the vegan black-bean chili is a standard; the soup of the day (sometimes vegan) might be spinach millet, split pea or potato herb. A bowl of either the soup or chili is $3.05; with a generous slice of bread, $3.55. Four salads (also $3.05 and $3.55 with bread) are offered daily: one pasta, one all-vegetable, one potato and one rice or grain. At 6 p.m. daily, a special is brought out. It might be a casserole, lasagna or pasta dish. Cornbread is offered after 6 as well.

Desserts, also a specialty, include all sorts of pastries and cookies. The honey-cashew cookie, tried on one visit, was a moist and chewy treat.

Kabul Afghan Cuisine

2301 N. 45th Street
545-9000

Lunch, dinner.
11:30-2 T-Sat, 5:30-10 M-Sat.
Several vegetarian and vegan choices.
Credit cards accepted.

The only Afghan restaurant in town (a new addition to Wallingford in 1992), Kabul serves some of the most delicious vegetarian fare in Seattle. Afghan cuisine is similar to Indian: both styles use an abundance of coriander, cumin and other hot spices, and rice and yogurt sauces also are important to Afghan cooking (if you're a vegan, Kabul often will substitute another sauce for yogurt). The place is full of charm and the prices are very reasonable. Kabul is named for the capital of Afghanistan, an ancient city of two million people at an altitude of 6,000 feet. Culture is important at Kabul: the menu includes a brief history of the city, the white and seafoam green walls sport several old black and white pictures of the capital, and jeweled Afghan caps are on display at the back of the small dining room. Music is featured on Wednesday nights.

Start with one of the six vegetarian appetizers ($2.25 to $4.75): ash is a soup made with noodles, yogurt, kidney beans and chickpeas, garnished with mint leaves. Bolani are delicious turnovers filled with scallions, cilantro and potatoes, served with a yogurt-garlic dip. Burta (cousin of the Indian bharta) is crushed eggplant blended with yogurt, sour cream, garlic, mint, cilantro, olive oil and lemon juice.

Five vegetarian entrées ($6.50 to $8) are available . The qorma-i sabzi is a medley of spinach, cilantro, parsley and scallions, cooked in spices and served over a bed of basmati rice. Qorma-i tarkari is a selection of seasonal vegetables flavored with dill, turmeric and cumin, served with basmati rice. Ashak are homemade dumplings filled with scallions, leeks and cilantro, with yogurt-garlic sauce, topped with a mildly spiced tomato and onion sauce and sprinkled with mint flakes. In badenjan borani, eggplant is sautéed in a light tomato sauce and placed on a bed of mint-yogurt sauce. The Kabuli palaw is a pilaf of basmati rice cooked in the oven with saffron, pepper, cardamom, coriander and cumin, topped with raisins, nuts and julienned carrots. It makes a better side dish than a main entrée.

By the end of our meals, we were too full to try the baklava, a Greek thin pastry layered with nuts and honey, or firni, a custard pudding flavored with cardamom and rosewater, topped with ground pistachios.

Julia's in Wallingford

1714 N. 44th Avenue

633-1175

Breakfast, lunch, dinner.
7-9 M-Sat, 7-2 Sun.
Several vegetarian and vegan choices.
Credit cards accepted.

Atmosphere is Julia's strength. The sister of Julia's Park Place in Ballard, it's a cozy restaurant with wood tables and plenty of hanging green plants -- a traditional American place with a healthful focus and a good selection of vegetarian dishes. There's a wine list, and your entrée is preceded by a basket of delicious bread.

Popular breakfast choices are the omelets and egg dishes. But the best option is the tofu breakfast special ($4.70 or $5.25, depending on whether you choose to accompany it with whole wheat or sourdough toast, or a bagel, cinnamon roll, coffee cake or pastry). It's made of tofu sautéed with mushrooms, scallions and a dash of soy sauce, and is served with grilled potatoes. Another good option is Karsten's sautéed veggies ($5.70 with grilled potatoes and toast, $6.25 with choice of pastry. Add $1.50 for tofu).

For lunch or dinner, you can get a nutburger made with eggs for $4.50 to $5.50, with optional toppings such as cheese, mushrooms and avocado. The dinner menu offers several other interesting vegetarian and vegan dishes ($7.50 to $8.25). There's the tofu and vegetable stir-fry, cooked in a light sauce of ginger, sesame oil and sake and served over brown rice. The pasta marisol mixes artichoke hearts, sun-dried tomatoes, pine nuts, olives, mushrooms and scallions with an herbed garlic-butter sauce, all tossed with fettuccine and topped with parmesan. The gado-gado — a traditional Indonesian dish — combines tofu and vegetables in a peanut and coconut-milk sauce, accompanied by brown rice. The vegetables dijonnaise is a medley of artichoke hearts and assorted vegetables cooked in a garlic, mustard, cream and wine sauce. It comes with a wild rice pilaf. If you want something simple, stick with the vegetables steamed with herbs and white wine, and served with brown rice. If salad's your thing, the Greek spinach salad ($6.25) is fine. A garden bowl salad ($5.50) can be topped with blue cheese, creamy dill, caesar, honey-dijon or peanut-lemon dressing.

At lunch, you also can order the Ed Hume sandwich ($4.25), with avocado, sprouts, cucumber, lettuce, tomato and choice of cheese.

The Rosebud Cafe

1411 N. 45th Street
633-0801

Breakfast, lunch, dinner.

8-10 Tu-Th, 8-10:30 F, 8:30-10:30 Sat, 9-3 Sun. Breakfast only Sun, and from 8:30 to 2:30 Sat.

Some vegetarian and vegan choices.

No credit cards.

Head chef Chris Stolte's culinary background is in French cuisine. Before coming to the Rosebud Cafe, a pleasant little restaurant in an old-fashioned Wallingford home, he hadn't had much occasion to cook meatless dishes. But so many vegetarians frequent the place (vegetarian specials strongly outsell their carnivore counterparts, Stolte notes) that he planned to change the menu in 1993, adding several more meat-free dishes.

You can get a filling breakfast here for $2.95 to $4.65, but mostly of the ovo-lacto variety. For example: two eggs served with hash browns and toast or two pancakes; pancakes, made with skim milk and plain yogurt; a side order of yogurt, granola and fruit, or the fruit cup.

For lunch ($4 to $6), vegans can savor the healthnut—an herbed tofu spread topped with lettuce, avocado, sprouts, toasted peanuts and fresh tomato, served on homemade pesto or garlic bread. The garden sandwich can be made vegan. It includes roasted peppers, zucchini and eggplant marinated in olive oil, garlic and herbs topped with fresh mozzarella, served on garlic or pesto bread with lettuce and garlic mayo. Quesadillas are marinated beans with green onions, mushrooms, diced tomatoes, and jack and cheddar cheese sandwiched between two whole wheat tortillas and topped with sour cream and salsa. Also ask about the specials of the day, which often are vegetarian or vegan.

The corn chowder is served daily. It's vegetarian, but includes dairy; a cup is $1.95, a bowl, $3.75. Ninety percent of the time, the soup of the day is vegetarian; half the time it's vegan. Choices might include curried pumpkin with ginger and wild mushroom chili. For lunch, try the soup and sandwich special ($3.95).

Salads at lunch and dinner include the house ($3.25), red-leaf and assorted organic greens tossed in a roasted garlic-honey dressing or a citrus vinaigrette; the wilted greens ($4.50), a mixture of spinach, assorted greens and radicchio that is quickly sautéed with garlic and balsamic vinegar and topped with goat cheese and caramelized pecans, and the Mediterranean ($6.95), a bed of couscous topped with organic greens, cucumbers, red onions, green peppers and feta cheese in a citrus vinaigrette.

Dinner includes many of the same lunch items, as well as some pasta dishes ($7.95 to $8.50). The angel-hair is herbed pasta with a sun-dried tomato and pesto sauce. The rigatoni is tossed in a sauce of gorgonzola cheese, cream and toasted walnuts. You also can get vegetarian enchiladas, an interesting-sounding dish with spaghetti squash, sun-dried tomatoes, mustard greens, fresh herbs and ricotta wrapped in corn tortillas, topped with a spicy molé sauce (made with onions, garlic, chile peppers, ground seeds and a small amount of chocolate) and served with a marinated bean salad.

Lotus Thai Cuisine

2101 N. 45th Street
632-2300

Lunch, dinner.
1:30 to 3, 5 to 9:30 Tu-Th, 11:30 to 10 Sat, 5 to 9 Sun.
Several vegan choices.
Credit cards accepted.

This popular Thai restaurant offers about ten choices for vegetarians. The tom kha-pug ($5.50) is a hot and sour soup with lemon grass and coconut milk. The rest of the vegetarian dishes (all $5.75) include garlic broccoli, spicy eggplant in a chile sauce with basil leaves and sautéed vegetables with cashew nuts.

The Juice Garden

4428 Burke Avenue N.
545-1061

Juice bar, with a few desserts.
9 to 7 every day.
No credit cards.

Come to this tiny juice bar for fine fruit and vegetable mixes. The produce is mostly organic, so there's no need to worry about pesticide residues. Juice choices vary with seasonal produce. Employees make hot and cold fruit juices, including apple, orange, lemon, grape, pineapple, grapefruit and tangelo. Vegetable options include the regulars. A 12-ounce juice costs $1.75; 16 ounces is $2.25.

Fruit smoothies include two fruits (choose among papaya, pineapple, cantaloupe, tangelo and banana), yogurt, seltzer and ice, and cost $2.75 for 16 ounces. The Juice Garden offers several specialties ($2.50 for 12 ounces, $3 for 16), such as the Kick-off, with tomato, green pepper and celery, and the Aloha, with pineapple, apple, lime and grapefruit. You also can get espresso here with soy milk or cow's milk.

For the hungry, Juice Garden sells Essential Sandwiches for $2.25. They're the popular vegan roll-up sandwiches available in refrigerators at health-food stores. You also can get some desserts here, straight from the vegan Globe Cafe on Capitol Hill.

India Cuisine

1718 N. 45th Street
632-5307

Lunch, dinner.

Lunch: 11:30 to 2:30 weekdays; 12 to 3 weekends. Dinner: 5 to 9:30 M-Th, 5 to 10 F-Sat, 5 to 9 Sun.

Several vegetarian choices.

Credit cards.

This small restaurant, which opened in 1992, apparently was catching on: It quickly filled up while we were there on a Sunday night. Despite the crowd, we found the food — especially the samosas — rather greasy. A better part of the meal was the curried okra dish, a spicy treatment of the delicate Southern vegetable.

Appetizers ($1.25 to $2.50) include vegetable pakoras, deep-fried vegetable and lentil-flour combinations served with mint chutney; papri chaat, seasoned flour crisps served with diced potatoes and chickpeas and garnished with homemade yogurt and special tamarind sauce, and pappadams, crispy lentil flour wafers served with mint chutney.

India Cuisine offers 10 vegetarian specialties (in the $6 range) for lunch or dinner. Kofta dilbahar are cream cheese and potato balls stuffed with dried fruit in a mild cream sauce. The khoya matar scrambles cheese with green peas and spices. Paneer ke phool sounds tempting: marinated vegetables and Indian cheese broiled on skewers. Dali bhalla ($3.95) is a ginger- and coriander-flavored lentil dumpling in yogurt with cumin and tamarind extract. You also can order one of several rice dishes (most $3.25), such as kashmiri rice with spices and fruit or mushroom rice with saffron. India Cuisine serves the usual assortment of Indian breads for a buck or two, among them naan, garlic naan and mint paratha, whole wheat buttered bread with freshly ground mint.

Other Choices

For vegetarian Japanese fare in Wallingford, you have two options. The better one is **Kitaro Japanese Cuisine** (1624 N. 45th Street, 547-7998), since it offers more choices. The vegetarian special bento box harbors tofu, hijiki and kappa roll and soup, salad and rice, all for $5.60 à la carte, or $7 for dinner (served with appetizers, salad and soup). The donburi ($4.95) tops steamed rice with beaten eggs and green onions boiled with a soy-based sauce. Ask for it without chicken. The kitsune udon soup ($4.50), served with salad, is made with noodles and bean curd. The hijiki seaweed can be ordered as a side dish.

So can the oshitashi, steamed spinach in a blend of soy sauce and ground sesame seeds. You also can order cucumber, pickle or tofu and rice sushi rolls. Open 11:30-2, 5-9:30 M-Sat. No credit cards.

At **Musashi's Sushi and Teriyaki Grill** (1400 N. 45th Street, 633-0212), choose the grilled vegetable skewers (80 cents or $1 each, including green onion, mushroom, zucchini, asparagus and mixed) or the veggie roll ($3.20 for 10 pieces). Open 11:30-2:30 Tu-F, 5-9 Tu-Th, 5-10 F, 5-9:30 Sat. No credit cards.

If Thai's your thing, stop at **Sea-Thai Restaurant** (2313 N. 45th Street, 547-1961). The Sea-Thai tofu ($4.50) makes an appealing appetizer — the tofu is browned and served with plum sauce. The Sea-Thai salad ($5.25) tops vegetables and sprouts with peanut sauce. The six vegetarian entrées (all $5.95) include priew wan (sautéed cucumbers, tomato, pineapple and onions in a sweet and sour sauce), g'ang pa' (mixed vegetables in curry and fresh basil) and Sea-Thai curry, a red curry with coconut milk. Open 11:30-3 and 5-10 Tu-Fr, 5-10 Sat, 5-9 Sun. Credit cards accepted.

Beso Del Sol (4468 Stone Way N., 547-8087) serves vegetarian-friendly Mexican food in an attractive dining room and bar. Beans here are cooked with vegetable oil. The nachos del sol ($5.25 if you ask for beans instead of meat) is a possible appetizer. So is the quesadilla ($4.25), a tortilla topped with cheese. For an entrée (most in the $7 range), you can get enchiladas or chiles rellenos — fresh stuffed peppers topped with sauce and served with rice and beans. Open 11:30-10 M-Th, 11:30-11 F-Sat, noon-9:30 Sun. Credit cards accepted.

Teahouse Kuan Yin (1911 N. 45th Street, 632-2055) is a wonderful place to sit with a friend and enjoy a pot of exquisite tea. Caffeinated black and green teas from China, Japan, India, Sri Lanka and Malaysia represent the biggest part of the menu. But there are some excellent herbal blends as well, with such names as world peace, haiku and wu-wei. A pot for one person is $1.75. Some foods also are available for $2.50-$4: hummus or baba ghanoush with pita bread, spanakopita, Chinese noodles with vegetables, quiche and humbow, a Chinese pastry filled with vegetables and little pieces of wheat gluten. Live music — perhaps classical guitar or sitar — is performed Thursday through Sunday evenings. Open 10-10 Sun-Th, 10-12 F-Sat. Credit cards accepted for purchases over $20.

Mari-Don HealthWay Natural Foods (1900 N. 45th Street, 632-7040), a health-food store, contains a small juice bar that serves carrot, celery, orange and apple juices, protein shakes and wheatgrass juice ($1.50 an ounce, $2.25 for two ounces). Carrot juice is 95 cents for a 7-ounce cup, and $2 for 14 ounces. Open 9-6 M-Sat.

Cold Mountain Juice Co. (2311 N. 45th Street, 632-0446) distributes bottled juices to area health-food stores and, on weekdays, doles out fresh-squeezed juices to customers in a small shop at the front of the plant. Smoothies ($2.25) include such goodies as pineapple-coconut, papaya-pineapple and strawberry-guava. Fifteen ounces of apple-carrot, carrot-celery or apple-pear juice will run you $2.25. A one-ounce shot of wheatgrass juice is $1.50; two ounces is $2.25. Decor is drab: a few $5 variety patio chairs grace the floor. Open 10-6 M-F. No credit cards.

Ballard

This largely Scandinavian neighborhood, to the northwest of Lake Union, does not have many vegetarian resources. The shopping district, centered mainly on Market Street, is dominated by restaurants that serve mostly high-fat dishes. Still, Julia's Park Place, a block south of Market, is a fine place to get hearty meatless meals.

Julia's Park Place

5410 Ballard Avenue N.W.
783-2033

Breakfast, lunch, dinner.
8-9 M-F, 7-9 S-S.
A few vegetarian, vegan selections.
Credit cards accepted.

Owned by Julia Miller, who runs Julia's in Wallingford, Julia's Park Place is an attractive, contemporary American restaurant that serves good international fare. Julia's features lots of eggs, chicken and fish, and some red meat. The eatery is expansive yet comfortable, with wooden country tables and chairs on three separate dining levels, and pretty woven tapestries and paintings of fish hanging on the walls. A little stand at the front offers espresso, as well as desserts and pastries from The Store Next Door in Wallingford. And you can take home Julia's Own Granola or Julia's Own Pancake Mix, made with whole wheat and buckwheat flours.

Breakfast ($3.50 to $5.95) involves such standards as french toast, made with sourdough bread and topped with powdered sugar or maple syrup, and omelets. The tofu breakfast blends sautéed mushrooms, scallions and tofu with a dash of soy sauce and a drop of sesame oil, and comes with grilled potatoes, pastry or toast. Jim's special combines grilled potatoes topped with cheddar, sour cream, ranchero sauce, scallions and salsa. A bowl of fresh fruit is $2.50. Pastries such as fruit coffee cake, cinnamon rolls, scones and bagels also are available.

Lunch ($4.25 to $6.25) includes sesame tofu, a stir-fried dish with mushrooms, scallions and celery in a sesame-sake sauce, and tofu chow mein with egg noodles. Or try cheese enchiladas, three corn tortillas stuffed with jack and cheddar cheese, served with black beans and rice. Vegetarian nutburgers (made with cheese and eggs) include grilled onions and cheese, mushroom and cheese or avocado and cheese. Or you can build your own burger.

The dinner menu ($6.95 to $8.95) yields cheese enchiladas again, as well as baked lasagna, pasta primavera in a rich garlic-cream sauce and sesame-tofu stir-fry with broccoli, carrots, green peppers, water chestnuts, mushrooms, celery and scallions. Nutburgers are $5.25.

Other Choices

Thai Siam Restaurant (8305 15th Avenue N.W., 784-5465), at the northern edge of Ballard, is a favorite of many fans of this spicy cuisine. At one visit, the tom kah mushroom soup with coconut milk and lemon grass was exceptionally tasty. The entrées we shared -- dressing rama (spinach and bean sprouts topped with tofu and peanut sauce) and vegetable curry -- were good, but not quite at the same level. The eight entrées are priced from $5.75 to $5.95. The homemade desserts also are held in high esteem: coconut ice cream, sweet sticky rice with Thai custard and bread pudding, among others. Open 11:30-3, 4:30-10 M-F, 4:30-10 Sat, 4:30-9:30 Sun. Credit cards accepted.

Thai Cafe (5401 20th Avenue N.W., 784-4599) offers a small assortment of vegetarian dishes ($4.50 to $6.25). Try the Thai salad with peanut sauce, always a favorite; the phad Thai noodle dish; rama garden, stir-fried vegetables with peanut sauce, or veggie lover, stir-fried vegetables in soy sauce and seasonings. Open 11-3, 5-9 M-F; 5-9 Sat. Credit cards accepted.

Fremont

The small business district of Fremont, a diverse (and, as one resident puts it, very unpretentious) neighborhood just north of the Lake Union Canal, has a surprising number of places that serve vegetarian food. You'll find artists, Bohemian-types, yuppies and working-class folks living and dining here.

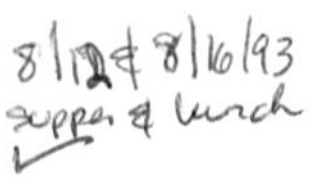

Still Life in Fremont Coffeehouse

709 N. 35th Street

547-9850

Breakfast, lunch, dinner.
7:30-9 Sun-Th, 7:30-11 F-Sat.
Some vegetarian options.
No credit cards.

If ever there were a good eatery for kicking back and watching life go by, Still Life is it. The coffeehouse, which serves a limited number of food options (about half of them vegetarian), is in a wonderful, huge open room full of wooden tables of different shapes (almost like an antiques shop), wooden chairs and benches. The diners and coffee drinkers are as likely to be reading or writing a book as they are to be carrying on casual conversation. Blues or jazz is played at moderate levels over the speakers; from 8-10 Thursday night, there's live music. Paintings by local artists hang on the walls.

The soup, salad and open-face sandwich specials of the day are usually vegetarian, but not vegan. Soups ($2.25/$3.60) such as carrot-potato-cashew curry with ginger, orange and cilantro are likely to contain small amounts of cream, and the open-face sandwich, perhaps roasted eggplant and hummus with a lemon-walnut spread, probably has cheese or butter. A veggie sub is $2.75 for a half, $4.75 for a whole if you're really hungry. It's good fare that was inspired by Mollie Katzen's vegetarian *Still Life* cookbook.

YooHoo

607 N. 35th Street

633-3760

Juice bar.
6:30-4:30 M-F, 8:30-5 weekends. Possibly open later in summer.
Some vegan foods.
No credit cards.

YooHoo is a tiny place to relax and chat with the friendly servers who make good fresh juices and caffeinated drinks. It's a favorite of Fremont artists, who come early in the morning for orange or carrot juice. The juice bar is likely to be playing loud jazz, new wave rock or Mexican music.

The juices are the best-sellers. An eight-ounce carrot juice is $2; 12 ounces will run you $2.50. Fruit smoothies ($3.25) are made with orange juice, bananas, yogurt and your choice of blueberries, strawberries or raspberries.

You can also order bagels (75 cents), pre-made vegan Essential Sandwiches ($2.25), vegan Imaginary Deli sandwiches ($3.25) that use meat analogs, and an assortment of pastries, including vegan and sugar-free options.

Other Choices

For a pleasant lunch in a tiny cafe, try **Spencer's Bistro** (3411 Fremont Avenue N., 632-3602), which keeps adding more vegetarian selections. Spencer's lunch menu ($4.25 to $5.25) lists vegetable lasagna, pasta primavera, a veggie sandwich with mayonnaise and cream cheese, and a garden burger made with cheese, eggs, nuts and grains. The soup of the day is always vegetarian, but usually includes dairy products. Fresh-squeezed juices ($1.75 for 10 ounces, $2.50 for 15) are a good addition to a meal. For dinner ($5.95 to $7.25), chef Michael Swanberg makes a garden sauté using olive oil with herbs and garlic, and white wine. It's topped with parmesan cheese. You can also get pesto tossed with angel-hair pasta or pasta primavera. Sit in the casual main dining area with local artworks hanging on the walls, or in the enclosed deck at the rear with a view of a parking lot and the backs of Fremont shops. Open for lunch 11-4:30 M-F, 10-6 Sat-Sun; dinner, 5-closing Tu-Sat. Credit cards accepted.

Costas Opa Greek Restaurant (3400 Fremont Avenue N., 633-4141) is a large Greek restaurant with several rooms full of plants and Greek ornaments. A lot of vegetarian food is served for lunch, including fakes soup, made with lentils, bay leaves, onions, garlic, olive oil and vinegar. (But vegetarians should stay away from the fasolada bean and vegetable soup, made with beef stock). You can get hummus, tzatziki, peppers and olives, grilled baby eggplant or feta cheese and tomatoes for $2.25 to $3.50. Prices for appetizers are a few cents extra for dinner. A hummus vegetarian sandwich, served in a pita with rice pilaf, is $3.75. The stifado sandwich ($4.25) wraps grilled baby eggplant with lettuce, feta and sauce in a pita. Or order spanakopita. There are only a couple of vegetarian dinner entrées: sautéed vegetables with rice pilaf ($8.25) and spanakotyropeta ($8.50), made of spinach, feta and eggs in a phyllo pastry, served with potatoes and vegetables. Lunch is served 11-4 M-Sun; dinner, 4-10 every day. Credit cards accepted.

Greenwood/Phinney Ridge

Predominantly residential areas on a hill with great views of mountains both east and west, Greenwood and Phinney Ridge claim a handful of good choices for meatless fare. The Santa Fe Cafe offers stylish Southwestern dining with several vegetarian choices. Sitar is the area's Indian restaurant. Rasa Malaysia prepares good Southeast Asian cuisine on weeknights. A sign of the relative progressiveness of the two adjoining neighborhoods is that the 74th Street Ale House serves a veggie burger.

The Santa Fe Cafe

5910 Phinney Avenue N.
783-9755

Lunch, dinner, Sunday brunch.
11-2 W-F, 5-10 M-Sun, 9-2 Sunday brunch.
Several vegetarian choices.
Credit cards accepted.

Like its namesake on N.E. 65th Street in Ravenna, The Santa Fe Cafe serves wonderful Southwestern food, much of it vegetarian. The dishes contain lots of cheese, so vegans won't feel too comfortable here. The Phinney restaurant -- unlike the Ravenna one -- offers a Sunday brunch.

Start lunch with chips and salsa ($1.75; $2.75 with tomatillo salsa) or a green salad. The fiesta corn salad ($3.75) includes corn, red and green peppers, olive oil, green chile and spices. It's topped with gruyere cheese and served with french garlic bread. Artichoke ramekin ($5.75) is a baked spread of artichoke hearts, green chile and kasseri cheese. The chile relleno tart ($9.25) combines hot green chile, mozzarella and gruyere, baked in a blue-corn pastry with a montrachet custard. The red enchilada plate ($7) brings a blue-corn tortilla rolled with colby cheese and onion, covered with red-chile sauce and served with pinto beans and a fresh flour tortilla.

The dinner menu includes eggplant encantado ($8.75), an appetizer of grilled eggplant filled with montrachet cheese, sun-dried tomato and fresh rosemary surrounded by tomato and green chile sauce, served with a baguette. The artichoke ramekin ($5.75) also is available for dinner; garlic custard, served with blue corn chips, is $5.75. The chile relleno tart is $10.25 for dinner.

Sitar

8518 Greenwood Avenue N.
782-7890

Lunch, dinner.
11:30-2:30 M-F, 5-9 Sun-Th, 5-10 F-Sat..
Several vegetarian choices.
Credit cards accepted.

A highlight of this Indian restaurant that opened in 1993 is the live sitar music presented here on occasional evenings. A beautiful sitar (an Indian relative of the guitar) rests in the front corner, waiting to be played. As for the food, it is very good (with a minimum of grease that often accompanies Indian dishes), although we found the portions rather small. The expansive dining room with peach and purple walls contains green-cushioned wicker chairs. Small, colorful Indian figures and wood-carved elephants rest on a ledge of one wall, and Indian tapestries hang from the ceiling and the walls.

Start a meal with one or two of these traditional Indian appetizers ($1.25 to $2.95): vegetable samosas, vegetable pakoras or pappadams (crispy, spiced lentil wafers). The samosas, pastries filled with potatoes and peas, are especially good.

The lengthy menu of vegetarian entrées (with a dozen choices from $5 to $5.95) embraces standards such as aloo ghobi, cauliflower and potatoes cooked with a mild sauce; a very spicy but tasty vegetable curry; channa masala (chickpeas spiced with ginger), and saag paneer (homemade cheese and spinach simmered with onions, tomato and a mild gravy). Other choices include bhindi masala, a delicious dish of okra cooked with onions in a tomato sauce; dal turka, a northern Indian specialty of lentils cooked in butter and garlic, and brinjal bhajee, eggplant cooked in ghee. Breads are a must with your meal: try naan, a leavened bread of fine flour cooked in the tandoor oven; roti, a whole wheat bread, or onion kulcha, a leavened bread stuffed with onion, dry mango and spices.

Other Choices

Phad Thai (8530 Greenwood Avenue N., 784-1830) serves a small selection of vegetarian dishes, each for $5.25, including hot summer jay, stir-fried vegetables and tofu in a red curry sauce; swimming tofu, deep-fried tofu with steamed vegetables topped with peanut sauce; phad Thai, and vegetables in wine sauce. Open 11:30-2:30 M-Tu, Th-F, 5-9:30 M-F, 4-9:30 S-S. Credit cards accepted.

Rasa Malaysia (6012 Phinney Avenue N., 781-8888) is one of five restaurants and food stands in Seattle that make up the Rasa Malaysia chain. This one is a tiny restaurant with posters of Malaysia on the walls. Choices (all under $5) include vegetarian potstickers, mee goreng (wheat noodles with vegetables and peanut sauce), sayur lodeh (vegetarian curry with tofu over saffron rice) and vegetarian combo (potstickers, curried vegetables, stir-fried noodles and rice). It's open only on weeknights. (Nearby is the Green Lake Rasa Malaysia, which is open for lunch and dinner daily, and has a larger selection.) Open 5-9 M-F. No credit cards.

74th Street Ale House (7401 Greenwood Avenue N., 784-2955) is a tavern that serves more healthful fare than usual. Here you can order a veggie-nut burger ($6.50) made with roasted hazelnuts, peanuts, almonds, cumin, bell peppers, carrots and onions. "The ultimate alternative!" boasts the menu. A vegetarian friend who eats here a few times a week calls it delicious. Also available is a vegetarian sandwich ($6), with montrachet, cream cheese, sun-dried tomatoes, artichoke hearts, roasted garlic, mayonnaise and Greek olives on a country loaf. Open 12-10:30 Sun-Th, 12-11 F-Sat. Credit cards accepted.

Green Lake

Green Lake, with its three-mile scenic walk (almost invariably crowded with pedestrians, bikers and roller bladers who love to circle the water), is a Seattle treasure. Beautiful homes and trees line the lake, and perhaps no other spot in town is better for relaxing and catching a few rays. But for such a great people place, Green Lake falls short on vegetarian dining options, lacking as it does a good full-service restaurant that serves vegetarian food.

However, there are a few places for herbivores in this eclectic neighborhood, most notably The Living Room Juice Bar and Coffee Company, which has an all-vegetarian (and mostly-vegan) assortment of dishes as well as refreshing juices.

The Living Room Juice Bar and Coffee Company

7104 Woodlawn Avenue N.E.
526-1520

Breakfast, lunch, dinner.

6:30-7:30 weekdays, 7:30-5 Sat, 8-5 Sun in winter. In summer, open until 10 most nights.

Strictly vegetarian, mostly vegan.

No credit cards.

Vegan owner Brenda Bailey worked for a time at Ed's Juice and Java on the other side of the lake, but broke away to start her own place in 1992. She's added a small assortment of mostly vegan dishes for those who want solid food along with a refreshing fruit or vegetable juice or a caffeinated drink.

Her place has style: antique radios sit atop every table, pictures of old-time Seattle hang on the peach-colored walls and 1940s jazz is likely to be playing over the stereo system. In the back is a cozy "living room" with sofas and lounge chairs. The Living Room is two doors down from the Seattle School of Massage, and Brenda reports that the mostly vegetarian clientele there represent some of her best customers.

A 10-ounce glass of a single juice, such as apple, pineapple, orange, grapefruit, carrot, cucumber or celery, costs $1.75; 16 ounces is $2.50. Another quarter lets you add beet, celery, kale, parsley, garlic or ginger to the vegetable drinks; pay 30 cents to add strawberry, kiwi, papaya, banana, lemon, lime, cantaloupe or honeydew to the fruit drinks. A one-ounce shot of wheatgrass costs $1.25 ($2 for two ounces). The produce is almost always organic.

Breakfasts ($2.25 or $2.50) are served until 11 a.m. and make a satisfying complement to a glass of fruit juice. The mixed fruit bowl will keep you feeling light and energetic through the morning. Or try the hot cereal, consisting of seven grains, raisins, sunflower seeds and apples; fat-free granola or organic corn flakes with banana, or toasted raisin bread topped with raspberry preserves.

After 11, you can get a more hearty meal ($3.25 to $4.75). On one visit, a bowl of brown rice topped with steamed vegetables, greens and a thick lemon-tahini sauce proved a delicious choice. The pasta salad with pesto, sun-dried tomatoes and olives, served with fresh bread, sounds interesting. Or try the hummus plate or a hummus roll-up, filled with sprouts and veggies. There's also a daily special roll-up. A veggie sandwich with avocado, hummus, tomato and sprouts is tempting. The soup of the day with bread might be lentil, spicy tomato or black bean.

Rasa Malaysia

7208 E. Greenlake Drive N.
523-8888

Lunch, dinner.
11-9 M-Sun.
Several vegetarian choices.
No credit cards.

This is the biggest of the Rasa Malaysias, a Seattle chain of five fast-food Malaysian eateries. Here you can actually sit down (after ordering in the cafeteria line by the front door) in a standard American cafe filled with posters and artifacts from Malaysia.

The menu is much more extensive than at the other Rasa Malaysias; the food is adequate (though not stellar), and the portions large for the money. Start your meal with potstickers (six for $2.50) or egg rolls (two for $2.50), or the gado-gado salad of steamed vegetables served with rice and hoisin or peanut sauce ($3.50). The hot and sour soup with tofu ($1.25/$2) is another good choice.

For the main course, you can pick from five meatless dishes ($3.50 to $4.75): mee goreng (wheat noodles with peanut sauce), goreng meehoon (rice noodles with brown or peanut sauce), sayur lodeh (vegetable curry with tofu and rice), Buddhist delight (tofu with vegetables and rice) or vegetarian combo, with stir-fried noodles, potstickers and curried vegetables. Rasa Malaysia also serves fresh fruit smoothies and juices.

Ed's Juice and Java

7907 Wallingford Avenue N.
524-7570

7-6 daily; in summer open later, until about sunset.
Juice bar and desserts.
No credit cards.

Ed is Ed Ives, who opened his tiny juice bar and coffee house a half-block from Green Lake in 1990. He wanted to create a business that would combine many of his loves, including raw, healthful foods (in the form of fresh-squeezed juices) and eclectic music. Eating represents our most intimate connection with Earth, he says; most people are unplugged from Earth. "In my small way, I'm trying to help people plug in." Ed's is a favorite of mothers with children who stroll around the lake, so he decided to offer an array of children's books for the kids to read while drinking some juice. The side wall is covered with changing drawings by kids, perhaps promoting recycling and other earth-friendly endeavors.

The juices are more popular here most of the year, but in the winter, caffeinated drinks dominate. The juice makers at this haunt (which has only a few seats) often encourage coffee drinkers to try the more healthful, natural pick-me-ups; Ed says the place is not so much a coffee shop, but a conversion clinic.

To order juice, pick a base, such as orange, apple, grapefruit or pineapple, or carrot, cucumber or celery (10 ounces $1.90, 16 ounces $3). Then add such goodies as strawberries or coconut (75 cents), papaya, kiwi or mango (60 cents), lemon, honeydew melon or frozen banana, or beet, cucumber, spinach, kale, celery, cabbage, garlic or ginger (30 cents). To be really energized, add spirulina, vegetable protein or exhilara to your drink for 75 cents. You also can order shots of wheatgrass ($1.25 for one ounce, $2 for two). A few baked desserts are offered.

Other Choices

L'Emir Restaurant (1400 N. 80th Street, 523-4196) dispenses standard Mediterranean fare in a classy setting. Order the falafel ($6.50) or other appetizers ($3 to $4) such as Lebanese salad or zahrah, which is deep-fried cauliflower with tahini sauce. Hummus, baba ghanoush, tabbouleh and the falafel sandwich also make fine choices. If you and your eating partner feel ambitious, try the L'Emir vegetarian mezze tray for two ($15.95): it includes tabbouleh, baba ghanoush, falafel and grape leaves stuffed with onion, tomato, rice, lemon juice and spices. Open 11:30-9 M-Th, 11:30-10 F, 4-10 Sat, 4-9 Sun. Credit cards accepted.

Greenlake Vietnamese Foods (7906 E. Green Lake Drive N., 525-0842) is a tiny and informal restaurant that dispenses three vegetarian entrées for $4.50: curry vegetables, tofu vegetables and tofu mushroom. Open 11-9 M-Sat. No credit cards.

University District

This college community, playground of the University of Washington Huskies, easily ranks as the best neighborhood in Seattle — if not the Pacific Northwest — for vegetarian fare. Here, interspersed with new age and used book stores, imported clothing boutiques and unique record and poster shops, are restaurants serving almost every imaginable kind of cuisine. And an unusually large number of them offer multiple meatless dishes.

Silence-Heart-Nest is the only strictly vegetarian Indian place in town. If Mexican food's your thing, Macheezmo Mouse serves healthful fast-food burritos and tacos. Thai aficionados have several great choices, most notably the Little Thai Restaurant, which serves only vegetarian and seafood dishes. Middle Eastern, Indian, Ethiopian and Greek restaurants also flourish here.

The restaurants mentioned in this chapter are found mostly along University Avenue (known simply as the Ave), Brooklyn Avenue and Roosevelt Way, and fall south of Ravenna Boulevard.

Morningtown Restaurant, a popular Roosevelt Avenue haunt for international vegetarian fare since the 1970s, closed unexpectedly in the spring of 1993.

Silence-Heart-Nest

5247 University Way N.E.
524-4008

Lunch, dinner.
11-9 M-Sat, 11-3 W.
Strictly vegetarian.
No credit cards.

Silence-Heart-Nest is a restaurant with a mission: to promote the teachings of Sri Chimnoy, an Indian teacher. In front of the restaurant, the owners even planted a Sri Chimnoy peace tree in 1991. The Indian eatery's unusual name is derived from an esoteric Sri Chimnoy phrase:

Eternity's silence:
The silence that embodies vision, light and delight.
Infinity's heart:
The universal heart that expands and expands.
Immortality's nest:
The nest of birthless and deathless nectar-delight.

Some might be put off by the spiritual nature of this place (you can browse through Sri Chimnoy books and literature from a tiny library near the front door while you eat your meal). But the food makes it worthwhile for disciples and non-believers alike. The dedicated folks who run Silence-Heart-Nest know how to put a good meal together.

For starters, try the soup of the day (often vegan) or lentil dal made with dairy ($1.50/$2.50). You can get a house salad for $1.95, or the much larger garden salad ($4.95). Dressings include a somewhat bland sesame-herb, infinite blue cheese, Italian and lemon-garlic. Be sure to order some of the appetizers, such as samosas, so you can sample a Silence-Heart-Nest trademark: its chutneys. The best are the coriander and the garlic-coconut, although some prefer the tamarind-raisin or the garlic-tomato.

Entrées are mostly the same at lunch and dinner, although pappadam (a wafer-thin East Indian bread made with lentil flour), chutney and a choice of soup or salad accompanies dinner. Lunch items come with soup or salad. The menu denotes vegan entrées with a (v), and most of the dishes are $4.75 for lunch, $6.95 for dinner. You can get a chapati roll-up (lunch only) — an East Indian burrito stuffed with salad, sprouts, cheese and choice of curry and dressing. Calananda, an East Indian calzone, is filled with spinach, mushrooms, tomato, cheeses and Indian spices. The curry of the day gives you a choice from three curries and is served with basmati rice. Masal dosai are tasty sourdough crepes made from rice and lentils, filled with curried potatoes and served with coconut chutney. The neat-loaf sandwich (lunch only) blends wheat cereal, eggs, ricotta, rice and herbs and is served on whole wheat bread with lettuce, tomato, mayonnaise, pickle and barbecue sauce. The bliss-burger mixes beans, nuts, soy, grains and herbs on a whole wheat bun with a special onion sauce and other fixings. Desserts (most $1.25) include double-chocolate brownies, vegan "mahvelous" chocolate pudding and fresh fruit pie.

Silence-Heart-Nest sporadically offers an all-you-can-eat Sunday brunch from 9:30 to 1:30; $6.95 ($3.50 for kids under 12) gets you blueberry pancakes, waffles, scrambled eggs or tofu, baked rosemary potatoes and other treats. Call to find out when the next one is.

Little Thai Restaurant

4142 Brooklyn Avenue N.E.
548-8009

Lunch, dinner.
11-9 M-F, 4-9 Sat, 12-9 Sun.
Half vegetarian.
No credit cards.

You won't find the usual beef and chicken dishes at this unique Thai place, a small cafe ensconced below street level. Here, fully half of the dishes are vegetarian, and the rest, seafood.

Little Thai is a vegetarian's bonanza. The broad-ranging dinner menu lists seven vegetarian appetizers, three salads, five soups, four curry plates, 15 à la carte entrées and seven noodle dishes. And unlike most Thai restaurants, here you can enjoy your meal over brown rice at dinner (at lunch, only the usual steamed white rice is offered). The tiny dining room's decor is nothing special, but the quality of the food and the low prices more than compensate. One dish not to be missed is the grilled eggplant with peanut sauce ($4.50).

Among starters (under $4), try the tofu satay, marinated and grilled tofu served with a sugary peanut sauce and cucumber salad; golden Thai lotus, crispy golden cups stuffed with vegetable curry; mee grob, crispy rice noodles stir-fried with sweet and sour sauce, or the unusual-sounding corn patties, fried corn mixed with Thai herbs and served with cucumber sauce. Soups ($4.95 each) are enough for two to four people, and include tom yum (a hot and sour vegetable soup); tom kha coconut; mixed vegetable with tofu in a clear broth, and glass noodle and seaweed with vegetables. The Thai ya salad ($3.95) mixes greens with cashew nuts and sesame seeds, while the yum woon sen ($3.95) blends bean thread with nuts, lime juice and Thai herbs.

Be sure to try the Thai red or green curries ($4.95) during one of your visits, as curries are a staple of the cuisine. Ask for mild if it's your first time, hot if you're a veteran of spicy foods. Steamed brown rice is an extra 65 cents per person (white rice is 50 cents). Stir-fried à la carte dishes are $4.50 each. Some examples: spicy mint leaves with mixed vegetables, chilies and garlic; chile-fried eggplant with black-bean sauce, chilies and egg; ginger Thai-style (black mushrooms with black-bean sauce and vegetables); chop suey (veggies in a brown sauce); baby corn and vegetables in a brown sauce, and the lotus plate (mixed vegetables and lotus seeds from the water lily in a brown sauce). The noodle dishes ($4.50 each) include such favorites as vegetarian phad Thai, big noodles with soy sauce and egg noodles with black mushrooms.

For lunch, you can choose from 20 vegetarian lunch specials for $3.95 each.

Flowers Bar and Restaurant

4247 University Way N.E.
633-1903

Lunch, dinner.
11-10:30 M-Sat, bar until 2 a.m.
Vegetarian lunch buffet.
Credit cards.

One of the more exciting events for Seattle vegetarians was the 1992 opening of Flowers, with its $4.95, all-you-can-eat vegan lunch buffet — an almost unimaginable feast of 25 to 30 mostly Middle Eastern grain, pasta and vegetable dishes sprawled across a table in the center of the trendy restaurant. For awhile, the pasta dishes were not vegan, made as they were with egg pasta. But owner Fadi Hamade planned to change over to whole wheat pasta as soon as he could find a reliable supplier. The buffet, offered from 11 to about 4 M-Sat, has been well received by both vegetarians and meat-eaters (witness the large lunch crowds). If people have one complaint, it's that the food is so good and plentiful that they find it almost too easy to overindulge and go home feeling, well, stuffed. What makes the vegan buffet all the more unusual is that Flowers' à la carte menu includes plenty of meat dishes, such as burgers, sandwiches and seafood. Fadi, a New York City transplant who ran a similar vegetarian restaurant on Manhattan's Upper West Side for 14 years and whose mother is a 35-year herbivore (he's not 100 percent vegetarian), says he likes to offer people a choice.

Buffet dishes might include cauli-tarafor (cauliflower with tahini), sesame soy noodles, sautéed okra with tomato and onion, mudardara (lentils with cracked wheat and sauteed onion and spices), curried bulghur wheat, sautéed zucchini with a mint-tomato sauce, roasted garlic potatoes, and standards like hummus and baba ghanoush. You won't be able to sample all the dishes in one sitting — there are simply too many.

If the buffet seems overwhelming, the straightforward lunch menu ($4.50 to

$5.95) offers a respite. The soup of the day is always vegan, and might be tomato-lentil, garlicky mushroom, vegetarian gumbo or spinach and broccoli. The banquet salad tops mixed greens, cabbage and carrots with sprouts, and you can choose from three dressings: lemon-tahini, tangy soy and the house vinaigrette. The farmer's sandwich is a baguette with grilled eggplant, zucchini, tomato and hummus. Thin-sliced eggplant, mozzarella, tomato and sprouts make up the roma. Or get the montrachet or mediterranean omelet with salad and homefries, the former with spinach and goat cheese, the latter with gruyere cheese and fresh basil.

Dinner choices are priced from $5 to $7.50. Prince Mazza is a combination plate of hummus, baba ghanoush and tabbouleh with pita. Entrées include casablanca, whole wheat couscous with curried vegetables, spaghetti aglio olio with basil, red pepper flakes, olive oil and garlic, and Japanese eggplant (ask for it without the beef), garnished with a tomato, mint and yogurt sauce. Vegetarian lasagna is also available.

Fadi chose Flowers for a name because he moved into the old Flowers gift shop, a 60-year-old fixture of the U-District. He wanted to maintain a sense of history, so he kept the familiar yellow neon sign above the restaurant.

Macheezmo Mouse Mexican Cafe

4129 University Way N.E.

633-4658

Lunch, dinner.
11-10 M-Sat, 12-10 Sun.
Several vegetarian, vegan choices.
No credit cards.

Macheezmo Mouse is a great spot for a fast and healthful Mexican meal. It's part of a chain of 10 restaurants in Seattle and Portland. For a description of food choices, see Page 31.

Grand Illusion Espresso and Pastry

1405 N.E. 50th Street

525-9573

Breakfast, lunch, dinner.
About 8:30-10 or 11 daily.
Strictly vegetarian, a few vegan choices.
No credit cards.

This cozy haunt, attached to an artsy movie house, is frequented most often by University of Washington students, who sprawl out their books on Shakespeare or quantum mechanics while guzzling caffeinated drinks and eating sweet pastries. They should feel at home: the Grand Illusion cafe seems like a college dorm living room, what with its fireplace and a hodgepodge of large plush chairs and wooden seats. The fare may be vegetarian, but the orientation is less toward health than sugar and caffeine fixes. The glass counter displays slices of pie, muffins and popovers.

But you can get a pot of herbal tea for 75 cents, or hot apple cider. The garden salad comes with choice of dressing: lemon-tahini, green-goddess or vinaigrette. Two kinds of quiche are offered: artichoke-scallion or broccoli-mushroom. They cost $3.75 with fruit or $4.95 with salad. A pita egg salad sandwich costs $2.50. The soup choice ($1.55/$2.45) rotates daily, perhaps Hungarian mushroom, mushroom-barley, corn chowder or Russian borscht.

Bangkok Cafe II

4730 University Way N.E.
523-3220

Lunch, dinner.
11:30-10 M-F, 12-10 Sat, 5-10 Sun.
Extensive vegetarian menu.
Credit cards accepted.

What's most notable about Bangkok Cafe II (a relative of Bangkok Cafe on 15th Avenue East) is the huge selection of vegetarian soups, salads and entrées: 17 in all. And the prices are reasonable, ranging from $4.45 to $5.25.

Begin your meal with vegetarian soup, with or without tofu. The vegetarian larb appetizer ($4.75) is interesting: minced tofu and mushrooms are mixed with lime juice and chilies, and garnished with mint. Then try the vegetarian curry, a mixture of tofu and bamboo shoots in curry paste and coconut milk, or bathing rama, tofu and peanut sauce drizzled over spinach leaves. The phad krapoa is tofu sauteed with basil leaves, hot pepper, onion and curry paste topped with peanuts. Phad Thai with egg is popular; in phad kha-na, broccoli is stir-fried with bean sauce.

Neelam's Authentic Indian Cuisine

4735 University Way N.E.
523-5275

Lunch, dinner, Sunday brunch.
10-10 M-Sat, 11-8 Sun.
Several vegetarian and vegan choices.
Credit cards accepted.

Another of several Indian restaurants in North Seattle, Neelam's serves good food in a pleasant dining room that affords a view of bustling University Way. As with most Indian eateries, the highlight here is the lunch buffet ($4.95, M-Sat). The Sunday brunch ($6.95) offers multiple items, too. The menu stresses the prominence of vegetable dishes in India. Since many Indians are vegetarians and vegetables can be "boring," the menu reads, Indian chefs have "spent centuries developing ways to cook vegetables and finding just the right spices" to accentuate their natural flavor. Needless to say, the cuisine here is colorful and full of flavor, and ranges in heat from mild to hot.

Start your meal with two vegetable samosas for $1.95, or eight vegetable pakoras for the same price. Aloo chat — Indian potato salad — and vegetable or lentil soup are good starters. There are nine vegetarian entrées ($5 to $6), such as dal makhani, black beans cooked in butter, cream and spices over rice; aloo ghobi, cauliflower and potatoes cooked with herbs; channa masala, a tasty dish of chickpeas cooked with onions, tomatoes and spices in a special sauce and garnished with coriander, and baingan bharta, eggplant baked in a tandoor oven, mashed and seasoned with spices and sautéed with tomato, onion, ginger and garden peas. Vegetable biryani blends basmati rice, saffron, nuts, spices and vegetables.

Neelam's breads ($1 to $2.50), baked in the tandoor oven, are excellent. Naan can be made with or without egg. Aloo paratha is a whole wheat bread stuffed with potatoes.

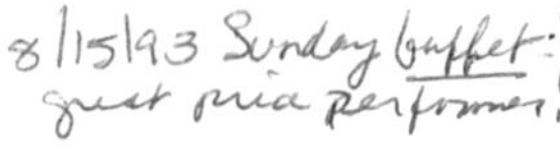

Tandoor Indian Restaurant

5024 University Way N.E.
523-7477

Lunch, lunch buffet; dinner; Sunday brunch.
11-2:30, 4:30-10 daily, to 10:30 F-Sat.
Several vegetarian options.
Credit cards accepted.

In a small, sparsely furnished room, the Tandoor serves up good vegetarian Indian fare. The best value is the all-you-can-eat buffet that so many Indian restaurants now feature. From Monday through Saturday, it's a great bargain at $3.95; almost as good at $4.95 on Sunday. That gets you salad, Indian bread, dal, a rice dish and one or two vegetable dishes.

If you order à la carte, be sure to start with everybody's favorite, vegetable samosas, fried triangular pastries filled with vegetables ($2.50 for two). Vegetable pakoras (deep-fried fritters) are also $2.50. Then enjoy Indian bread staples such as naan ($1.25). Entrées (most in the $6 range) include eggplant bharta; channa pindl, chickpeas made with spices and served with potatoes and tomato, and paneer makhni, homemade cottage cheese cooked in creamed tomato. Kashmiri rice cooked with spices and fruit and mushroom rice are each $3.25.

Ricardo's Espresso Cafe and Juice Bar

4217 University Way N.E.
633-1327

Breakfast, lunch, dinner.
7:30-7 M-F, 9-7 Sat, 9-6 Sun.
Several vegetarian and vegan choices.
No credit cards.

The owners of Ricardo's Espresso Cafe noticed a surprising lack of juice bars along the Ave (progressive in so many other ways), so they decided to add a juice bar to their store at 4725 University Way in 1991. When they expanded to a second cafe five blocks south in 1992, they equipped it with juicers, too, and closed the 4725 store in early 1993 to concentrate efforts at the newer juice bar and deli.

Ricardo's offers a large number of fruit and vegetable juices. You can select all kinds of ingredients for a nourishing juice or fruit smoothie: carrots, celery, cabbage, beet, spinach, ginger, lemon, orange, apple, grapefruit and so on.

Prices are $2 or so for a 10-ounce glass and $3 or so for 16 ounces. Popular drinks include the Picasso ($2.75/$3.75), with carrots, celery, cucumber, spinach, beets and cabbage, and the Mario Andretti ($2.25/$3.25), a blend of carrot, apple, beet and ginger.

If hungry, order a veggie roll-up, topped with a spicy garlic-cucumber-yogurt sauce, for $2.25 (with feta cheese, add 50 cents). A broiled lemon-tempeh burger with potato salad costs $4.95; by itself, the potato salad is $2.10. A black-bean burrito smothered in salsa and cheddar cheese is $4.75. Or, you can buy the ever-popular vegan Essential Sandwiches for $2.40. Vegetarian soups are made without dairy.

Hong Kong Golden City Restaurant

4228 Roosevelt Way N.E.
633-4350

Lunch, dinner.
11-11 daily.
Several vegetarian dishes.
Credit cards accepted.

A Chinese restaurant that doesn't cook its vegetable and tofu dishes in chicken stock is a rarity. There are plenty of pork, beef, chicken and seafood dishes on the 159-item menu here, which also offers Malaysian and Vietnamese dishes. But Mrs. Lee, as everyone calls her, a delightful woman who loves to chat with customers when she has a free moment, explains that her 15 or so vegetarian dishes are cooked only in corn oil and spices.

The mixed-vegetable tofu potte ($8) is an interesting dish with three kinds of mushrooms and a side soup. Scrambled eggs with tomato is $4.25. Hung sui tofu ($5.50) is deep-fried tofu with vegetable sauce. The chestnuts with black mushrooms ought to be good: the treat costs $12. From the Malaysian menu, vegetarians have one choice: the curry vegetables and rice ($4.50). None of the Vietnamese entrées is meatless. Mrs. Lee notes that if you call ahead, she'll prepare meat-analog dishes made out of wheat gluten.

Shalimar Restaurant

1401 N.E. 42nd Street
633-3854

Lunch, dinner.
11-9 M-Sat.
Several vegetarian dishes.
Credit cards accepted.

Fine Pakistani cuisine is the specialty of this small but attractive restaurant, with white linen-covered tables, pink walls with a purplish-blue trim and large windows looking onto both the Ave and 43rd Street. Shalimar, which opened in 1988, appeals mostly to University of Washington students and faculty, who study and work on campus a block away.

Vegetarian entrées (most in the $5 range) include dal; palak, a dish of creamed spinach with a spicy butter sauce, and matar paneer, green peas cooked with homemade cheese and simmered in a curried cheese sauce. Vegan choices are aloo palak, spinach and potatoes in a curry sauce; tori, a plate of zucchini simmered in a mildly spiced curry sauce; shulgam palak, an interesting-sounding dish of baby turnips and chopped spinach, and began ki bhaji, eggplant cooked slowly in a creamy curry sauce.

Cedars Restaurant on Brooklyn

4759 Brooklyn Avenue N.E.
527-5247

Lunch, dinner.
11-10 M-Th, 11-10:30 F-Sat, 11-9 Sun.
Several vegetarian choices.
Credit cards accepted.

Here's an unusual twist: a restaurant that combines Indian and Middle Eastern cuisines. Owner Muhammad Bashir Bhatti, who hails from Pakistan, explains that one of the two main chefs comes from India, the other from Lebanon. The food here was nothing above average at our visit; the decor was fairly nice.

Cedars is located in an old Seattle home. The main dining room is attractive, with cushioned chairs, tables topped with pink tablecloths and pretty artificial flower arrangements, a large wine cabinet against the wall and large windows looking onto the street (unfortunately, the main landmarks out the window are a Safeway grocery store and its expansive parking lot and a Jack in the Box fast-food joint). There's a patio with a few seats for warm-weather dining outside. Attached is a tiny store that sells Indian and Middle Eastern food products.

The lentil soup is tasty, but loaded with butter. It comes with buttered naan, an Indian bread. The Middle Eastern combination plate ($6.95) includes hummus, baba ghanoush and four falafel balls smothered with a tahini sauce and placed atop a bed of lettuce and salad dressing. Pita bread is provided on the side. The Middle Eastern vegetarian plate ($7.95) includes vegetables cooked with curry sauce and seasonings, served with bulghur wheat, grape leaves, spinach and cheese pie. Tabbouleh ($3.50) is a fine salad. Vegetable cutlets ($3.95) combine vegetables, herbs and spices into lightly breaded patties that are sautéed in butter and served with chutney and cilantro sauce. Indian vegetable curry costs $5.95.

Other Choices

Sala Thai (5004 University Way N.E., 522-2297), a full-service restaurant and adjoining take-out deli, offers 12 vegetarian entrées, and two soups and salads. Start with tum kah tofu ($4.75), a mild hot and sour soup with tofu, mushrooms, lemon grass and coconut. The Sala Thai salad ($4.75) is traditional: lettuce, tomatoes, carrots and cucumber topped with a fine peanut sauce. Entrées cost $5 each at dinner and range from kang pate pug, a red curry with vegetables, tofu and coconut milk, and tofu stir-fried with basil and vegetables to preow whan tofu, a sweet and sour stir-fried tofu and vegetable dish. Open 11-3, 4:30-9 M-Sat, 4-9 Sun. Credit cards accepted.

Thai Kitchen (4112 University Way N.E., 545-6956) is a tiny Thai cafe at the back of House of Rice, an Asian market. The tom yum ($4.50), a spicy hot and sour soup, blends chile paste, lemon grass, mushrooms, lime leaves, lime juice and cilantro. Stir-fried vegetables with tofu is $4.50. The rest of the menu is comprised of meat dishes, but the cook will substitute tofu in many. Open 11-8 M-Sat. No credit cards.

Nyala Ethiopian Restaurant and Lounge (5261 University Way N.E., 524-8871) serves a good selection of vegetarian dishes in one of the more authentically decorated Ethiopian restaurants in town. The main room has American-style tables, but a room in back harbors the traditional rimmed stools and tables that are so much a part of the Ethiopian eating experience. The entrées (each $6.50) bear unusual names: yemisir wott combines lentils in a red pepper sauce; yekik alicha blends yellow split peas in a mild sauce. Yeatkilt kilkil wott is a gently spiced vegetable stew. The atkilt beyeaynetu combines smaller portions of all three. Each of these dishes is served on spongy injera bread; you break off pieces and scoop up the food. It may be messy, but that's a small price to pay to enjoy one of the world's more interesting cuisines. Open 12-10 M-W, 12-11 Th-Sun. Credit cards accepted.

Axum Ethiopian Restaurant (4142 Brooklyn Avenue N.E., 547-6848) is in the basement of a church converted into a shopping center. Joe Nemee, a native Oklahoman who traveled to Ethiopia and married the current chef, Alganesh, in 1970, opted for an American-diner feel rather than traditional Ethiopian furniture. The result is a hodgepodge restaurant with yellow and orange paint, typical booths and an assortment of Ethiopian decorations (check out the display case in the middle of the restaurant with Ethiopian baskets and crafts). The few vegetarian dishes here are cooked without butter or other dairy products, but most of the menu is for carnivores. The lone meatless entrée, atakilt aleecha ($5.25 for lunch, $5.75 for dinner), includes five of the six vegetable side dishes (separately, $1.75 each): your choice of spiced greens, onions and bell peppers; cabbage, carrot and onion blended with spices; red lentils pureed and simmered in a hot berbere sauce; yellow split peas cooked with spices; spinach and onion, and potatoes spiced with rosemary. Open 11-9 M-Sat, 5-9 Sun. Credit cards accepted.

India House Restaurant and Lounge (4737 Roosevelt Way N.E., 633-5072) offers dishes from many regions of India. Beyond soups, salads and appetizers, you can choose from nine meatless specialties. Dinners are served with soup, rice pilaf with almonds and raisins, dal and puri (deep-fried puffy bread made with white flour). Or you can order the dishes à la carte . Eggplant bharta ($9.50/$5.50) seasons whole eggplants baked over an open flame with herbs and then sautées the mixture with onions. Vegetable kofta ($9.50/$5.50) are vegetable balls served in a sauce. Breads include naan and tandoori roti, made with whole wheat flour. Open 5-9 Tu-Th, Sun, 5-10:45 F-Sat. Credit cards accepted.

Sergio's Poco Loco Burrito Express (4518 University Way N.E., 548-9877) is a tiny take-out stand serving lard-free bean dishes like crisp tacos, soft tacos, burritos and tostadas in the $1.50 to $3 range. Open 11-7 M-Sat, 11-5 Sun. No credit cards.

Tarantula Jack's Championship Chili Parlor(4543 University Way N.E., 632-0089) provides a $3.89 vegan chili (cheese is optional). It is served with rice. Open 11-9 M-Sun. No credit cards.

Costas Greek Restaurant (4559 University Way N.E., 633-2751) offers such Greek standards as hummus ($2.75), tzatziki ($2.50) and spinach salad ($6), as well as a vegetarian pita sandwich ($3.75) with lettuce, tomatoes, cucumbers, mushrooms and sprouts. Or try one of the omelets or pasta dishes. Open 8-10:30 Sun-Th, 8-11:30 F-Sat. Credit cards accepted.

Sahara Mediterranean Cuisine (4752 University Way N.E., 527-5216) offers a few interesting vegetarian dishes, most notably the vegetarian grape leaves ($6.95), stuffed with rice, parsley, tomato, onions and mint leaves, and served with hummus and yogurt. The falafel dish, including soup, costs $6.50. Among appetizers are hummus, tabbouleh and tzatziki, a yogurt salad ($2.95 each), and baba ghanoush ($3.50). The appetizer tray ($11.95) brings all four plus falafel. The vegetarian tray ($19.95) yields a sample of all the vegetarian options and easily feeds two. Open 4-9:30 M-Th, 1:30-10 F-Sat, 12-8 Sun. Credit cards accepted.

The **Korean Kitchen Restaurant** (4142 Brooklyn Avenue N.E. #104, 548-1527) is a small cafe with a couple of good vegetarian dishes. The vegetable combination is a stir-fried blend of mushrooms, broccoli, onions, carrots, cabbage and a house sauce ($3.99; with tofu, $4.25). The vegetable curry, served with salad, soup and rice, is $3.99. Open 11-8 M-Sat, 12-7 Sun. No credit cards.

Persian cuisine is the specialty of **Persepolis** (5517 University Way N.E., 524-3434), which opened in 1992. There are just a few vegetarian appetizers here (under $2.50) and no meatless entrées, but it's interesting fare. The spicy lentil soup combines lentils, garlic, mint, onions and turmeric with lemon juice. Or try the pinto bean soup. Mirza ghosemi blends barbecued eggplant, tomato, garlic and turmeric with an egg. The coo-coo is a baked egg dish with scallions, spinach, crushed walnuts with wild zershk berries, parsley and cilantro. Open 11:30-10 every day. Credit cards accepted.

For Middle Eastern food, sit-down or take-out, try **Cedars Restaurant** (1319 N.E. 43rd Street, 632-7708). The Samira's Lentil Soup ($1.75 for a cup, $2.50 for a bowl and pita bread) and ful mudames ($3) — fava beans with Cedars' special dressing and pocket bread — are good starters. Hummus, baba ghanoush, tabbouleh or a falafel sandwich are $3 to $3.25. The vegetarian plate ($5.50) includes grilled onions, mushrooms, green peppers, tomato, zucchini, carrots and eggplant served on a bed of rice and drenched with tahini sauce. Open 11-8:30 M-Sat, 2-7 Sun. No credit cards.

Mid-City Cafe (5509 University Way N.E., 623-7979), a fully vegetarian restaurant specializing in American cuisine, closed its doors at its old downtown location in May 1993, and planned to reopen on the Ave in the late summer or early fall. Kanti Mati and Von Paul Read opened in their original site in 1991. They planned to maintain the same menu, with a few additions, offer longer hours and bring the same American diner decor, complete with jukebox, to the site formerly occupied by the vegan restaurant, The Healing Earth. Lunches and dinners were to include the same garden burgers and tofu hot dogs ($4.50 to $6.85), nachos, Texas chili cheese fries, organic stir-fry vegetables, grilled tofu and grilled cheese sandwiches and quesadillas. Brunches were to bring 10-grain pancakes, tofu veggie scramble, granola and organic oatmeal. A frequent complaint is that the ownership is unfriendly to vegans. Open 11-7 Tu-F, 11-2 Sat, 10-2 Sun brunch.

University Village

The area down the hill to the east of the University District is a haven for students and young professionals, but contains few vegetarian resources. Be sure to visit the **Great Harvest Bread Co.** (5408 Sand Point Way N.E., 524-4873), which makes delicious whole food breads that contain no oils or fats, milk, eggs or preservatives. It's open 6-6 M-Sat, 7-5 Sun.

Marlai

3719 N.E. 45th Street
523-3200

Lunch, dinner.
11-10 Sun-Th, 11-10:30 F-Sat.
Several vegetarian selections.
Credit cards.

Marlai just might be the prettiest Thai restaurant in town. In a modern commercial building up the road from the University Village shopping center, the eatery has green carpeting and tables with purple chairs. A giant statue of a Thai angel — directly underneath a sunroof in the center of the dining room — greets visitors, and is encircled by plush green plants. Large windows look out onto the busy street. Two dining rooms on the side allow private dining for larger groups. The open kitchen at the back is separated from the dining room by an eating counter with stools.

Six vegetarian dishes ($5.75 to $6.50) are offered. They include rama tofu (tofu sautéed with a curried peanut sauce and served over spinach), pud Thai tofu (fried rice noodles, tofu, ground nuts and vegetables in a tamarind sauce), eggplant with basil and shiitake mushrooms in a black-bean sauce, and pineapple fried rice.

Roosevelt

Roosevelt, dominated by the intersection of 65th Street N.E. and Roosevelt Avenue N.E., packs a lot of great restaurants and shops into a small area. The neighborhood is among Seattle's most interesting and progressive: there are several great ethnic eateries here and a number of fine bookstores (including three specializing in new age titles). Sunlight Cafe, one of Seattle's oldest vegetarian restaurants, serves good soups and salads; Ethiopian, Thai, Mexican and Japanese cuisines are also popular here.

Sunlight Cafe

6403 Roosevelt Way N.E.
522-9060

Lunch, dinner, weekend brunch.
11-9 M-F, 10-9 S-S.
Strictly vegetarian.
No credit cards.

One of the first vegetarian restaurants in town, the Sunlight Cafe is a Seattle institution. It's almost always crowded, and you often have to wait for a seat — especially for brunch, which is offered from 10 to 2 on weekends. Sit in the lower of the two dining rooms if you can: it's more spacious and sunny. The high walls sport the works of local artists. Bulletin boards declare plenty of daily specials, including soups, salads, entrées, baked goods and desserts. Both the food and the atmosphere give the Sunlight Cafe a 1960s granola feel.

The food here is mostly American with some international influences — nothing especially imaginative, but pleasing to the palate. It's a little pricey compared to other restaurants of similar caliber. Stay away from the juices: coming from the refrigerator, they cannot compare to fresh-squeezed.

The most interesting item on the brunch menu (priced in the $3 to $6 range) is the eggless sesame crunch waffle (bananas, blueberries or yogurt are extra). It, the blueberry-yogurt hotcakes and the tahini toast — two slices of french toast with a layer of sesame tahini — are served with Vermont maple syrup and fresh fruit. The Sunlight scramble is a vegan steamed vegetables and tofu dish with homefries and half a seven-grain English muffin. There is a daily quiche.

Lunch, served 11-3 weekdays, includes several sandwiches (from $3 to $5.50), among them egg salad with green onions, tomato and lettuce; avocado-cheese, with swiss or raw milk cheddar, and peanut butter with bananas and raisins. A nutburger topped with melted cheese, served on a seven-grain bun, comes with soup or salad. Hummus with pita bread is $2.05. The bean burrito ($6.35, $7.60 with avocado) includes cheddar cheese, vegetables and rice, and comes topped with enchilada sauce and sour cream.

Salads (most in the $4 to $6 range) are available for lunch and dinner. They include a tofu salad, spinach, blushing lettuce, and fruit salad, the last with chopped almonds, walnuts and coconut. Among dressings are lemon-tahini, herbal and a daily special. The changing special salad usually includes grain, bean or pasta. The hearty legume and vegetable soups ($1.35/$2.10) also rotate; a soup, salad and bread combo costs $4.65.

The dinner menu (in the $6 to $9 range), served from 4 to 9 daily, includes sautéed vegetables with a Thai-style peanut sauce (tofu optional), served over organic brown rice. A separate sautéed vegetables dish comes with a tamari-ginger sauce with yogurt and cheese. The vegetarian lasagna is made with three cheeses, fresh spinach and whole wheat spinach noodles. The nutburger and bean burrito are also available, as are rotating daily specials (check the blackboard), which include vegetable pies, casseroles, curries and pasta dishes.

Lucy's Guadalajara Mexican Restaurant

1205 N.E. 65th St.
524-0717

Lunch, dinner.
11:30-9 M-Th, 11:30-9:30 F-Sat, 4-9 Sun.
Separate vegetarian menu.
Credit cards accepted.

Vegetarians are such a presence in the Roosevelt district that it's no surprise Lucy's has a separate menu for them, a fact the restaurant advertises in large letters on the window. It's a very colorful place (what Mexican restaurant isn't?) with two dining rooms and friendly owners.

On two separate visits, we found the portions huge and the food delicious, especially a bean burrito with a zesty red sauce. The meal always starts with chips and salsa. Most combination items on the vegetarian menu are $6.50, including one chile relleno and one bean chalupa; two cheese and onion enchiladas, with a green sauce; tamale, taco and cheese enchilada, and crazy burrito with guacamole and sour cream. The deluxe bean enchilada ($5.95) includes onions and bell peppers, and is topped with a green or red sauce. Side dishes also are available: nachos, a bowl of boiled beans and guacamole.

Wanza Ethiopian Cuisine

6409 Roosevelt Way N.E.
525-3950

Lunch, dinner.
11:30-2:30, 5-9 M-Sat, 5-9 Sun.
Several vegan options.
Credit cards accepted.

For those who like spicy food, Ethiopian can be among the most interesting of cuisines. It's best enjoyed when shared with a small group of friends. Vegetable preparations are served atop spongy, rounded injera bread, which you break off into pieces and use to scoop up bites of the vegetable stews. Wanza handles the cuisine very well, in a tiny, unpretentious space that has more of an American than African feel. (Most of the increasing number of Ethiopian restaurants in town have rather drab decor in lieu of the traditional Ethiopian stools and tables, due to the high cost of importing the African furniture.) Owner Daniel Wakgira, one of the founders of Kokeb on First Hill in the early 1980s, opened this restaurant in 1986.

Wanza is a particular hit with local vegetarians, and its menu leans to vegan entrées. For lunch, you can order any three dishes served on injera for $5.50, an excellent value. Choose from 10 vegetarian items, such as azifa (lentils mixed with green chile and a dash of lemon), yabesha gomen (collard greens cooked with ginger and garlic), bederjan (eggplant baked in a homemade sauce with cinnamon) and yefasolia alicha (green beans and carrots in a sauce).

The procedure for ordering dinner is a little different. For each main entrée you order, you get your choice of two side dishes to fill out your injera bread. Yemisir wott ($9.25) is one hot main dish — red lentil puree stirred with fiery berbere sauce. Another is ingudie wott ($9.75): mushrooms cooked in sunflower oil with berbere sauce. Most of the side dishes come from the lunch menu.

Other Choices

Royal Palm Thai Restaurant (6417 Roosevelt Way N.E., 523-2400) is an elegant second-floor restaurant at a corner of one of Seattle's liveliest intersections. Choose from eight vegetarian lunch and dinner options (in the $4.50 to $6.25 range), such as vegetable rolls with plum sauce, phad Thai tofu, eggplant with tofu and basil leaves in a black-bean sauce and Royal Palm salad with tofu, a salad layered with thinly sliced fried tofu, rice noodles, shredded cucumber and carrots, topped with ground peanuts and an oriental pineapple dressing. Open 11-10 every day. Credit cards accepted.

Himalaya Cuisine of India (6411 Roosevelt Way N.E., 526-9670) dispenses 11 vegetarian entrées, including dum aloo ($5.95), fried potatoes and spices; vegetable zhalfrezi ($5.95), a dish of potatoes, tomatoes, green peppers, carrots, peas and spices, and dal maharani ($3.95), a combination of three lentils. Breads include naan ($1.50), onion kulcha ($2) and chapati ($1.25). Open 11:30-3, 5-9:45 M-Sat, 12-3, 5-9:45 Sun. Credit cards accepted.

Taj Mahal India Restaurant (6510 Roosevelt Way N.E., 524-8834), a counterpart to Taj Mahal in Lake City, opened in 1993 in the former, strictly vegetarian Original King Restaurant site. The Taj Mahal lists 14 vegetarian specialties, which you can order as a dinner ($6.95 to $9.95, with soup, rice pilaf and naan bread) or à la carte ($5.50 to $7.95). They include vegetable biryani, a rice dish; aloo ghobi (spiced potatoes and cauliflower); eggplant bharta and malai kofta, a dish of vegetable balls. You also can get vegetable samosas, dals, the Taj Mahal spinach salad and any number of breads. The all-you-can-eat lunch buffet (M-Sat, $5.95) involves three vegetarian dishes plus breads and salads. Open for lunch 11-3 M-Sat; dinner, 4:30-10 Sun-Th, 4:30-11 F-Sat. Credit cards accepted.

Tanooki Cafe (6311 Roosevelt Way, 526-2935) is a posh, contemporary Japanese restaurant that serves a few vegetarian items, such as chilled tofu ($2), yakisoba with tofu ($4.25), the yaki bowl of stir-fried vegetables and tofu with rice ($4) and stir-fried vegetables ($2.75). Open 11-9 M-F, 12-9 Sat. Credit cards accepted.

Ravenna

A pleasant residential neighborhood that extends from the University District and University Village to Roosevelt, Ravenna offers a few places for vegetarians, most notably the Corner House.

Corner House

4758 19th Avenue N.E.
526-9859

Breakfast, lunch, small dinner.
7-11 Tu-F, 8-11 Sat, 8-2 Sun.
Strictly vegetarian, some vegan dishes.
No credit cards.

"Coffee, breads and things" is what the Corner House — an appealing vegetarian eatery at the southern edge of Ravenna (just north of University Village) — specializes in. Opened by Susan Cole in the summer of 1992, it is like a giant living room, full of old tables and chairs, a plush army-green couch, bookshelves and many plants. Order your food by the cash register at the back of the room. Main dishes are available only until 2 p.m., but the daily special soup and salad, as well as pastries and desserts, are served all day. The Corner House is frequented mostly by people from the neighborhood. On Thursday nights, live acoustic music is featured. Cole hopes to broaden the menu in the future, possibly adding a full dinner.

Soups ($2.95) range from french onion to tomato-vegetable to miso-tofu. Salads ($3.95) might be a garden, spinach or pasta variety. Omelets ($3) are served with homefries; you also can get a good tofu scramble with homefries. Other entrées are under $6 and include Noah's mess, a heaping pile of home fries with tomato, sprouts, salsa, guacamole and cheddar cheese; the funky special (a double-decker grilled cheddar sandwich with tomato, avocado and sprouts), and the corner club, made with cucumber, spinach, onions, tomato, sprouts and hummus on wheat bread.

Baked goods ($1 or so) might include orange-walnut or lemon-poppyseed muffins, banana bread, herb cheese scones or chocolate brownies. Among the caffeinated drinks, soy milk lattes are available; so are herbal teas.

The Santa Fe Cafe

2255 N.E. 65th Street
524-7736

Lunch, dinner.
11-2 Tu-F, 11-4 Sat, 5-10 Sun-F, 4-10 Sat.
Several vegetarian choices.
Credit cards accepted.

The Santa Fe Cafe serves creative, wonderful Southwestern food that draws raves from many vegetarians. The dishes contain lots of cheese, so vegans won't feel too comfortable here. The cafe is divided into two rooms, painted in peach and lighter shades; one has a bar. Roasted chilies hang in clusters from the dark blue ceiling; colorful tapestries and paintings are displayed on the walls.

Start lunch with chips and salsa ($1.75, $2.75 with tomatillo salsa) or a green salad. The fiesta corn salad combines corn, red and green peppers, olive oil, green chilies and spices. It's topped with gruyere cheese and served with garlic french bread. Artichoke ramekin ($5.75) is a baked spread of artichoke hearts, green chilies and kasseri cheese. The chile relleno tart ($9.25) includes hot green chilies, mozzarella and gruyere cheese, baked in a blue-corn pastry with a montrachet custard. The red enchilada plate ($7) has a blue-corn tortilla rolled with colby cheese and onion, covered with red-chile sauce and served with pinto beans and a fresh flour tortilla.

The dinner menu lists eggplant encantado ($8.75), an appetizer of grilled eggplant filled with montrachet cheese, sun-dried tomatoes and fresh rosemary surrounded by tomato and green chile sauce, served with a baguette. The artichoke ramekin ($5.75) also is available for dinner; garlic custard, served with blue corn chips, is $5.75. The chile relleno tart is $10.25 for dinner.

Other Choices

The 65th Street Deli (2615 N.E. 65th Street, 525-7747), owned since 1988 by a couple from Israel's West Bank, dispenses hummus, baba ghanoush, tabbouleh, falafel, spanakopita, veggie lasagna and eggplant parmesan (along with plenty of meat dishes), for $2.29 to $3.99. Seating consists of a counter by the large window looking onto 65th St. and a summer cafe out back. Open 9-10:30 M-Sat. Credit cards accepted.

Puget Consumers' Co-op (6514 40th Avenue N.E., 526-7661) is a health-food store that offers a deli with several interesting vegetarian salads to go. Open 8-10 M-Sun.

Northern Seattle

The Seattle neighborhoods north of Ballard, Wallingford, Green Lake and the University District are more suburban and have fewer vegetarian opportunities, but there is a scattering of interesting places that offer Indian, Indonesian, Thai and Middle Eastern cuisines.

India Palace (13025 Aurora Avenue N., 361-9710) is in an old American pizza parlor that later became a Chinese restaurant. In 1992, the India Palace took over. The decor is minimal with white-clothed tables and black-rimmed chairs with green cushions, and booths by the windows. The $4.99 all-you-can-eat lunch buffet, offered every day, includes two or three vegetarian dishes, naan bread, salads and chutneys. Dishes are cooked in vegetable oil instead of butter. On the à la carte menu, appetizers include samosas and pakoras; breads consist of naan, onion paratha and others. Then choose from 11 vegetarian specialties ($4.50 to $6.50), among them shahi paneer (Indian cheese and dried nuts in a tomato sauce), eggplant bharta and aloo bhindi (diced potato and okra cooked with freshly ground spices). Open 11:30-3, 4:30-10 M-Sun. Credit cards accepted.

Hello Belly (10002 Aurora Avenue N., 526-5130) represents an unusual blending of culinary forces, offering an array of burgers as well as Middle Eastern food. The little diner, in the Larry's Market shopping plaza, serves falafel ($5.95), hummus ($3.45), baba ghanoush ($3.95) and Greek salad ($3.45). Open 11-8 M, 11-10 T-Th, 11-11 F-Sat, 1-8 Sun. No credit cards.

The decor won't draw you to the **Siam Wok** (15221 Aurora Avenue N., 368-8517), in a converted fast-food burger restaurant on Highway 99, where you still order at the counter. But perhaps the Thai food will. Available is a handful of vegetarian dishes for $4.95 each, including tofu and vegetables, spinach topped with peanut sauce and vegetable fried rice. Open 11 to 9 M-Sat. No credit cards.

Java Restaurant (8929 Roosevelt Way N.E., 522-5282) is the lone Indonesian restaurant in Seattle. In this elegant eatery in a house in a semi-residential neighborhood, you can get two interesting vegetarian dishes for about $8 each. The sayur campur stir-fries mushrooms, onions, cauliflower, tomato, bell peppers and zucchini in a tomato sauce. The gado gado istimewa tops steamed garden vegetables with a peanut sauce and a hard-boiled egg. Open 5-10 daily. Credit cards accepted.

Omar Al Khyam Restaurant (7617 Aurora Avenue N., 782-5295), the older sibling of the Renton restaurant of the same name, opened in 1976. It dispenses Lebanese-style Middle Eastern food (in the $5 range), including hummus, baba ghanoush, tabbouleh, falafel, zahra (deep-fried cauliflower) and vegetarian grape leaves stuffed with rice, parsley, tomatoes and spices. Open 4-10 M-Sat. Credit cards accepted.

Charlotte's Bakery (124 N. 103rd Street, 789-8969) is a wholesale bakery specializing in vegetarian and vegan breads and desserts (it sells to such places as Gravity Bar, Puget Consumers' Co-op and Central Co-op Grocery); in addition, it offers a vegetarian soup for lunch. The $2.25 cup or

$3.25 bowl each come with two slices of fresh bread. A sunken dining area in the modern office building includes five tables with country chairs; above, at street level, is a corner that looks like a living room, with sofas and a coffee table. The place is wheelchair-accessible. Taking off on buy-10-get-one-free espresso punch cards, here you can get a loaf of bread free after you've bought 10. Open 6:30-4 M-F, 8-4 Sat.

Lake City

Lake City is a suburban-like Seattle neighborhood several miles north of downtown. There are only a few restaurant choices of note for vegetarians here.

Taj Mahal India Restaurant

12343 Lake City Way N.E.
367-4694

Lunch, lunch buffet, dinner.
11:30-10 M-Th, 11:30-11 F-Sat, 4:30-10 Sun.
Several vegetarian and vegan choices.
Credit cards accepted.

On balance, Taj Mahal offers decent vegetarian fare in a dining room that's somewhat drab. The $4.95 lunch buffet includes two vegetable dishes (on one occasion they were vegetable jalfraize, vegetables sauteed with spices and tomato, and navratan vegetable curry, both excellent), a nondescript iceberg lettuce salad, a mediocre tabbouleh salad and naan, the standard Indian bread.

If you order from the menu, you can ask for an entrée solo ($4.95 to $6.25), or as part of a full dinner ($6.95 to $7.95), with lentil soup, Indian salad, rice pilaf, and choice of chapati or puri bread. The most ordered dishes from the 14-item vegetarian menu include navratan curry, eggplant bharta and chole pindi — garbanzo beans cooked with spices and served with potatoes and tomatoes. Aloo palak combines potatoes and spinach in a curry sauce. Dal Maharaja, a spicy lentil soup, is $3.50.

Appetizers and breads ($1.65 to $3) are an important part of an Indian meal. Vegetable samosas and pakoras are favorites. Dahialoo chaat (potato patties in spicy yogurt with tamarind sauce) and potato vada (spiced potatoes deep-fried in chickpea batter) are interesting choices. Paratha is buttered and leavened whole wheat bread. A more adventurous choice is the stuffed paratha, filled with potatoes.

Finish your meal with one of the four sugary-sweet desserts, including ras malai, Indian cream-cheese patties in cream with almonds, or perhaps shrikand, a homemade yogurt in sweet syrup.

Other Choices

Meenar Restaurant (12359 Lake City Way N.E., 367-5666) serves Pakistani, Indian and Middle Eastern food. An added attraction for some is live music and belly dancing Thursday through Saturday evenings. The menu blends disparate appetizers such as vegetable samosas and hummus or baba ghanoush. An appetizer plate of hummus, baba ghanoush, tabbouleh and Indian naan bread is $6.95. The daily lunch buffet includes vegetable dishes, bread and salads. From the menu, you can order à la carte ($5.95 to $6.95) or full dinners ($7.95 to $10.95) served with salad, basmati rice, pilaf, chapati bread and hot mint chutney. Among vegetarian specialties are eggplant bharta, aloo chole curry (a blend of chickpeas and potatoes sauteed in curry sauce), bujia (sauteed spinach and potatoes in curry sauce) and moussaka (dinner only), layers of eggplant and other vegetables on a bed of rice pilaf topped with toasted pine nuts. Open 11-10 M-W, 11-2 Th-F, 4-2 Sat, 4-10 Sun. Credit cards accepted.

Cafe Long (12517 Lake City Way N.E., 362-6259) is a small Vietnamese place in an old American diner that touts its half-dozen vegetarian dishes. The prices are dirt-cheap: $3.75 gets you curry tofu, with garlic, onion and roasted peanuts, or sweet and sour tofu. The chow mein tofu is $3.50 and the tofu with vegetables, $3.25. Open 10:30-3, 5-9 M-F, 5-9 Sat. No credit cards.

West Seattle

Driving along West Seattle's main drag, California Avenue, you might feel as though you're passing through the 1950s: the two or three main concentrations of shops along the road have that middle America, small-town feel. Unfortunately, the restaurants here also seem largely as if they come from that era: you're much more likely to see people feasting on a side of ribs than a garden burger. Even along festive Alki Beach Drive, which feels so Californian, there are precious few opportunities for vegetarians.

But there are some. Best bets here are Phoenicia, Maharaja's Indian Cuisine, Pallin Thai Cuisine and Miyake Japanese Restaurant.

Phoenicia Restaurant

2716 Alki Avenue S.W.
935-6550

Dinner.
Tu-Sat, hours unavailable at presstime.
Several vegan, vegetarian choices.
Credit cards accepted.

Hussein Khazaal, a native Lebanese, opened Phoenicia in West Seattle in 1974 before moving to Lower Queen Anne. The building that housed Phoenicia a stone's throw from the Seattle Center was to be replaced by a Larry's Market, and Hussein planned to return to a new location in West Seattle in mid-1993.

The friendly owner claims that he serves the best meatless fare in all of Seattle. In a city full of good vegetarian restaurants, that's a debatable point. After all, much of Phoenicia's emphasis is on lamb and other meat dishes. However, the pure vegan food certainly is good, and his enthusiasm commendable. He planned to retain much the same menu.

The appetizers boast enough good selections to create a meal: tabbouleh and baba ghanoush ($3.95 each); ful mudamas ($3.95) — fava beans cooked with garlic, cumin, cilantro, olive oil and salsa; Egyptian Caesar salad ($2.95/$6.95), with garlic, pepper, lemon, olive oil and goat cheese (and no anchovies); and poor man's caviar, a dish of broiled and mashed eggplant with English cucumber, roast garlic, parsley, basil, olive oil, cilantro and balsamic vinegar.

Main dishes (most $8.95) include steamed fresh vegetables and rice; a falafel plate; vegetarian couscous, a tasty dish of couscous topped with eggplant, chickpeas and onions in a mildly spicy sauce, and the Mediterranean plate ($9.95) — hummus, baba ghanoush, salad and poor man's caviar.

Khazaal proudly mentions the three vegetarian specials he offers every night. One time, the choices were fresh angel-hair pasta with roast eggplant, tomato and garlic ($9.95); shiitake mushrooms, sun-dried tomatoes, garlic and pepper served with roasted garlic, roasted shallots and fresh tomato with brown rice or pasta ($10.95); and roasted eggplant, baby zucchini, baby squash, asparagus and green beans served with a sauce of mushrooms, chestnuts, chickpeas and pine nuts ($9.95).

Sugary-sweet desserts include the Mediterranean staple baklava ($2.50); knafi ($2.95), crisp shredded wheat filled with nuts, honey and orange flower water, and a cheese pastry oozing honey, cream cheese and cinnamon ($2.50).

Maharaja Cuisine of India

4542 California Avenue S.W.

935-9443

Lunch, dinner.
11 to 2:30 M-Sat, 11-2 Sun; 4-10 every day.
Several vegetarian choices.
Credit cards accepted.

The American steakhouse decor won't make you think you're in India, but if you close your eyes, the aromas and tastes certainly will. This is quality Indian food. Maharaja is owned by the folks who run another Indian restaurant by the same name in Federal Way. This one used to be a combination steakhouse/lounge. The new owners retained the lounge.

Maharaja's best deal is the all-you-can-eat lunch buffet for $5.95. You get dal, the lentil soup that's a staple of Indian cooking, as well as two other vegetarian entrées (often, at least one is vegan). Help yourself to the cucumber, carrot and green pepper salad to cool your palate after the spicy entrées. Be sure to take a slice or two of naan, the Indian pastry-flour bread cooked in a tandoor oven. And the vivid green mint-coriander chutney, hot and spicy, is not to be missed.

The restaurant offers 11 vegetarian entrées for both lunch and dinner (prices are the same for each, in the $4 to $6 range.) Matar paneer is made of homemade cheese and peas cooked in a mildly spicy gravy. Bharta mixes eggplant pulp, roasted in a tandoor oven, with peas, onions, tomatoes and fresh seasonings. In sag paneer, cubes of cheese and spinach are combined in a spicy sauce. Malai kofta is vegetable balls cooked in exotic Indian herbs and spices. Vegetable biryani, basmati rice with mixed vegetables, is a meal in itself.

Also try vegetable samosas ($1.95 for two) — Indian pastries deep-fried and stuffed with delicately spiced mashed potatoes and peas. Also excellent are the Indian breads (about $2), including garlic naan, paratha (a multi-layered whole wheat buttered bread), aloo paratha, stuffed with mildly spiced potatoes and peas, and onion kulcha, leavened bread filled with minced onions and baked in the tandoor oven.

Other Choices

Pallin Thai Cuisine (2223 California Avenue S.W., 937-8807) offers a dozen vegetarian choices, including eight entrées. Spring rolls, served with plum sauce, are $3.95. Tom yum phug ($4.50) is a hot and sour soup with mixed vegetables. Entrées (under $5) include sweet and sour vegetables; sautéed fresh eggplant with chile paste; sautéed zucchini, carrots, snow peas and broccoli served with garlic sauce and a touch of white pepper, and phad Thai. Open 11:30-10 M-F, 5-10 S-S. Credit cards accepted.

Miyake Japanese Restaurant (2605 California Avenue S.W., 938-8515) is a fine place for meatless Japanese dishes priced from $2.95 to $5.45. Lunch choices (each $3.45) include vegetable tempura; ten don, which is fried vegetables over rice; tempura udon (deep-fried veggies on noodle soup) and kitsune udon (fried tofu and onion on noodle soup). The miso soup ($1) is excellent, bearing green onion and little pieces of tofu. Agedashi deep-fried tofu is served for both lunch and dinner; so is yutofu, boiled tofu in a soup with a citrus-infused ponzu sauce. The avocado rolls, sandwiched between sticky white rice and seaweed, are delicious. Open 11:30-2:30, 5:30-10 M-Sat. Credit cards accepted.

For a quick weekend breakfast or weekday lunch, stop at **Peace Cafe** (2352 California Avenue S.W., 935-1540), a quaint espresso joint with a small kitchen. Here you can get a vegan Egyptian lentil soup ($1.50/$2.50) or a vegetable soup — although more often than not, the chef uses chicken stock for the latter, so ask before ordering. Hummus is $2; boreks — spinach and feta wrapped in phyllo pastry — are $3.95. Also under $5 are a falafel sandwich and a spinach and feta quiche. Breakfasts ($3.75 to $5.50), served weekends only until 2 p.m., include apple pancakes or waffles, french toast, eggs florentine and "eggless," sautéed veggies over potatoes.

A Taste of Vietnam (4453 California Avenue S.W., 933-9521) is a tiny 1950s-style diner that, somewhat out of character, serves Vietnamese and Chinese dishes. Among the eight interesting vegetarian entrées (in the $5 to $6 range) are sweet and sour tofu with tomato, garlic, onion, green pepper and pineapple; tofu with lemon grass, peanuts and hot pepper, and tofu with saté and hot pepper. Open 11-9 M-Sat. No credit cards.

Beach House Espresso & Juice Bar (2620 Alki Avenue S.W., 935-4221) is a fine place for a refreshing drink on a warm summer day. You can sip your juice inside, or outdoors on the deck. Besides the usual array of fruit and vegetable juices ($2 for 10 ounces, $3 for 16) and caffeinated drinks, you can get pastries or baked potatoes here, and the soup of the day is usually vegetarian. Open 8-10 or 11 daily in summer; in winter, 10-6 W-F, 9-8 Sat, 9-6 Sun. No credit cards.

Georgie Cafe (9214 45th Avenue S.W., 933-8413) serves Greek food on the lower floor of a trendy blue apartment building, two blocks east of the West Seattle ferry landing. Here you can order hummus, tzatziki (a yogurt, cucumber and garlic dip) or melizanosalata (a mixture of eggplant, garlic and herbs) for $3.50 each; a vegetarian lentil soup with lemon, garlic and butter ($2.25/$3.75) or Greek salad ($3.95/$5.95). Entrées ($6.95 for lunch, $8.95 for dinner) include George's combination plate (but be sure to ask for a substitute, which they will provide, for the shish kebab); moussaka, a traditional Greek eggplant dish baked with garlic, tomato, spices and pine nuts and topped with feta cheese, and spanakopita, a spinach and cheese pie with phyllo pastry. Breakfast includes omelets and french toast. Open 11-9 M-F, 9-10 weekends. Credit cards accepted.

Eagles Thai Restaurant (4510 California Avenue S.W., 938-6708) serves five vegetarian dishes, each a bargain at $3.75: vegetables in wine sauce, hot summer jay (stir-fried tofu in red curry sauce), eagle garden (soft tofu in a light soy gravy), swimming eagle (tofu and steamed veggies topped with peanut sauce) and vegetable curry in coconut milk and red curry sauce. Spring rolls are $3.25. Open 11-3, 5-10 M-Sat. Credit cards accepted.

Take Two (2341 California Avenue S.W., 932-8505), a tiny cafe right next to the Admiral Theater movie house, offers two vegetarian sandwiches ($4.95): the Anthony Quinn with eggplant, roasted peppers, feta cheese, greek olives, hummus and herbed olive oil, and the Whoopi Goldberg with cheese, artichoke hearts, roasted peppers and herbed olive oil. But they're not so savvy on vegetarianism, calling an Italian ham sandwich the Madonna (she gave up meat long ago). Open 11:30-8:30 T-Th and Sat, 11-9 F. No credit cards.

Taqueria Guaymas (4719 California Avenue S.W., 935-8970) is a small and informal Mexican eatery that dispenses a handful of vegetarian choices, including a veggie burrito with whole beans ($3) and a veggie taco ($1.85). Order at the back counter, then sit on one of the picnic tables in the restaurant or take your meal home. Open 11-10 M-Sun. No credit cards.

Puget Consumers' Co-op (2749 California Avenue S.W., 937-8481) has a small deli that serves several good vegetarian salads. You also can choose from an assortment of pre-made veggie sandwiches from the refrigerator. Open 8-10 M-Sun.

Capers (4521 California Avenue S.W., 932-0371) is a pleasant deli that provides caffeinated drinks as well as spanakopita, quiche and some other interesting (and occasionally vegetarian) salads. But the apple juice on one visit was a watered-down version dispensed from the soda fountain. Cookbooks and a limited stock of cooking supplies are also for sale. Open 6:30-7 M-Th, 6:30-8 F, 8-6 Sat, 8-5 Sun.

The Eastside

The Eastside — the several King County towns east of Lake Washington, including Bellevue, Kirkland, Redmond and others — may be the epitome of suburbia from housing and shopping centers to eating habits. But, surprisingly, there are lots of dining choices here for vegetarians. There are no fully vegetarian restaurants, but many ethnic places offer plenty of meatless fare.

Two of the Northwest's finest Indian restaurants are found on the Eastside: Shamiana in Kirkland and Raga in downtown Bellevue. The debate continues over which is better; Shamiana is slightly more vegetarian-friendly. The Bite of India, a small booth in the food court at Crossroads Mall in Bellevue, is no slouch either. Its masala dosa is one of the most delicious, and popular, meatless dishes in the Puget Sound area. The Pompeii is an elegant downtown Bellevue restaurant specializing in Italian cuisine, much of it vegetarian or vegan. Blacksheep Cafe and Catering in Bothell offers fine vegetarian fare for breakfast and lunch.

Circo Circo in Kirkland, a Mexican restaurant owned by a vegetarian, serves creative meatless choices among more traditional fare. Coyote Coffee Company is a coffeehouse that offers mostly vegetarian soups, salads and sandwiches.

Bellevue

Raga Cuisine of India

555 108th Avenue N.E.

450-0336

Lunch, lunch buffet, dinner.
11:30-2, 5-10 Sun-F; 5-10 Sat.
Several vegan and vegetarian items.
Credit cards accepted.

One of the best Indian restaurants in Washington, Raga epitomizes elegance yet simplicity. Here you won't find the garish ornaments and tacky paintings that clutter some Indian eateries. Raga's two dining rooms are decorated in pristine white and black colors. White linen tablecloths are set off by sleek black chairs. Sophisticated paintings of Indian scenes, done in the classic style, hang on the white walls. The restaurant, which serves North Indian cuisine (with some Western innovations), was opened in downtown Bellevue in 1991 by Bill Khanna and Kamal Mroke.

The best deal here is the $6.95 lunch buffet. You can make multiple trips to the two tables laden with Indian salads and entrées. The buffet always contains several vegan and vegetarian salads, based on vegetables, chickpeas and even pasta. The hot portion of the buffet always includes a dal or a chickpea dish, rice pilaf and, unfortunately, just one vegetable dish (most Indian buffets involve two or three). The buffet also comes with naan bread.

If you're ordering à la carte, from the appetizer menu (dubbed "The First Experiment"), try the vegetable samosas ($3.50) or pakoras. The Buddha salad

($3.95 or $6.95) combines lettuce, homemade cheese and cilantro flour crisps. Breads (in the $1.50 to $3 range) are always a must when eating Indian: try the naan with onion and cilantro or the garlic and basil naan.

Raga serves nine vegetarian dishes ($8 to $9). Most popular is the eggplant bharta — eggplant baked over charcoal and mixed with diced onion, tomatoes and hot Indian spices. An interesting dish with Italian overtones is the vegetable pastarama, curried fettuccine with vegetables in a cream sauce. More traditional is aloo ghobi, sautéed potatoes and cauliflower in curry. For those who don't mind a lot of cholesterol, there's paneer tikka masala, homemade cheese cooked in a sauce of tomato, yogurt, cream and butter.

Desserts (most $2.95) include mango ice cream with pistachios and nuts; gulab jammun, deep-fried balls of light cheese in sugar syrup and rose water, and kheer, a thick rice pudding.

Pompeii Ristorante

108th Avenue N.E.
646-6860

Lunch, dinner.
11-3, 4-11 M-F, 4-11 Sat, 4-10 Sun.
Several vegetarian and vegan dishes.
Credit cards accepted.

Pompeii, on the ground floor of Koll Center Bellevue, a downtown skyscraper, is an elegant Italian restaurant serving a variety of vegetarian and vegan dishes, along with meat, chicken and seafood. The dining room is hand-painted in shades of red. A large and beautiful scene of ancient Italy is painted on one wall. Many of the pastas are made with semolina flour instead of eggs.

Lunch antipasti ($3.95 to $4.50) include eggplant and mozzarella with basil and olive oil and herbed polenta served over a bed of sautéed spinach with roasted red pepper salsa. Salad choices ($2.95 to $6.50) are butter lettuce and finely diced vegetables with olive oil and red wine vinegar; cucumbers, baked beets and smoky roasted yellow peppers on a bed of spinach; ricotta and roma tomatoes over watercress dressed with olive oil, and grilled flatbread with cucumbers, kalamata olives, roma tomatoes, red onions and goat cheese. The minestra aromatica soup ($2.95) is cooked in a vegetable stock, adding new potatoes, arugula (a somewhat bitter salad green), herbs and rice. The housemade ravioli filled with roasted eggplant, roma tomatoes and basil is tossed in brown butter and sage, and garnished with roasted hazelnuts ($7.50, $9.95 for dinner).

Polentas ($6.95 to $7.50) are available for lunch and dinner. They include ground polenta served with gorgonzola and cream, and polenta sautéed with wild mushrooms, white wine and rosemary.

Dinner brings different appetizers, salads and soups. Start with grilled marinated eggplant layered with parmesan, fontina, gruyere and provolone, baked with herbs and marinara sauce ($5.50). Salads ($3.25 to $4.50) include organic greens, toasted walnuts and scallions tossed in a red wine vinaigrette; braised swiss chard sautéed in olive oil with pine nuts and black pepper, and thinly sliced radishes, carrots and watercress, drizzled with olive oil and parmesan. A soup of pureed white beans, herbs and squash with fresh rosemary is $3.50. A pasta dish of fresh baby artichokes and olives tossed with parmesan-reggiano cheese and black pepper is $8.50.

Vegetarian diners also may enjoy the (mostly vegan) daily antipasti dishes, including such treats as marinated, grilled eggplant and roasted bell peppers. For $7, you can get a plate full of the four or five daily choices; $1.75 pays for a side plate of one choice.

Bite of India

15600 N.E. 8th Street
643-4263

Lunch, dinner.
11-9 M-Sat, 12-6 Sun.
Several vegan options.
No credit cards.

It may be just a small food-court stand in the Crossroads Mall, but Bite of India serves a lot of good vegetarian fare. By far the most popular item on the menu is the masala dosa ($4.99), a sourdough lentil and rice crepe stuffed with spicy potatoes. The foot-long dosa spills over the edges of the extra-large plate and is accompanied by a spicy coconut chutney and a small bowl of sambar, the spicy Indian lentil soup. The electronic bulletin board overhead claims that more than 60,000 dosas have been served.

Other dosas include the mung dosa, made with mung beans sprinkled with onions and jalapeno pepper, and sada dosa vada, a deep-fried lentil dumpling. A bowl of sambar with pappadam (a giant chip made of beans and lentils) is $1.99. Vegetable curry with rice pilaf is $3.49 or $4.99.

Twelve Baskets Restaurant & Catering

825 116th Ave. N.E.
455-3684

Lunch, dinner.
11-3 M-Th, 11-9 F-Sat.
Several vegetarian, a few vegan choices.
Credit cards accepted.

Eastside vegetarians have been heading to Twelve Baskets for years, albeit to three different locations. John Bagge first opened the place in 1976 on Main Street in Old Bellevue, before moving it seven blocks away. In 1991, Twelve Baskets switched to its latest site, which he says is a better location. In the beginning, Twelve Baskets was mostly vegetarian, but John added meat dishes to attract more customers. In 1993, he planned to revise the menu, adding several more grain and bean dishes. Meatless entrées here tend to contain eggs or cheese, but some can be made vegan.

A cozy country place (on a very busy Bellevue street) with old mismatched wooden chairs and tables in two spacious dining rooms, the restaurant is most popular at lunch. Each of the more than 12 baskets here ($5.50 to $6.50 at lunch) is named for a Biblical character. In 1992, Paul's Basket was voted the best vegetarian dish on the Eastside by Eastside Weekly, an alternative newspaper. It is a mildly spicy chile and cheese burrito topped with black olives, avocado, sour cream and green onions, served with a brown and wild rice medley and chips and salsa. Samuel's Basket is a vegetarian burger (with cheese and eggs), topped with provolone cheese, lettuce, tomato and mustard. For Hannah's Basket, vegetables are steamed or stir-fried with teriyaki sauce, and are served with rice and a 12-grain roll. Naomi's Basket is another sought-after dish: a baked potato stuffed with steamed vegetables and covered with low-fat cheese sauce. The soup of the day ($2.35 or $3.15) is always vegan, says Bagge.

For dinner ($7 to $8), Hannah's Basket and Samuel's Basket are available. Or try Andrew's Basket, a casserole layered with brown rice, sour cream, zucchini and grated colby cheese, baked in the oven and topped with tomatoes and cashews. Several pastas and salads also are offered for lunch or dinner.

Juice Works

Bellevue Square Mall
455-0823

Juice bar.
9:30-9:30 M-Sat, 11-6 Sun.
No food.
No credit cards.

Here's a nice surprise: a store in a shopping mall that promotes good health. Juice Works is a pleasant, light place with a black and white checkerboard floor, a purple counter with several stools and cabinets full of fresh produce. Opened in late 1992 by two architects, Garrison and Tricia Bailey, Juice Works also sells Juiceman juicers and a selection of relevant books, such as John Robbins' *Diet for a New America.* Garrison's paintings of produce hang on the wall. It's a fun and funky place with an assortment of music — ranging from jazz to rock 'n' roll — playing over the speakers.

Smoothies, containing a variety of fruits and yogurt, are among the most popular items here ($3.75 for 16 ounces). Juices ($2 for eight ounces, $2.75 for 12 and $3.25 for 16) include orange, apple, pineapple, pear, melon, grape, carrot, celery, beet, spinach, cucumber, cabbage and tomato. Combinations are an extra 25 or 50 cents. Add garlic or honey to your drink for 50 cents; protein powder or amino acids are an extra $1.

Other Choices

King & I (10509 Main Street, 462-9337), on the southern edge of downtown Bellevue, serves 13 Thai vegetarian entrées ($5 to $6), as well as two soups, an appetizer and a salad. Start with King's spring rolls or tom yum pug, a hot and sour vegetable soup. The yum tofu is a salad with fried tofu, lime juice, chile, onion, tomato, chili paste and lettuce. Entrées include ginger tofu, stir-fried broccoli and vegetables with tofu and black-bean sauce, Anna's garden (vegetables stir-fried with wine and garlic) and vegetables in a red curry sauce. Open 11-10 Sun-Th, 1-11 F-Sat. Credit cards accepted.

River Kwai Cafe (10666 N.E. 8th Street, 637-1185), in downtown Bellevue, is a Thai restaurant that offers four vegetarian dishes for lunch ($4.95 each), including phad Thai jay (stir-fried noodles with egg, tofu, broccoli, snow peas and sprouts), cashew jay (stir-fried tofu and vegetables with cashews) and curried vegetables. For dinner, choose from 11 vegetarian dishes (all $4.95), among them spicy tofu, ginger tofu and fried rice jay. Yum tofu is a salad with fried tofu, lemon juice, herbs, chile paste and lettuce. Open 11-10 M-Sat, 11-9 Sun. Credit cards accepted.

Andre's European and Vietnamese Cuisine (14125 N.E. 20th Street, 747-6551) wins acclaim from local vegetarians and food critics (it won second place in the Eastside Weekly's 1992 survey for favorite restaurant). A bar and saté bar take up the center of the elegant restaurant; plush booths line the walls on either side. At lunch (under $5), try the vegetarian egg noodles; vegetarian delight, with tofu and vegetables over rice, or vegetarian ca-ri — stir-fried curried vegetables and tofu. Vegetarian choices at dinner ($8.25 to $8.75) include a curry crepe made of tofu, vegetables, bean sprouts and mushrooms; da nang tofu, a fried tofu sandwich with vegetables, basil, mushrooms, a special sauce and steamed rice, and ha long noodles, stir-fried vegetables and tofu with coconut milk and curry paste. Open 11:30-3 M-F, 5:30-9:30 T-Th, 5:30-10 F-Sat. Credit cards accepted.

Thai Chef (1645 140th Avenue N.E., 562-7955) offers three vegetarian appetizers, two soups and six entrées in the $4 to $6 range. Start with Thai spring rolls or vegetarian mee krob, crispy rice noodles mixed with tofu in a Thai sauce. Tom yum pak includes cabbage, mushrooms and baby corn in a hot and sour soup with a touch of lemon grass. Vegetarian curry and spinach delight — spinach and tofu with a spicy peanut sauce — are tempting choices. Patpong veggies combines broccoli and cashews. Open 11-2:30, 5-9:30 M-F, 5-9:30 S-S. Credit cards accepted.

The Thai Kitchen Restaurant (14115 N.E. 20th Street, 641-9166), the twin restaurant of the Thai Kitchen II in Kirkland, has an extensive vegetarian menu, with five appetizers, five soups and 12 entrées (most $4 or $4.50). Favorite appetizers are spring rolls or fried wontons, as well as corn patties. Soups include hot and sour vegetable, bean curd and coconut with mushrooms. Among entrées are eggplant with curry and sweet basil, stir-fried bean sprouts and vegetables, and stir-fried vegetables with tofu. Open 11-10 M-Sun. Credit cards accepted.

Karim's Kitchen (2115 Bellevue-Redmond Road, 641-1174) was known as Marco Polo until a name change in 1993. It still serves the same Pakistani and Middle Eastern cuisine. During one visit here, our food was mixed: onion naan bread ($1.50) was drizzled with excessive amounts of butter and the eggplant bharta ($2.50) was cold and soupy. But the aloo ghobi ($4.95), cauliflower and potatoes simmered in a light sauce of tomatoes, onions and spices, was delicious. You can also order a hummus sandwich ($3.95); Sabz curry ($4.95), seasonal vegetables simmered in tomatoes, onions and spices, served with yogurt and chutney, and matar paneer ($4.75), green peas and tomatoes tossed with mild Pakistani cheese. The decor involves Pakistani accessories in a typical American dining room. Open 11-2 M-F, 4-10 Tu-Sat, 4-9 Sun-M. Credit cards accepted.

Ebru Mediterranean Deli (in the Crossroads Mall food court, 15600 N.E. 8th Street, 641-4352) serves several vegetarian standards, including sandwiches and salads. Good choices (all $3.99) are the vegetarian delight sandwich, combining hummus, avocado, tomato and sprouts in a pita; the hummus croissant, and Ebru's veggie sandwich with baked eggplant. The changing specialty salads are $2.09. No credit cards.

Yonny Yonson's Yogurt and Sandwich Shop (14725 N.E. 20th Street, 641-6206) serves two meatless burgers. Vegans will enjoy the tofu burger ($3.40), a patty made from tofu, soybeans, carrots, potatoes, whole wheat, sunflower seeds, oil, tamari and spices. Those who don't eat dairy should ask them to skip the cream cheese and Thousand Island dressing. Others will like the garden burger ($3.60), made from mushrooms, onions, oats, mozzarella, cottage cheese, cheddar cheese, bulghur wheat and walnuts. You can also get a vegan garden salad with assorted vegetables, avocado and sprouts for $3.80, a standard vegetarian sandwich with avocado, cucumber, cream cheese, sprouts, sunflower seeds, mayo, lettuce and tomato ($2.75 for half, $3.90 for full) or a sticky adam ($2.50/$3.60), peanut butter with bananas, raisins, cream cheese and sunflower seeds. Open 9-7 M-F (until 9 in summer), 11-6 Sat, 11:30-5 Sun. No credit cards.

Casa D's Taqueria (102 Bellevue Way N.E., 462-8410) is a small Mexican eatery that offers lard-free bean dishes. And unlike most Mexican restaurants, the rice here is not cooked in chicken stock. You can order a garden burrito with guacamole for $4.25 (a "super," made with two lard-free flour tortillas, is $5.95). Other options include garden tacos, tostadas and a garden taco salad ($3.75 to $4.90). Open 11-8 M-Sat, 12-8 Sun. Credit cards accepted.

Nature's Pantry (10200 N.E. 10th Street, 454-0170), a full-service health-food store, has a serve-yourself deli, including soups ($1.10/$1.65), and several microwavable vegetable and tofu salads in the cooler. Seats are available in back. Open 9-7 M-F, 9:30-6 Sat, 12-5 Sun. No credit cards.

Factoria

O'Char (in Loehmann's Plaza, 3700-F N.E. 128th Avenue, 641-1900) serves a variety of Thai vegetarian dishes. Meatless lunch choices ($4.50) include steamed spinach topped with spicy peanut sauce, phad Thai, fried rice with egg and three others. For dinner, you can order five spring rolls for $3.95, or one of eight vegetarian entrées for $5.50, such as cucumber, pineapple, tomato, onion and bell pepper in a sweet and sour sauce; ginger vegetables; steamed vegetables with black pepper and garlic, or veggie lover — sautéed vegetables with soy sauce. Open 11-3 M-F; 4:30-9:30 M-Th, Sun; 4:30-10:30 F-Sat. Credit cards accepted.

Kirkland

Shamiana
10724 N.E. 68th Street
827-4902

Lunch, lunch buffet, dinner.
11-2:30, 5-10 M-F, 5-10 S-S.
Several vegetarian and vegan choices.
Credit cards accepted.

"Elegant" is the best word to describe Shamiana — a surprise, since the Indian restaurant is located at the edge of a nondescript shopping center, around the corner from the Kirkland Puget Consumers' Co-op. Sleek black tables grace the bi-level dining area, which has large windows and colorful banners hanging from the red ceiling. A collection of tiny, colorful Indian slippers, arranged in concentric circles, adorns one wall. Restaurant critics rave about the food here; some call Shamiana the best example of Indian cuisine in metropolitan Seattle. Service is quick and personable.

The vegan-friendly menu places a diamond next to each item (vegetarian and meat alike) that contains no dairy products. From the vegetarian specialties, four of eight entrées (in the $5.75 to $7 range) are vegan: vegetable curry, eggplant bharta, saag (spinach pureed with coconut milk and spices served with potatoes or cheese) and chickpeas gujarati, simmered in a light tomato and fennel sauce.

Other vegetarian dishes include matar paneer — peas, tomatoes and spices tossed with homemade Indian cheese; butter masala paneer, a tasty dish of cheese cubes in a smooth cream sauce; aloo dum kashmiri, potatoes simmered in a spicy yogurt, onion and tomato sauce ("Vegetarian Nirvana!" proclaims the menu), and eggplant hashmet, thick slices of grilled spiced eggplant topped with a cool yogurt sauce.

The dal ($1.75) is dairy-free. Vegetable samosas and vegetable cutlets (both $4.25) also are listed as vegan. Chapati and pappadam breads ($1 each) are vegan; naan ($1.50), brushed with ghee and nigella seeds, is not. Desserts include an assortment of sorbets and other palate cleansers.

At lunch, try the all-you-can-eat buffet ($5.95), with two or three vegetarian dishes, dal, naan, salad and rice pilaf. All the buffet items are labeled as dairy or non-dairy.

Circo Circo
12709 N.E. 124th Street
821-9405

Lunch, dinner.
11-10 M-Th, 11-11 F-Sat, 3-9 Sun.
Several vegetarian options.
Credit cards.

Circo Circo is a boon for vegetarian fans of Mexican dining. Although the festive restaurant -- opened in 1993 in the Totem Place shopping plaza -- offers the usual meat and chicken dishes, here you'll find lard-free beans and rice that is not cooked in chicken stock. Owner Kim Mora, a vegetarian, has created a menu with many tempting meatless options. Circo Circo's theme is the circus, and Kim went on a shopping spree in Guadalajara to purchase the dozens of authentic clown puppets that hang from the ceiling. Before opening Circo Circo, she operated Mexican places in Factoria and Lynnwood.

A lengthy listing of appetizers ($3.25 to $5.95) includes nachos, quesadillas, potato skins, hongos à la Diabla (the Devil's mushrooms, cooked in butter and a zesty sauce) and high-wire veggies (cold Mexican vegetables with seasonings). Those trying to avoid the fat in guacamole can order mockamole, a tasty substitute made out of asparagus. The burrito vegetarian special ($6.75) during our visit was delicious, smothered in a spicy ranchero sauce and filled with beans. Even better was tacos rancheros, corn tortillas filled with seasoned potatoes (an unusual but welcome variation). Kim said the potato filling can substitute for meat or beans in many of the dishes.

Coyote Coffee Company

111 Main Street
827-2507

Lunch, dinner.
6-8 M-Tu, Th, 6-9 or 10 W, F, Sat, 9-6 Sun.
Several vegetarian options.
Credit cards accepted.

A 1992 addition to downtown Kirkland, the Coyote Coffee Company is a mostly vegetarian establishment that concentrates on coffees but also sells soups, salads and sandwiches. Martha and Carl Austin, owners of this informal, modern place filled with local artwork, books by Native-American authors and other gifts, are not vegetarians. But in recent years, they've gradually changed their diets to include more meatless foods. When they opened the coffee house, they wanted to serve the kinds of meals that they were eating.

Thus the menu harbors such things as an Italian herb bread sandwich filled with artichoke hearts, tomato, fresh basil, lettuce and feta cheese ($3.50), a mixed green salad with artichoke hearts and feta ($3.95) and tortilla Santa Fe or garden vegetable soup ($1.35 a cup, $2.50 a bowl). Perhaps the favorite sandwich here is the tuffolo, hearty Italian bread brushed with olive oil, garlic and fresh herbs and stuffed with mozzarella, tomato, green pepper, onion and sweet basil. On the menu, it's completed with salami. But the Austins report that many of their customers are vegetarians, and they gladly substitute artichoke hearts for the salami more than half the time. A "mostly muffuletta" sandwich is a mixture of Spanish green manzanilla olives, California black olives, capers, artichoke hearts, garlic and Italian herbs, served in a crusty Italian roll with provolone cheese.

Many of the rich desserts are made with Seattle's Dilettante Chocolates. You might try hazelnut-chocolate mousse topped with whipped cream and bittersweet chocolate ephemere sauce, or one of the dessert specials in the front pastry counter. Wednesday, Friday and Saturday nights are music nights here, and the coffee house -- which ordinarily closes at 8 -- remains open until 9 or 10.

Other Choices

Portofino Cafe (107 Lake Street, 822-2176), in downtown Kirkland, has a juice bar and serves vegetarian soups and a sandwich. A 10-ounce juice is $2; 16 ounces cost $3. Choose from carrot, celery, cucumber, apple, grapefruit, melon, orange or pineapple. The soup of the day is usually vegetarian, but not vegan. A vegetarian sandwich ($4.50) with herbed cream cheese, cucumber, zucchini and mushrooms is served on nine-grain bread. Three or four salads range from $1.35 to $3. White walls are adorned with funky local art; the black and white checkerboard floor holds just a few tables. A tiny patio in back offers a couple of seats. Open 6-4 M-W, 6-6 Th-Sat, 7-4 Sun. No credit cards.

The Thai Kitchen Restaurant II (11701 124th Avenue N.E., 821-5335), the twin restaurant of the Thai Kitchen in Bellevue, offers an extensive vegetarian menu, with five appetizers, five soups and 12 entrées. Favorite starters include spring rolls or fried wontons ($3.95 each), as well as corn patties ($4.50). Among soups ($4.50) are hot and sour vegetable, bean curd and coconut with mushrooms. Entrées, also $4.50, include eggplant with curry and sweet basil, stir-fried bean sprouts and vegetables and stir-fried vegetables with tofu. Open 11-10 M-Sun. Credit cards accepted.

Thai Place (136 Central Way N.E., 828-0808), in downtown Kirkland, offers a small vegetarian selection. The lunch menu ($4.95 to $5.50) includes tofu rama with spinach and peanut sauce, spicy tofu with curry paste and panang tofu, a deep-fried tofu dish with coconut milk and red curry. Dinner brings five choices ($4.95 each), including pra ram puk (vegetables with peanut sauce), puk wine (vegetables sautéed with white wine) and puk preo wan (sweet and sour vegetables). Open 11-3, 5-10 M-F, 5-10 S-S. Credit cards accepted.

Tommy Thai Restaurant (8516 122nd Avenue N.E., 889-2447) dispenses four vegetarian entrées ($5.50 to $5.95), including Tommy Thai's garden (stir-fried vegetables in Thai soy sauce with bean-thread noodles), sweet and sour vegetables, tofu swimming angels (deep-fried tofu topped with peanut and chile sauce on a bed of spinach) and pa-nang puk (vegetables in Thai red curry and coconut milk with deep-fried tofu). Open 11:30-2:30 Tu-F, 5-9:30 Tu-Th, Sun, 5-10:30 F-Sat. Credit cards accepted.

Puget Consumers' Co-op (10718 N.E. 68th Street, 828-4621) is a huge health-food store with a small deli and a few tables. You can order a variety of nutritious salads, among them marinated tofu, for a reasonable price. Open 8-10 M-Sun.

Redmond

Temasek Restaurant (16421 Cleveland Street, 867-1171), in downtown Redmond, serves six Thai and Singapore vegetarian dishes for $5.25 to $5.75, including stir-fried vegetables and garden delight vegetables topped with peanut sauce. But the most interesting dishes are the Singapore ones: tahu goreng, deep-fried tofu served over a bed of vegetables topped with peanut sauce, and sayor lodeh, a Malaysian-style vegetable stew in a spicy coconut gravy. Open 11-2:30, 5-9 M-F, 5-9 Sat. Credit cards accepted.

Dos Jalapenos (15163 N.E. 24th Avenue, 644-4522), an informal fast-food restaurant in the Overlake Square shopping center near Sears, serves some vegetarian Mexican dishes. The refried beans here are cooked in lard, but the whole beans are done in vegetable oil. You can get a vegetarian burrito for under $4, stuffed with beans, rice, salsa and sour cream, or tacos ($4.45 for one, $6.45 for two). Open 11-8 M-Sat. No credit cards.

The Bento Box (15119 N.E. 24th Avenue, 643-8646), a small Japanese deli, offers a vegetarian menu as well as the usual Japanese meat and fish items. The vegetable stir-fry is $4.95; with tofu, $5.50. Vegetable yakisoba, a noodle soup, is $4.95. Open 11-8:30 M-F, 12-8:30 Sat. Credit cards accepted.

Bothell

Blacksheep Cafe and Catering

18132 Bothell Way N.E.
485-1972

Breakfast, lunch.
8-3 Tu-Sun.
Several vegetarian, vegan selections.
Credit cards accepted.

In an area with few places for so much as a vegetarian bite, the Blacksheep stands out. It's a pleasant little cafe with an open kitchen and tables by the window; on top of the piano sit several stuffed sheep in country clothes. Paintings of sheep adorn the walls.

Breakfast, served until 10:30, includes several egg dishes such as three-egg omelet ($4.75) and huevos rancheros ($5.50); also available are fruit salad, granola with seven grains, nuts, seeds and raisins, sweetened with honey and served with milk or yogurt, and fruit bran muffins. Sunday brunch ($4.25 to $5.95), served until 2, adds tofu scramble with potatoes and toast, Szechuan noodle salad with corn chips, pancakes and french toast.

Lunches (under $5) include a vegan sunburger and marinated tofu burger, both of which can be topped with cheese and are served on a whole wheat bun. The Mexi-burger, with avocado and cheese, is not vegan. A garden veggie sandwich and a bagel and cream cheese also are available. You can get twice-baked potatoes, smothered with cheese, butter and scallions, or tostadas with lardless refried beans. There's always a vegetarian soup (often, vegan) ($1.75/$2.50). The Blacksheep generally has one or two vegetarian daily specials.

Woodinville

Thai Woodinville (17610 140th Avenue N.E., Woodinville, 481-5114) offers seven vegetarian dishes ($5.95), among them pra ram puk (sautéed vegetables topped with peanut sauce), tofu curry with broccoli, basil leaves and coconut milk, and phad Thai puk (pan-fried rice and noodles with vegetables, egg and bean sprouts topped with ground peanuts). Open 11-9 M-Th, 11-10 F, 5-10 Sat. Credit cards accepted.

Issaquah

The Art House Cafe Bakery and Gallery (317 N.W. Gilman Boulevard, 392-2648) is a friendly little place in Gilman Village, an artsy collection of shops and restaurants just south of downtown. The Art House always serves a black-bean soup ($1.50/$2.50) with three-grain bread; the soup of the day is often vegetarian, usually with cheese. You can order a grilled vegetarian sandwich ($4.25) with artichoke hearts, fontina cheese, sun-dried tomatoes, basil and other herbs, or the veggie ($4.40), with avocado, roma tomato, cucumber, sprouts and cream cheese. Open 8-6 M-Sun; later on Fridays and Saturdays. No credit cards.

The Good Little Food Store (55 W. Sunset Way, 391-1584), is a full-service health-food store with produce, vitamins and a small, windowless deli in the back. The deli always has a vegan soup, such as marinated tofu and potato or split pea, for $3.25 with a slice of bread. Egg salad, veggie with avocado and garden pattie sandwiches are each $2.75. Pre-made vegan Essential Sandwiches may be ordered here for about $2.25. Quiche and low-fat pastries also are available. The deli includes a juice bar, which is on the pricey side compared to others (most of the juices are organic). Four-and-a-half ounces of anything from the produce department cost $1.75; eight ounces cost $3.50. Open 9-7 M-F, 10-6 Sat, 11-4 Sun. Credit cards accepted.

Mercer Island

Pon Proem Thai Restaurant (3039 78th Avenue S.E., 236-8424) is an especially friendly place that dispenses eight vegetarian dishes for $6.25 to $6.95. Top choices are gang pak (vegetables cooked in red curry and basil leaves), phad tofu (stir-fried tofu, onions, mushrooms and carrots) and phad lad na (rice noodles topped with tofu, broccoli and bean sauce). Open 11-9:30 M-Th, 11-10 F, 5-10 Sat, 5-9 Sun. Credit cards accepted.

Thai on Mercer (7691 27th Street N.E., 236-9990), in the Tabitt Village shopping center near Interstate 5, includes no vegetarian section on its menu, but will make dishes such as phad Thai, mixed vegetables with garlic or vegetable curry ($6.50 to $8.50) without the usual shrimp or chicken on request. Open 11:30-2 M-F, 5-9 Sun-Th, 5-10 F-Sat. Credit cards accepted.

South King County

Vegetarian food is harder to come by once you leave the friendly confines of Seattle and travel south into the Federal Way/Kent Valley areas. The cities that make up South King County are largely bedroom suburbs or blue-collar towns with an abundance of strip malls and fast-food restaurants and few places for a truly healthful meal.

But there are some treasures, most notably on rural, pristine Vashon Island. There, visit Sound Food Restaurant and Bakery for tempeh burgers or Dog Day Cafe and Juice Bar for a selection of sandwiches and specials. Perhaps the best Thai restaurant in the area is Thai Thai in White Center; it offers a number of meatless choices. In Federal Way, Marlene's Market and Deli serves wonderful lunches.

White Center

Thai Thai

11205 16th Avenue S.W.
246-2246

Lunch, Dinner.
11:30-2:30 M-F, 5-9:30 M-Sat.
Several vegetarian choices.
Credit cards accepted.

Here's one of the better Thai restaurants in the Seattle area, located in a former Kentucky Fried Chicken building along a busy street with many fast-food outlets. The 112-item menu contains several meatless choices. The owners are savvy about vegetarian preferences, and will substitute tofu for meat or chicken in many dishes. If you so choose, they'll make sure not to include oyster sauce in your dish. And they'll be glad to take the egg out of the phad Thai if you prefer. Another good thing about this restaurant: the bargain prices (mostly under $5 per vegetarian entrée), the same for lunch and dinner.

Our party enjoyed the tom yum pug, a delicious hot and sour vegetable soup in a spicy broth of lemon grass, kafir lime leaves, spices and lime juice. The bowl easily served three people. Spring rolls are wrapped around cabbage, bean thread, onion, carrot and bean sprouts, and served with a sweet plum sauce. The bathing rama mixes spinach with a powerfully hot peanut sauce. In phad Thai jay, pan-fried Thai rice noodles are mixed with dried tofu, egg, ground peanuts, green onion and bean sprouts.

Other vegetarian choices include pud ped pug jay (sautéed vegetables with a spicy sauce), vegetable fried rice and priew wan jay (sautéed cucumbers, onions, bell peppers, tomatoes, pineapple and celery topped with a sweet and sour sauce). But feel free to stray to the portions of the menu reserved for meat entrées, and exchange tofu for chicken, pork, beef or seafood. There you'll find red ginger curries and other fine dishes.

Burien

Thai Dusit Restaurant (653 S.W. 153rd Street, 431-1491) does not have a separate section for vegetarian items on its menu, but a majority of entrées and soups can be made with tofu instead of chicken, pork or beef. Most dishes (huge portions) are a bargain at $5.50 or less. At one visit, the som tum salad of shredded cabbage and carrots, tomatoes and ground peanuts was topped with a delicious spicy sauce with hot peppers, while the Thai spicy rice was full of chunks of tofu, corn and onions. Other possibilities include stir-fried chile-garlic sauce with basil and tofu, sautéed tofu with cashew nuts and vegetables and phad Thai. Open 11:30-2:30, 5-9:30 M-F, 5-10 S-S. Credit cards accepted.

Seeda Thai Restaurant (14816 1st Avenue S., 246-5889) dispenses six vegetarian dishes for $5 to $6, including fried rice with broccoli and egg, sweet and sour vegetables and vegetables and fried tofu in hot Thai curry. Open 11-3, 5-10 M-Sat, 2-10 Sun. Credit cards accepted.

Saigon Garden (202 S.W. 152nd Street, 431-9493) offers five Vietnamese vegetarian meals ($4.25-$4.50), including garden delight, house special tofu, vegetable chow mein and vegetarian fried rice. Open 11-9 M-F, 9-9 S-S. Credit cards accepted.

Mr. Ed's Cafe (15101 Ambaum Boulevard S.W., 246-5568), a standard American diner offering mostly meat dishes, began serving a vegan burger in mid-1993. The owners were talking about adding other vegetarian dishes to their menu. Open 6-9 M-F, 7-9 S-S. No credit cards.

Renton

Omar Al-Khyam Restaurant (354 Sunset Boulevard N., 271-8300), an ornate Mediterranean restaurant since 1979 just northwest of downtown Renton, provides several vegetarian appetizers that are filling enough to make a meal. For lunch ($2.50 to $4.25), try hummus, baba ghanoush, tabbouleh, zahra (deep-fried cauliflower) or falafel. The same choices are available for dinner ($3.50 to $4.95), along with the vegetarian grape leaves entrée ($7.95). Open 11-9 M-Th, 11-10 F, 4-10 Sat. Credit cards accepted.

Tukwila

Zoopa

393 Strander Boulevard
575-0500

Lunch, dinner.
11-9 S-Th, 11-9:30 F-Sat.
Giant salad bar.
Credit cards accepted.

Zoopa is a big hit with the health-conscious crowd (what little there seems to be of it) in the Tukwila area. The bright, festive salad bar restaurant, opposite the southeast corner of Southcenter Mall, is especially crowded at lunch, but dinner seats can be hard to come by, too. People are drawn here by the low price for all-you-can-eat soup, salad, pasta, bread and dessert, as well as the fun atmosphere. For $6.95, you get as much salad, soup, pasta, fresh bread, muffins, fruit and dessert as you can eat. (For $6.45, you choose between salad, soup or pasta and you get the rest. You might as well pay the extra 50 cents for all three.)

Ambience here is à la Disneyland. It's clean, bright, colorful and full of character. Vivid signs proclaim "Colorful Fruits," "Unlimited Espresso — free refills" or "International Pastries." Several large trees dominate the spacious interior, and lots of plants hang from the ceiling. The expansive dining room is painted in beige with red and green trim. The tables are bright red, with green-cushioned seats. Check out the interesting Greg Brown paintings of personalized vegetables in the about-to-be-cooked stage. The quality of the prepared food tends to the institutional rather than the inspirational, as the place does such a high volume.

It's all serve yourself, from the salad bar (with what seems to be a thousand items) to the pasta and soup bars. The salad bar offers an excellent variety of veggies, from green or yellow zucchini and blue or green cabbage to cauliflower and peas. On one visit, Zoopa even had jicama, the exotic Mexican root vegetable. Toppings range from standard salad dressings (including low-cal) to honey-mustard and salsa. Also available: soy bacon bits and three kinds of bean sprouts. Side salads include three-bean, a very sweet Asian noodle salad with almonds and a vinegary mint-cucumber concoction with orange zest. Soups always incorporate a vegetarian choice. At the pasta bar, choose from two dishes: at our visit, one had cheese, the other was shells and tomato sauce. The bread bar involves two breads (perhaps a sourdough and a sweet multi-grain), as well as several muffins. Desserts are fruit and standard American cakes and pastries, as well as self-serve frozen yogurt.

SeaTac

Bai Tong Restaurant (15859 Pacific Highway S., 431-0893), a stone's throw from SeaTac International Airport, is reputed to be one of the most authentic Thai restaurants in the region. Six vegetarian choices are available (in the $6 range): hot tofu soup, tofu and vegetables, bean sprouts with spring onion, spinach topped with peanut sauce, phad Thai and fried rice with vegetables. Open 11-3, 5-10 M-Sat, 5-10 Sun. Credit cards accepted.

Erawan Thai Cuisine (3423 S. 160th Street, 241-1122), located in the Orchid Inn a block east of Bai Tong, offers six meatless choices in the $4.50 to $5.50 range, including fried rice with broccoli and egg, sweet and sour vegetables and mixed vegetables in Thai hot curry. Open 11-3, 5-10 M-F, 1-10 S-S. Credit cards accepted.

Des Moines

Spyro's Gyros & Etc. (21851 Marine View Drive S., 870-1699), ensconced in a tiny hut at the front of the Food Giant shopping center, prepares Greek food with a healthful bent. Here you can order such standards as falafel ($3.75), Greek salad or hummus, baba ghanoush or tzatziki with pita bread ($1.75 each). At least one of the two daily soups is vegan: perhaps black bean, lentil or vegetable. The cluttered eatery harbors four indoor tables and a counter, as well as a few picnic tables outside. Open 10 to 9 M-Sat. No credit cards.

Kent

Maharaja Cuisine of India

21608 Pacific Highway S.
946-0664

Lunch, lunch buffet, dinner, Sunday brunch.
11 to 2:30 M-Sat, 11-2 Sun, 4-10 every day.
Several vegetarian choices.
Credit cards accepted.

South King County vegetarians cheered when this Indian restaurant -- a companion to the one in West Seattle -- opened in 1992. Atop a plateau between the Kent Valley and Puget Sound, it bears a Kent address, but really is identified more with Des Moines and Federal Way. In an area short on good meatless ethnic foods, Maharaja offers welcome relief. But don't come here for the decor: it's located in a former Arby's fast-food restaurant in an Albertson's supermarket shopping center. Although Maharaja may feel like a Burger King or a Taco Bell (they took the prices down behind the counter, but left the grid), the food is quite good. Maharaja's best deal is the all-you-can-eat lunch buffet ($5.95). The menu is the same as at the West Seattle operation (see Page 83).

The Bittersweet (211 1st Avenue S., 854-0707) is a pleasant restaurant with a cavernous dining room and country decor. Specialties include a daily broccoli pie ($6.50 with salad), spinach salad ($5.50) and a lengthy dessert list of pies and cakes. One of the three daily soups usually is vegetarian, perhaps potato-dill or wild rice. A cream cheese and avocado salad is available, and sometimes vegetarian lasagna is offered. Open 10-4 M-Sat. No credit cards.

Chao Praya (21222 84th Avenue S., 395-7777), a Thai restaurant, does not have a vegetarian section in its menu, but can substitute vegetables for meat on most orders ($4.25 at lunch, $4.75 at dinner). Tofu, if substituted for meat, is 50 cents extra. Open 11-8:30 M-F, 2-8:30 Sat. Credit cards accepted.

Saya (8455 S. 212th Street, 395-7987) dispenses several vegetarian Thai dishes for $4 to $5. Among them are curried vegetables, spinach topped with peanut sauce and vegetable fried rice. Open 10:30-9 M-F, 10:30-8 Sat. Credit cards accepted.

Singwah Cafe (308 W. Meeker Street, 854-2526), in downtown Kent, incorporates seven vegetarian dishes ($2.75 to $4.25) on a menu of Chinese, Vietnamese and American foods. Try curried vegetables over rice, Buddhist delight or bok choy ginger stir-fry. For breakfast, pancakes, omelets and other egg dishes are available. Open 9:30-6 M-Sat. Credit cards accepted.

Nature's Market (26011 104th Avenue S.E., 854-5395) on Kent's East Hill is a fancy, modern health-food store with a small juice bar. Apple, orange, carrot and a few other goodies from the market's organic produce section are available for juicing ($1.75 for eight ounces, $3 for 16).

Federal Way

Marlene's Market and Deli

31839 Gateway Center Boulevard S.
839-0933

Lunch, dinner.
9-9 M-Th, 9-10 F, 9-7 Sat, 11:30-6 Sun.
Mostly vegetarian.
Juice bar.
No credit cards.

Marlene's is a jewel in a community known more for traffic gridlock and fast-food burger outlets than for healthful eating places. And people know it: lunches are especially crowded as devotees flock here for great soups, salads and baked goods. The deli is at the back of the contemporary market, which in 1993 was named best medium-size health-food store in the nation by a trade magazine. It's a bright, sunny deli with large windows looking onto the plaza, fountain and movie theater across the way. Seats are available outside, too. Marlene's is in the Gateway Center shopping plaza just west of Interstate 5 at Exit 143.

At lunch, usually three soups are offered; two of those are likely to be vegan (perhaps tomato garlic, cashew chili, split pea or white bean with spinach). Wholesome breads to dip in your soup are available beside the register. Display cases are full of such homemade salads as tabbouleh, black bean and corn and greens with vegetables; vegetarian and vegan entrées such as pizza with soy cheese or curried tempeh over rice that can be microwaved by the deli staff; veggie burgers galore; vegan Essential Sandwiches and lots of other similar chapati roll-up sandwiches, and wholesome desserts that are often fruit-sweetened and dairy-free. Most items cost less than $5. Marlene Beadle's thriving establishment also has a juice bar. Wheatgrass juice is bought by large numbers of customers. At dinner, some of the soups and entrées may run out, and the kitchen closes at 8 on weekdays. Attached to the deli is a room serving espressos and regular or soy milk lattes.

Other Choices

Viable Products Co. (2335 S.W. 336th Street, 838-7576), a health-food store in the Safeway shopping plaza that specializes in vitamins and sells a limited stock of natural foods, has a deli in back with a juice bar. You can order an ovo-lacto garden burger or a vegan tofu burger ($2.95), a veggie sandwich with cream cheese ($3.95), a salad or juice (carrot, celery, beet or wheatgrass).

Carrot juice is $1.80 for nine ounces, $2.75 for 16. Smoothies with seasonal produce also are available. Open 5 a.m.-8 p.m. M-F, 9-8 Sat, 9-6 Sun.

BB Roasters (31675 Pacific Highway S., 946-7282) is a fast-food restaurant with a more healthful focus than some. Here, along with hot-air roasted chicken and burgers, you can get a vegetable burger (with dairy) for $3.50. The place, which opened in 1993, also has a juice bar, where you can get orange or apple juice, or fruit "dizzys" made with fruit juice and french-vanilla yogurt. Open 10:30-10 M-Sun. Credit cards accepted.

Vashon Island

Sound Food Restaurant & Bakery

20312 Vashon Highway
463-3565

Breakfast, lunch, dinner.
7 to 9 or 10 M-F; 8 to 10 Sat.; 8 to 9 Sun.
Several vegetarian items.
Credit cards accepted.

This is a Vashon original, founded in 1974 as a simple place offering the best and freshest fare, cooked from scratch — "sound food," the genuine article. Back then, you couldn't get a fried egg and the other egg dishes at breakfast came with alfalfa sprouts. What one principal called a "mellowing" slowly set in and Sound Food expanded, upscaled and added variety, to the point where it has become an all-around island dining favorite and the board of specials proclaimed prime rib at a Friday visit. But vegetarian foods and healthful breads remain a hallmark. The spacious, L-shaped dining room is serene and restful, its large rear windows looking onto garden and woods, with a canopied deck for outside dining taking full advantage. Decor is country pretty: rich wood tables left bare except for blue napkins and vases of fresh flowers, and wood floors covered with blue carpeting and an oriental rug.

There's a meatless special every night: curried nutty noodles ($11.95) when we stopped by, full of noodles, vegetables, curry and light cream plus — "the best part," according to the hostess — walnuts, pecans and coconut. Tempeh burgers ($4) are a specialty here, and can be topped with cheese, grilled mushrooms and onions or sprouts and avocado. Or try the black-bean burrito or eggplant parmesan. Veggies on a skewer are another option showing how the chef will alter the menu to suit individual tastes. All the soup stocks here are vegetable based and homemade.

Desserts are said to be fantastic: you could try blackbottom peanut-butter pie, mixed fruit cobbler or peach pie, along with such goodies from the pastry case as coconut-orange butterflies, fruit-filed scones and pecan sandies. At the counter are dog-eared copies of the restaurant's 1984 cookbook, *Recherché Recipes from Sound Food Restaurant and Bakery* ($9.95). It contains a handful of vegetarian recipes: mushroom moussaka, aloo ghobi curry (with lentil dal, lemon rice and banana raita) and vegetable couscous. The bakery displays such bread treats as seven-grain, Swedish hearth, anadama, three-seed (poppy, sesame and sunflower), all $1.95 a loaf. A special might be fagasa, an unusual and good-looking round presentation made of French bread dough accented with tomatoes, onions and bell peppers.

Dog Day Cafe & Juice Bar

Vashon Highway at S.W. Bank Road
463-6404

Breakfast, lunch, dinner, Sunday brunch.
Summer: 9-9 M-Th, 9-10 F-Sat.
Winter: 10-6 Tu-Th, 9-9 F-Sat, 10-4 Sun.
Mostly vegetarian.
No credit cards.

Opened in 1991, this pure establishment shows owner Steve Shanaman's love for Italy. He did the painting, sponged the walls, found the striking iron gates that stand at the entrance of the tiny arcade, and came up with an inviting Italian trattoria and bar, with eight tables and a stand-up counter. The white-linened tables are covered with butcher paper, the better for doodling with the box of crayons available. The juice bar has two big juicers, so the juice is really fresh. Juices ($2.25 for 10 ounces, $3.25 for 16) include orange, apple, pear, melon, pineapple, carrot, celery, beet and spinach; ginger root, spirulina and protein powder are optional add-ons. Everything is vegetarian except for the obvious, which at one visit was a night's special of chicken. Soup choices ($2.75 or $3.50) might be miso-vegetable, borscht, Italian-pesto vegetable or cream of broccoli. Country-style moussaka with salad costs $6.25. Breakfast, served all day, includes an assortment of fresh baked goods, granola, breads and nut and seed pancakes. If you start with a double shot of wheatgrass ($2.25), maybe you'll feel virtuous enough to order a slice of chocolate oblivion torte.

Mary Martha's

17520 Vashon Highway
463-3720

Breakfast, lunch, dinner.
10-7 M-F, 9-5 Sat.
Some vegetarian choices.
No credit cards.

"Good Things to Eat" is the logo of this tiny takeout deli and espresso bar at the Thriftway Shopping Center. And indeed they are. The restaurant offers a blackboard vegetarian menu in addition to the usual soup/salad/sandwich/pizza suspects (most dishes in the $2.75 to $5.50 range). There's always the Vashon veggie sandwich, full of carrots, cucumber, avocado, cream cheese, tomato, sprouts and sunflower seeds on your choice of bread. Or try the veggie burrito. Specials could be vegetable strudel, hot pesto croissant, vegetarian pizza ($10.75 or $14) and steamed rice with sautéed vegetables, with choice of toppings: lemon-tahini, soy sauce, gourmet teriyaki or cinnamon and sugar. An interesting breakfast menu offers rice and sautéed veggies, among other dishes.

Other Choices

Minglement (20316 Vashon Highway S.W., 463-9672), a health-food store and gift shop next door to Sound Food, offers a large selection of veggie sandwiches, as well as the usual bulk grains, herbs and homeopathics. The store also sells locally made Island Spring tofu. Island-made and Guatemalan crafts are featured here, too. Open 10-6 M-F, 10-7 Sat, 10-5 Sun.

Pierce and Thurston Counties

Vegetarian offerings are sparse in Tacoma and abundant in Olympia, the cities that dominate these adjoining counties in southern Puget Sound. Tacoma is more of a blue-collar city, and is the home of only a few ethnic restaurants that offer meatless fare. Almost all of those are west or south of downtown, which has lost much of its clout to Tacoma Mall to the south. Be sure to visit Cedars III in western Tacoma, which prepares wonderful baba ghanoush, tabbouleh and other Middle Eastern favorites. A few miles to the north, the Antique Sandwich Company — just south of Tacoma's scenic Point Defiance Park — offers vegetarian sandwiches and salads with organic greens.

The purest vegetarian place in the Tacoma area is at the Lakewood Natural Foods store, just south of Tacoma. Enjoy its luncheon deli, which serves mostly vegan food.

Olympia, though smaller than Tacoma, offers vegetarians many more choices. The state's capital city seems to have more of a new age, earthy tone; there's a great co-op and The Evergreen State College just west of the city is home to many environmentalist types. The Corner restaurant there dispenses cheap, strictly vegetarian food during the school year. Downtown, Saigon Rendez-Vous offers dozens of simulated meat and seafood dishes. The Urban Onion, a classy American eatery, has several vegetarian choices.

Just west of Olympia, check out the **Blue Heron Bakery** (4935 Mud Bay Road, 866-2253, open 6-6 M-Sun), where granola, breads, pastries, cookies and bars are served. It specializes in dairy-free and wheat-free diet alternatives. The rebel crunch granola is unusual in that it is free of oil, honey and wheat. The chocolate-chip cookies are vegan, sugar-free and made with wheat. Breads include ten-grain, three-seed, toasted blue corn and sourdough spelt.

Tacoma

Cedars III

7104 6th Avenue
564-0255

Lunch, dinner.
11-2, 4-9 Tu-Sat, 4-9 Sun.
Several vegetarian and vegan items.
Credit cards accepted.

Cedars III was opened to rave reviews in 1992 by the brother of the owners of Cedars and Cedars on Brooklyn in Seattle's University District. "One of the all-time great places!" proclaims a personal note from Tacoma's Morning News Tribune restaurant reviewer Bart Ripp, which Nadim Alawar proudly displays on the wall at the bottom of the three-star review Ripp gave his place. The stars seem warranted: the food is outstanding and the decor pleasant. The white walls are covered with Persian carpets that contain scenes of the Middle East (look for the very interesting one of skiers at a Lebanese winter resort), paintings and large color photographs. The tables feature pink cloths and black chairs, and wine racks hold elegant brands. Giant windows allow a view of the busy but rather nondescript corner of 6th Avenue and Oxford.

The lunch menu includes plenty of traditional Middle Eastern favorites ($3 to $6). Start with hummus, baba ghanoush or tabbouleh. The Greek salad mixes greens, feta cheese, mint, Greek olives and a dressing of olive oil, lemon juice, garlic and herbs. The hot vegetarian plate is an assortment of vegetables and herbs sautéed in olive oil and served over rice. Or you can get the falafel dish, topped with tahini sauce. The vegetarian Cedars delight ($15.99 for two) includes falafel, hummus, baba ghanoush, stuffed grape leaves, fatoush (a tomato-cucumber salad with mint), spinach pie and rice.

Dinner appetizer prices run from $3.75 to $5 and include the same choices as lunch, along with jebneh — a combination of feta cheese and olives topped with mint and olive oil and served with pita bread. At one visit, the baba ghanoush was superb, served with several pieces of pita bread to scoop up the tasty eggplant and tahini mixture. That and the large tabbouleh appetizer were plenty to satisfy most appetites. Dinner entrées ($7.50 to $7.95) include falafel and spinach delight (marinated spinach and onion cooked between layers of phyllo dough served with grape leaves and rice with a cucumber-yogurt-mint sauce). The vegetarian Cedars delight is $22 for dinner. End your meal with baklava, which is said to be very good here.

Antique Sandwich Company

5102 N. Pearl Street

752-4069

Breakfast, lunch, dinner.
Open 7 a.m. to 8 p.m., except 7-9:30 Tu and F. Opens at 8 Sun.
A few vegetarian and vegan choices.
No credit cards.

When you ask Tacoma residents where to go for vegetarian food, they'll say either Seattle or the Antique Sandwich Company. Well, much of the food here is for carnivores, but the friendly folks who run this neighborhood institution (opened in the mid-1970s) make a conscientious effort to dispense organic and whole foods. Desserts, for example, use whole wheat flour and honey or fruit sweetener instead of sugar. But the real draw to this establishment — more so than the food, even — is its terrific character. The cavernous deli and dining room contains an eclectic range of artifacts, such as a statue of an Indian woman, Chinese drawings, Persian carpets, a samovar and antique mirrors. Live music is featured on Tuesday and Friday nights. A display cabinet contains cassettes and compact discs by featured musicians for sale. Lines can be especially long here on weekends, when people stop by before or after a visit to Tacoma's finest treasure, Point Defiance Park.

Breakfast involves an assortment of pastries, caffeinated drinks, herbal teas and juices. The lunch and dinner menu offers seven vegetarian sandwiches for $2 to $5; each comes with a salad that can be topped with lemon-tahini, blue cheese or oil and vinegar dressing. Most interesting is the hummus, sprout and tomato sandwich. Among the options are peanut butter and jam, avocado and cheese or sprouts and tomato. Specials cost under $6 and include salad.

Usually, the quiche of the day is vegetarian (perhaps artichoke and black olive); so is the spinach lasagna. Spanakopita also is available. If the soups don't include meat in the title (listed on the chalkboard), they're vegetarian. An organic wild green salad usually is available. Among desserts are cheesecake, peanut-butter fudge, sundaes and whatever specials might be in the pie case.

Other Choices

Bua Thai Restaurant (758 S. 38th Street, 474-5001), in a largely Asian neighborhood a short drive across the freeway from the Tacoma Mall, offers 11 vegetarian selections. Thai salad costs $3.50, and the following entrées are $4.75: glass noodles with tofu, basil tofu, ginger tofu and curried tofu with vegetables. Open 11-8 M-F, 12-8:30 Sat. Credit cards accepted.

It's Greek To Me (1706 6th Avenue, 272-1375), a tiny fast-food place, offers four vegetarian dishes for $5 or less: spanakopita, Greek village salad, veggie gyros or falafel sandwich. Open 10-10 M-Sun.

Freighthouse Square Food Court

Freighthouse Square, a short walk from the Tacoma Dome just off Interstate 5 near downtown, is a warehouse building that has been converted into an excellent collection of small stores. Here you'll find new age book stores, arts and crafts shops and a good food court. Lots of people come here on the weekends.

The Palace (430 E. 26th Street, 272-0845) serves Mediterranean cuisine, including hummus, tzatziki, tabbouleh, grape leaves stuffed with rice and herbs, falafel and spanakopita. Prices range from $3 to $4.25. Open 10-6 M-Sat, 12-5 Sun.

Wendy's Vietnamese Restaurant (430 E. 25th Street, 572-4678) is a decent place for a quick bite. There are four vegetarian choices ($3.25 to $4): stir-fried vegetables with rice, vegetable curry, vegetable chow mein and hot and spicy tofu with vegetables. Open 10 to 6 or 7 M-Sat.

Murph's International Burgers (2501 E. D Street #206, 572-7374): It may be a stretch to include a burger stand in a guide for vegetarians, but Murph's offers an ovo-lacto vegetarian burger for $3.75.

Fife

Jewel of India (3518 Pacific Highway E., 922-2697) is located beside the lobby of the Hometel Inn a few miles east of Tacoma, alongside Interstate 5. Nine vegetarian specialties ($5 to $7.75) include eggplant bharta, matar paneer (homemade cottage cheese cooked with peas and spices) and kofta lajavab (cottage cheese and potato balls stuffed with chutney and dry fruits in a butter sauce). The most popular dish is the navratan sahi korma, vegetables cooked with cheese, almonds, raisins and cashews. Appetizers such as samosas and pakoras, and breads including naan and onion kulcha, also are available. The decor here feels more like an American country inn than an Indian restaurant. Open 10-10 M-Sun. Credit cards accepted.

Lakewood

Lakewood Natural Foods

5808 100th Street S.W.
584-3929

Full-service lunch; dinner to go.
10-3 M-Sat, soups and salads to go 3-9.
Mostly vegan.
Credit cards accepted.

Lakewood Natural Foods is a gem. In a town whose stores and restaurants show little health consciousness, this large health-food store and deli more than compensates. Owner Marie Foxton, a member of EarthSave Seattle and a dedicated vegetarian, started the place in 1990 to the raves of local vegetarians and health-food fans. People drive from all over northern Pierce County to enjoy the store's large selection of organic produce, bulk foods and vitamins.

The deli at the back is tiny, but pure: the blackboard declares, "Our food is prepared with organic ingredients, pure water and much love." Sit at one of the two round tables or at the green counter and chat with the staff or other customers, or just kick back and enjoy the pleasant health-food-store ambience.

The deli serves three to five vegan soups a day ($2.50): they might include such temptations as split pea or black bean. Two entrées ($4.75) are generally offered. One is always the tofu veggie stir-fry. Other choices, depending on the mood of the chef, might be burritos, enchiladas, tofutillas or tofu parmesan. You also can order sandwiches ($4.75, with green salad), including hummus, avocado, tofu paté or a pesto bagel. Fresh carrot juice is available.

Tillicum

It's Greek To Me (14623 Union Avenue S.W., 582-1557), in a former Taco Time fast-food building at Interstate 5's Exit 122, dispenses a variety of vegetarian items for under $5. Try a Greek village salad, veggie gyro or falafel sandwich or spanakopita. This restaurant is the sibling of It's Greek To Me in Tacoma. Open 10-9 M-Sat, 11-8 Sun. Credit cards accepted.

Olympia

Saigon Rendez-Vous

117 W. 5th Avenue
352-1989

Lunch, dinner.
10:30-10:30 M-Sat, 12-10 Sun.
Several vegan choices.
Credit cards accepted.

The highlight at Saigon Rendez-Vous is the huge selection of delicious

Vietnamese and Chinese vegetarian dishes, made without any hidden animal products. Buddhism has had a strong influence in Vietnam, and many Vietnamese follow its strict vegetarian diet regimen. The fake meat dishes here originate from that group. Mui Nguyen, the owner, has always offered many vegetarian choices since she opened her restaurant in 1989. But in 1993, she created a separate vegetarian menu that contains a whopping 40 main dishes. (The only thing on the menu of meat and seafood look-a-likes that is not fake is the prawns — Nguyen said her staff is still working on a vegetarian substitute.)

The Saigon Rendez-Vous decor isn't as inspiring as the food: the establishment, in downtown Olympia, feels like an American diner, with its Pepsi case in the back, neon beer signs and a string of Christmas lights along one wall. Baskets of fake green plants hang from the ceiling among the booths. Some Vietnamese pictures and paintings show the home of the cuisine, which is good enough to make you overlook the decor.

One of the best dishes on the menu (entrées, $5 to $8.50) is the tofu with lemon grass in spicy sauce. Tofu is often a bland accompaniment to a stir-fry dish. But not here: it's deep-fried so that it can absorb lots of flavor from the sauce. Also a treat is the almond soy chicken, a meat analog that had our party of four reminiscing about the times when we ate the real stuff. This fake poultry will fool you: it has the taste and substance of chicken, and comes with a brown gravy that further promotes the illusion. We found the stir-fried broccoli and vegetables tasty, but not exceptional. Other options include meatless lo-mein with egg noodles, pepper steak with steamed rice, stir-fried squid with bamboo shoots and vegetables, vegetable fried rice and Mongolian tofu.

The Urban Onion

116 Legion Way
943-9242

Breakfast, lunch, dinner.
7-10 M-Th, 7-11 F-Sat, 7-9 Sun.
Several vegetarian and vegan choices.
Credit cards accepted.

Adorning the menu of this classy semi-vegetarian restaurant in the Olympian Hotel in downtown Olympia is a picture of vegetables wearing shades, carrying briefcases and marching down the street. The image fits the hip nature of the enterprise: here you'll find a busy restaurant that serves interesting American and ethnic meatless dishes. The high ceiling towers over the elegant booths, tables and a breakfast counter, which combine to make a nicely polished eating environment. It used to be all-vegetarian, but a few years ago, the ownership decided to add chicken, seafood and burgers to draw a larger crowd. The Urban Onion is pricey as far as vegetarian dishes go, but the portions are huge, so you can take part of your meal home for leftovers. The lunch and dinner menus are the same, with most dishes in the $7 to $11 range.

The place hops for weekend breakfasts, when you can get french toast, omelets or fruit salad. During one visit, two plate-size whole grain and granola pancakes with real maple syrup ($3.95) were delicious.

During another trip for dinner, the gado gado — the Urban Onion's own spicy

Indonesian peanut sauce poured over an assortment of sautéed vegetables and steamed brown rice, served with salad or the daily soup (in this case, a hearty lentil) and fresh-baked herb and onion bread — was superb. If that doesn't tempt your palate, try gorgonzola cheese and walnut ravioli, wrapped in fresh spinach and roasted garlic, gently sautéed with vegetables and tossed in an asiago sauce, or pasta puttanesca — sautéed vegetables with garlic, capers and black olives simmered in a provencal sauce, tossed with fettuccine and garnished with parmesan cheese. Or order the vegetable sauté, cooked with dill and garlic. You can get a vegetarian burrito with cheese, served in a whole wheat chapati, or a bean and rice enchilada, homemade refried beans and fried rice in a soft corn tortilla, served with olives, sour cream, white cheddar cheese and salsa. The UO nut burger ($6.25) is a vegetable and nut mixture sprinkled with sprouts, carrots and a celery root vinaigrette. It comes with your choice of two accompaniments: hash browns, fried rice, a cup of soup, cottage cheese or salad.

Start your meal with one of seven vegetarian appetizers ($3 to $5), such as blue corn tortilla chips served with a black-bean and corn salsa or a spicy bean and cheese dip, the fresh vegetable plate accompanied by hummus and pita triangles, and "the veggie" — sautéed mushrooms, zucchini, onions, green chiles and melted cheese. The dessert list, including such choices as chocolate mousse, espresso cake and chocolate peanut-butter torte looked impressive, if not particularly healthful. But by that time we were too full to try any.

The Corner

The Evergreen State College
866-6000, Ext. 6343

Breakfast, dinner, Sunday brunch.
Breakfast: 8-10:30 M-F, 10:30-1 Sun.
Dinner: 5-9:30 M-Th, 5-9 F, Sun.
Closed during Christmas and spring break, and during summer (mid-June through mid-September).
No credit cards.

The Evergreen State College, an experimental four-year school founded by the state in 1971, is seven miles west of Olympia (take Highway 101 to the Evergreen Parkway exit). Here, students spend most of their time in seminars and independent learning situations, and receive written evaluations rather than grades. The emphasis is on cooperative learning rather than competition.

The Corner, which shares space with a laundry room, student mail boxes and the Java Junkies coffee stand in the Housing Community Center that borders the sports fields and dormitories, fits in perfectly with this progressive attitude: it's a strictly vegetarian, student-operated cafeteria whose produce comes from the college's organic farm in season. The food is bountiful and cheap — which the student-managers attribute to the low rent owed to the college. Although the place is frequented chiefly by students, anyone is welcome to eat here.

The dishes change with the whims of the student cooks, but always include homemade breads, salads, a soup, a beans and rice plate, two or three entrées and rich desserts (at least one non-dairy dessert is always available, a manager said). At one visit, $3 paid for a plate overflowing with organic greens, cabbage and sprouts topped with tahini, and savory vegetables with tofu over rice.

Breakfast brings waffles, granolas, coffee and tea.

Red Apple Natural Foods
400 Cooper Point Road N.W.
357-8779

Lunch, early dinner.
10-5:30 M-Sat.
Juice bar, several vegetarian and vegan selections.
No credit cards.

Tempeh and tofu burgers in the midst of a Safeway shopping plaza? You'll find them at Red Apple Natural Foods, on Olympia's west side. Tucked away in the back of the small health-food store, which concentrates more on supplements and vitamins than food products, is a small deli that serves a surprising amount of good chow. The three-bean chili is vegan; and the soup of the day almost always is, too. Each costs $1.59 for a cup, $1.89 for a bowl.

A number of sandwiches are available for $4.25: The tofu, tempeh and garden burgers come with avocado, tomato, sprouts and cheese on a whole wheat bun, along with blue corn chips. The pocket hummer sandwich includes avocado, black-bean paté, hummus, cucumber, tomato, cheese and sprouts. The "no mama" is so named because none of its ingredients come from an animal: it's about the same as the pocket hummer, without the cheese and with olives and sunflower seeds. The juice bar dispenses carrot juice ($1.60/$2.60) and wheatgrass juice ($1/$1.75). Smoothies are available, including one with organic apple cider, bananas and strawberries.

Other Choices

Smithfield Cafe (212 W. 4th Avenue, 786-1725), an informal place with the menu on a blackboard behind the cash register, a comfy sofa and country tables and chairs, offers mostly vegetarian fare for $5 and under (everything's meatless except for a sandwich and salad with turkey). Two veggie sandwiches with tomatoes, sprouts and cucumbers are offered; one has cream cheese, the other avocado. Order a deluxe burrito (with the usual fillings) or, if adventurous, a hummus burrito (which contains avocado, sour cream and salsa). A basic salad ($2.10) combines green leaf and romaine lettuces, cabbage, carrots, tomato and sprouts; you can add avocado, raisins, artichokes and cheese. Nachos, tabbouleh, carrot juice and caffeinated drinks also are available. Breakfast brings egg dishes, granola and bagels. Open 7-8 M-F, 8-8 S-S. No credit cards.

Sweet Oasis Mediterranean Bakery and Cafe (113 W. 4th Avenue, 956-0470) in downtown Olympia offers several vegan Middle Eastern dishes ($2.25 to $4) in a small diner setting. Vegan spinach triangles are made with onions, walnuts, olive oil, lemon juice and sumac. Triangles with cheese also are available. Hummus, tabbouleh and falafel are other favorite items here. The combination plate includes falafel, tabbouleh, hummus and pita on the side. None of the desserts — made with lots of butter and sugar syrup — are vegan. Open 6:30-8 M-F, 8-6 Sat. No credit cards.

Mekong Thai Restaurant (125 N. Columbia Street, 352-9620) is a two-room eatery with pink tablecloths, bright red cafeteria chairs and lots of ornate Thai decorations hanging on the walls and from the ceilings. Locals say it is a consistently good place for vegetarian fare. Mekong makes 11 meatless dishes and salads (most in the $5 to $7 range). During one visit, the tao-hoo ped — tofu, green beans and mixed vegetables sautéed in a hot sauce and coconut milk — was a fine choice. Other possibilities include tofu ginger, phad Thai and phad ka-na (broccoli fried with black-bean sauce and tofu). Open 11-10 M-F, 3-10 S-S. Credit cards accepted.

Thai Dish Restaurant (2010 Black Lake Boulevard S.W., 352-3484), in west Olympia, claims a menu more interesting than most Thai places. It offers eight vegetarian choices ($6 to $7). Massaman tofu is a curry with sweet potato, onions, peanuts and coconut milk. In pak pasom, vegetables are sautéed in a soybean sauce. The tom kha tofu is a spicy tofu soup with coconut milk, mushrooms and lime juice. Open 11-10 every day. Credit cards accepted.

Thai Pavillion (303 4th Avenue, 943-9093) features four vegetarian choices ($5.75 to $6.50): green curry tofu, veggies and bean thread, phad Thai tofu and the daily house special. Dinner brings six choices ($6.25 to $6.95): coconut lime mushrooms, chef's choice veggies, stir-fried tofu, veggies and bean thread, vegetarian pad prik khing (tofu, stir-fried with green beans in spicy sauce) and spicy eggplant. Open 11-2 M-F, 5-8:30 M-Th, 5-9:30 F-Sat. Credit cards accepted.

Fuji Japanese Restaurant (214 W. 4th Avenue, 352-0306) includes a "Vegetarian's Delight" section on its menu, with five choices ($4 to $6): veggie rice bowl, veggie tempura, veggie yakisoba or veggie nabe udon. A 10-piece veggie sushi combo is $6.50. Open 11-9 M-Sat. Credit cards accepted.

The Cottage Garden (119 W. 5th Avenue, 786-1099), a restaurant/gift store, serves a daily vegetarian or vegan soup, Indonesian salad (with brown rice, water chestnuts, cashews, raisins, almonds, sesame seeds and red peppers), spinach pasta salad with a honey-mustard dressing, fruit salad, quiche and a vegetarian sandwich with cheese. Prices range from $2.25 to $5.25. Open 9-6 M-Th, 10-4 F. Credit cards accepted.

J-Vees Health Food Bread Board Restaurant (3720 Pacific Avenue S.E., 491-1930) combines 1950s decor and a couple of meatless options for under $5. You can get an avocado sandwich or one of two vegetarian burgers with cheese and mayo. A garden green salad includes cheese, sprouts and sunflower seeds. The accompanying health-food store has plenty of bulk and frozen products. The deli is open 11-3 M-Sat. No credit cards.

Olympic Peninsula

There is nothing quite like driving along the Olympic Peninsula. Extraordinary scenery dominates: deep blue water and lush green forests please the eye, and majestic mountains peek over foothills. The peninsula is one of the state's most popular tourist destinations, with Olympic National Park, numerous state parks and plenty of hiking and boating opportunities.

The peninsula is far more rural than Puget Sound's east side. You can drive long stretches and pass few restaurants, shops or services. If you're trekking out here, you ought to bring plenty of good food in your cooler or knapsack. Health consciousness is slowly creeping onto the peninsula, although vegetarians won't be as happy eating here as they are in Seattle.

Health-food fans will do especially well in Port Townsend, a resort town full of Victorian architecture and shops at the northeast corner of the peninsula. Its bustling downtown supports a juice bar, a Thai restaurant, health-oriented American cafes and a Mexican restaurant that doesn't use lard. Top choices include The Salal Cafe and the Silverwater Cafe. The city's main drag, Water Street, also harbors one of the best new age bookstores in the Puget Sound region, Phoenix Rising.

The vegetarian scene in Port Angeles, a small city that depends heavily on the logging industry, is improving, due largely to the efforts of Robyn Miletich and Linda May, the owner and the manager of **The Country Aire Grocery** (117 E. 1st Street, 452-7175, open 9:30-5:30 M-F, 10-5:30 Sat., and in the summer on Sundays from 12-4), a fantastic downtown health-food store. Stop here for all the basics, such as organic produce, bulk foods, tofu, tempeh and cereals, as well as massage oils, incense, books and eco-friendly products. Robyn and Linda have persuaded some of the local restaurants (a carnivorous lot) to sell vegetarian burgers and other meatless dishes. The Coffee House, just across the street from The Country Aire, serves plenty of vegetarian and vegan fare.

On U.S. 101, just west of downtown Sequim, is the **Sunny Farms** natural foods and produce market (1546 Highway 101 West, 683-8003, open 8-7 daily, until 8 in summer), a peninsula establishment. It offers a gigantic selection of fresh produce and most of the health-food store basics. Purists try to ignore the butcher's shop in the back.

Bremerton vegetarians fare poorly for a city of its size. There are only a couple of choices here, most notably the Royal Thai Restaurant in northwest Bremerton, across the bridge from downtown. To the south, in Gig Harbor, visit Le Bistro Coffee House for a few vegetarian selections and a juice bar in one of the most characterful restaurants around.

Port Angeles

The Coffee House

18 E. First Street
452-1459

Breakfast, lunch, dinner.
7-7 M-Sat, 8:30-3 Sun (open until 9 in summer).
Several vegetarian, vegan selections.
No credit cards.

The Coffee House is a vegetarian's paradise in an area largely barren of meatless fare. In this friendly little downtown diner across the street from The Country Aire, an outstanding health-food store, you'll find plenty of good, hearty soups, sandwiches and entrées. The restaurant is peppy, spacious and sunny. Purple dominates: it's in the carpet, the ceiling and the mosaic pillars that separate the main dining room from the small deli and espresso section. Every month, the works of a different local artist are featured. When The Coffee House opened in 1984, it was mostly vegetarian, but since has found it necessary to add more meat dishes. It supports local organic farmers, and uses as much organic produce as possible.

Breakfast is mostly an ovo-lacto affair: plenty of omelets, eggs and pancakes. A vegetable omelet costs $4.25 (add 50 cents for cheese); also $4.25 are the Coffee House flapjacks, a multi-grain cake with pecans and honey. Total granola ($4.95) includes yogurt and fruit, and is topped with blueberries. It's served with a fresh-baked muffin or biscuit.

The lunch menu is a bonanza. Appetizers ($2.50 to $4.50) include chips and salsa, nachos, pesto toast and classic white pizza topped with olive oil, garlic and fontanella cheese. One of the two daily soups ($2.25 or $3) is always vegan. The veggie burger ($4.25) is a vegan, mixed-grain patty served with mustard, tomato, lettuce, sprouts and grilled onion, on a whole wheat onion bun. The veggie burrito ($4.95) combines vegetables, lardless beans, jalapeno peppers and jack cheese in a flour tortilla. There are several vegetarian sandwiches (about $5). The South of the Border is made with avocado, mild green chilies, jack cheese and tomato; the Middle Eastern combines hummus, cucumber, purple onion and feta cheese.

Dinner involves the same appetizers and soups, as well as eggplant parmesan and pasta primavera (both $8.95).

Other Choices

Harbor Deli (102 W. Front Street, 452-8683), a sandwich shop, sells a vegetarian burger for $3.95, as well as meatless lasagna ($5.95 or $7.95) and meatless ravioli ($6.95). A sandwich with cream cheese, avocado, green pepper, cucumber, black olives and sprouts costs $4.50, or $3.25 for a half. Open 7 a.m.-10 p.m. daily April through August, 8:30-9 the rest of the year.

Joshua's Restaurant (136 E. Front Street, 457-7473) is a typical burger diner that sells a vegetarian burger for $3.95, with a side of fries. Open 6-3 daily.

Port Townsend

The Salal Cafe
34 Water Street
385-6532

Breakfast, lunch.
7-2 W-M.
Several vegetarian choices.
No credit cards.

A big hit with the twentysomething granola crowd, The Salal offers a large menu of soups, sandwiches and Mexican dishes. It's a cozy and unpretentious restaurant, with two small dining areas (one non-smoking) in front, and a modern, sunny solarium in back with a view of a garden. In the summer, outdoor dining is also available out back.

Breakfast brings numerous omelets and egg dishes. The vegetarian omelet is $5.25. For $3.95, you can get marinated tofu, green peppers and tomatoes sautéed in garlic butter on top of an English muffin with sharp cheddar and sprouts. The tofu and vegetables sauté ($6.25) includes sprouts and sunflower seeds. A tofu-scramble dish ($5.50) is cooked in garlic butter and comes with red potatoes and choice of blueberry oat muffin, English muffin or toast.

Lunch includes a tofu reuben sandwich ($4.95), a blend of swiss cheese, sauerkraut, mustard and mayonnaise. The vegan nature burger on an onion-dill bun ($4.50) is topped with jack cheese. A burrito ($3.75) is made with beans cooked without lard. Tofu stroganoff ($6.75) is sautéed in garlic butter and white wine with mushrooms and broccoli in a cream sauce. It comes with garlic bread and salad. A vegetarian soup ($1.75/$2.95) is available every other day, served with bread. Miso soup is offered daily ($1.50, $1.75 with sautéed veggies).

Khu Larb Thai
25 Adams Street
385-5023

Lunch, dinner.
1-9 M-F, 11-10 S-S.
Several vegetarian choices.
Credit cards accepted.

Paul Itti, who moved to the States from Thailand in 1982, first opened a Thai restaurant in Kelso, sold it and moved to Port Townsend to open Khu Larb Thai in 1989. Locals rave about the food here, and the decor of the two dining rooms in the old Victorian building is pleasant, too. There are many tastefully placed Thai ornaments including butterflies, tapestries and plates on the walls. Look for the case of antique Thai silverware on one wall. An unusual touch: the beautiful xylophone in the corner is played on Friday and Saturday nights.

Ten vegetarian dishes (in the $5 to $6 range) grace the menu. Phad Thai, a standard of the cuisine, combines stir-fried clear noodles with tofu, bean sprouts, green onion and mixed vegetables, topped with ground peanuts.

Vegetable curry includes bamboo shoots, basil leaves and pineapple. Broccoli with garlic is the top-selling vegetarian dish.

Silverwater Cafe

26 Quincy Street
385-6448

Lunch, dinner.
1-9 M-Sun.
Some vegetarian items.
Credit cards accepted.

A trip to the Silverwater is worth it, if only for the homey atmosphere. The classy cafe, a half block east of Water Street toward the water, holds a large, high-ceilinged dining room with a pellet stove by the front door. Full of hanging plants, the restaurant rotates fascinating works by local artists monthly. The front wall is brick; the others are white. You can eat at a table or at the counter by the back wall.

A vegetarian soup ($1.75/$2.50) is offered daily; sometimes, it's vegan. Lentil and black-bean soups are often on the docket, as are chilled fruit soups in summer. The Silverwater also features a daily vegetarian special, perhaps spanakopita, a pasta, tofu dish or Mexican entrée. On the main menu, stir-fried veggies with wild and white rice is $4.50 for lunch, $7.50 for dinner. The pasta primavera is $4.95 ($7.95 for dinner). Almost everyone asks for the viola burger ($3.95), although it's not on the menu. It's a grilled mushroom burger topped with cheese, sprouts, onion, lettuce and tomato.

El Sarape

28 Water Street
379-9343

Lunch, dinner.
1:30-8 M-Th, 11:30-9 F-Sat, 12-8 Sun.
Several vegetarian dishes.
Credit cards accepted.

Mauricio Cisneros, a native Mexican, and James Gonzales, who grew up in San Diego, joined forces in 1991 to open this Mexican restaurant with a focus on healthful foods. The pair converted the 1892 Lewis Building (which has gone through various incarnations as an art gallery and different restaurants) into a festive place, full of bright, colorful Mexican paintings, shawls and artifacts. The menu contains a vegetarian section, and beans here are cooked in vegetable oil instead of lard. Gonzales has been toying with creating a separate vegetarian menu.

The deluxe tostada ($4.25) includes whole beans, lettuce, tomato and cheese topped with sour cream and guacamole. Other dishes are priced from $4.25 for a bean burrito to $7.65 for two chiles rellenos. Among them are nachos, a bean enchilada and a chimichanga.

Other Choices

Waterfront Naturals (810 Water Street, 385-3290) is a small health-food store with a well-stocked juice bar. Most of the produce used for juicing is organic. Orange, apple and grapefruit juices cost $2.25 each for eight ounces, $2.95 for 12. Carrot juice is $2/$2.75. A one-ounce shot of wheatgrass juice is $1.85. Eight combinations are offered, including sunrise ($3.50): OJ, lemon and garlic, ginger and a touch of olive oil; morning tonic ($2.50), including grapefruit and apple, and tropical tonic ($3.50): papaya, coconut, pineapple, orange juice and bananas. Waterfront Naturals also sells a veggie sandwich with cream cheese ($1.95) and a daily vegan soup ($1.95/$2.50). Open 9:30-5:30 M-F, 10-5 Sat, and in summers, 11-4 Sun. No credit cards.

Bread and Roses Bakery (230 Quincy Street, 385-1044), just off Water Street, is in a charming old beige Victorian home with green trim, a wooden fence and a garden in front and a deck extending from the front around the side to the back for outdoor dining. The sunny bakery serves plenty of the usual sweets and breads, as well as a hummus sandwich ($3.75) with tomato, lettuce, sprouts and red onion. A bagel with vegetables and havarti cheese costs $2.25. The daily soup is sometimes vegetarian ($1.95/$2.95). A slice of vegetarian pizza costs $1.75. Open 6:30-5 M-Sat, 6:30-4 Sun. No credit cards.

Burrito Depot (at the corner of Washington and Madison streets, 385-5856), a block from Water Street, serves Mexican fast food cooked without lard. You can order nachos, a veggie soft taco or a veggie fajita with tofu in the $1.85 to $3.75 range. Open 10-9 M-S, in summer 11-4 Sun. No credit cards.

Bainbridge Island

Natural Gourmet

Harold's Square
842-2759

Lunch.
Deli open 11-4:30 M-F, 11-3 Sat.
Some vegetarian and vegan dishes.
No credit cards.

Tucked away at the back of a small health-food store in downtown Bainbridge Island, Natural Gourmet dispenses good vegetarian and vegan lunch fare, along with some chicken dishes. The deli serves a veggie sandwich ($3.50) with cream cheese, cucumber, tomato and sprouts and a garden salad ($4.25). The soups change daily, but always include one vegan offering such as split pea or chili ($1.75 cup, $2.50 bowl). Salads are displayed in a glass cabinet; at our visit, the choices included a vegan five-spice sesame pasta and vegan gingered rice ($2.45 for half a pint). The daily hot specials might include black-bean and rice enchiladas with chilies, cheese and salsa or polenta with sautéed vegetables ($3.85). There are a few tables in front of the store, which sells the usual assortment of health foods and supplements.

Other Choices

Bainbridge Island fans of spicy foods were thrilled when **Sawatdy Thai Cuisine** (8780 Fletcher Bay Road, 780-2429) opened in 1992. No longer do residents have to take the ferry to Seattle or drive to Bremerton or Port Townsend to sample this exotic cuisine. A short hop from downtown, Sawatdy offers seven vegetarian dishes, including tom yum pug ($5.25), a hot and sour vegetable soup with lemon grass, magrood leaves and chile paste; gang hed ($5.75), a red curry dish with straw mushrooms, bamboo shoots and fresh basil, and eggplant with tofu and basil leaves in a black-bean sauce ($6.50). Open 11:30-2, 5-9:30 M-Sat (until 10 F-Sat). Credit cards accepted.

Cluckers (112 Winslow Way West, 842-0381) is a sit-down and take-out chicken place that also serves a vegetarian garden burger ($3.75), made with cheese. Open 7:30-7:30 M-Sat, 8-4 Sun. No credit cards.

Silverdale

Creative Juices

Kitsap Mall
698-3290

Juice bar.
Open mall hours, seven days.
A few food items, including vegan ones.
No credit cards.

When Kitsap Mall expanded in 1992, it gained a new tenant that has quickly become a hit with some mall-goers. Many go up to the sleek, modern juice bar near the new entrance to ask about juicing and try one of the more than two dozen varieties offered. Jeff and Lesli Dullum were inspired to open Creative Juices after visiting Seattle's Gravity Bar — the granddaddy of juice bars. The couple has built a contemporary place that impresses with its energy and commitment.

Most single fruit juices cost $1.75 for 10 ounces, $2.50 for 16. Choices include apple, orange, pineapple, grapefruit and lemonade. Cranana ($2.25/$3.25), Creative Juice's most popular drink, is a blend of cranberry, apple, banana and orange. Carrot or carrot-apple juice costs $1.50 or $2.50. V-6 — available only at 16 ounces for $3.25 — combines carrot, tomato, spinach, celery, parsley and apple.

Creative Juices, unlike most juice bars, does not serve espresso (the mall lease precludes that). It does serve a few food items, such as the good vegan Essential Sandwiches ($2.25), a bagel and cream cheese ($1.25) and assorted muffins and desserts.

Bremerton

Royal Thai Restaurant

3622 Wheaton Way
377-7909

Lunch, dinner.
11-3, 4:30-9 M-Th, 11-3, 4:30-10 F, 4:30-10 Sat, 4:30-9 Sun.
Several vegan dishes.
Credit cards accepted.

The Royal Thai is committed to healthful eating. Every weekday, the large and ornately decorated restaurant offers a "healthy lunch special" for $3.95, including an entrée, the vegetarian soup of the day, a salad and rice. The special might be cashew nuts with tofu, ginger tofu or tofu with sweet and sour sauce.

The à la carte menu lists 15 vegetarian dishes for $5.95 or $6.95, such as b.b. broccoli with tofu and black-bean sauce, pud Thai jay, and tofu with spinach and peanut sauce. The ginger tofu during one visit was superb, with tofu, mushrooms, green pepper, onions and celery mixed with thin strands of ginger root. The place even serves brown rice.

Other Choices

Saigon West (1208 Sylvan Way, 377-2611) is a tiny Vietnamese-American eatery that offers a good vegetarian menu with 10 choices for $5.55 each. The decor is minimal, the food ordinary. The stir-fried almond chicken-substitute, made with tofu instead of chicken, includes cubes of carrots, celery, green and red peppers and onions on top of white rice and made for a satisfying dish. "Heavenly tofu" combines roasted tofu nuggets with vegetables. You also can order curry tofu, veggie fried rice or "out-of-this-world" tofu salad. Open 4-9 weekdays, 12-9 weekends and holidays. Credit cards accepted.

Port Orchard

Hadi's Restaurant

818 Bay Street
895-0347

Lunch, dinner.
11-9 M-Sat.
Some vegan choices.
No credit cards.

Hadi's is short on atmosphere and decor, but long on good flavors, according to locals. It may be the only restaurant to offer Mediterranean cuisine on the peninsula — at least between Olympia and Port Townsend. Hadi's is located along the main shopping street in downtown Port Orchard.

Vegetarian appetizers are a bargain here, for lunch or dinner. Hummus, baba ghanoush and tabbouleh each cost $2.45 for lunch, $3.25 for dinner. Zahra —

a deep-fried cauliflower appetizer — is $2.75 by day, $3.75 by night. On the main menu, vegetarian grape leaves are $5.50 (lunch) or $7.25 (dinner), while the falafel dish is $5.25 or $6.25.

Other Choices

Natural Health (1700 Highway 160, South Kitsap Mall, 876-1134), a large health-food store with all the standards, offers a juice bar with carrot, celery, beet, spinach and apple juices. Carrot juice is $1.25 for 8 ounces, $2 for 16. Other juices are $1.75 or $2.50. Open 10-8 M-F, 10-6 Sat, 12-5 Sun. No credit cards.

Gig Harbor

Le Bistro Coffee House

4120 Harborview Drive
851-1033

Breakfast, lunch, dinner.

Opens at 6 a.m. weekdays, 7:30 a.m. weekends; closes at 10 every night in summer, 6 in winter (except 7 F-Sat).

A few vegetarian and vegan options.

Juice bar.

Credit cards accepted.

It's hard to find an eatery with more character than Le Bistro. In an old yellow house down near Gig Harbor's waterfront, it is a hustling and bustling place where everyone seems to know owner Debi McAlpine. She's a friendly woman who loves to chat with the regulars between making espressos and lattes. Handsome art posters from around the world grace the walls. Behind the main counter is an appealing mural that glorifies the benefits of juicing with smiling pineapples, oranges and pears. Two diminutive dining rooms contain small round parlor tables and green-cushioned wooden chairs.

Le Bistro is known more for meat dishes, but popular demand has prompted it to make at least one vegetarian special — perhaps lasagna or a pasta — each night. Le Bistro always serves a vegetarian quiche ($4 with fruit) and a sandwich of avocado, cream cheese, lettuce, onion, tomato and sprouts ($4.25 full, $2.75 half). The daily chili occasionally is meatless. And about once a week, there's a vegetarian or vegan soup.

Le Bistro seems especially popular at breakfast, when locals come in for a pick-me-up coffee before work. You can choose from an assortment of egg dishes, muffins, scones, fruit cups and granola.

The full-service juice bar blends a variety of fruit and vegetable concoctions. Tropical morning, for example, consists of pineapple, papaya, banana, coconut and yogurt. Party punch blends pineapple, pear, banana and ginger. Those drinks cost $2.75 for eight ounces, $3.75 for 16 ounces. The martini marinara ($2.50/$3.50), made with carrot and beet, is especially refreshing.

Snohomish County

This county just north of Seattle, including the bedroom communities of Edmonds, Lynnwood and Mukilteo, and Everett, a largely blue-collar city that depends heavily on Boeing, is scenic. The views of Puget Sound, the Olympics and the Cascades from these cities are awesome.

The vegetarian scene is less satisfying, since just a handful of places offer appropriate fare here. Best bets include Chanterelle Specialty Foods in downtown Edmonds, an appealing deli that serves a vegetarian falafel burger; Indian Palace in downtown Everett, with decent Indian food, and a number of Thai places scattered throughout the area.

Edmonds

Chanterelle Specialty Foods

316 Main Street
774-0650

Breakfast, lunch, dinner.
8-9 Tu-Sat, 8-4 Sun-M.
Some vegetarian and vegan items.
Credit cards accepted.

A charming little restaurant and deli in downtown Edmonds, Chanterelle offers a small selection of vegetarian fare. The floor is wood, as are the tables and chairs; greenery hangs from a wooden rack extending along the wall above all the tables. Large windows open to the active street life in front. The deli is in the center of the dining room of what is a great people place.

Breakfast (served 8-11 M-Sat, 8-1:30 Sun) involves standard egg and pancake dishes. Lunch offers more for herbivores. One of the two soups of the day ($1.95/$2.95) always is vegetarian and often vegan. The falafel salad ($6.25) contains greens with alfalfa sprouts, cucumber, red onion, tomato, falafel patties and lemon-tahini dressing. The vegetarian sandwich ($5.25) yields hummus, sprouts, cucumber, cheddar and swiss cheese on whole-grain bread. The hottest seller is the Chanterelle burger ($6.25), made of falafel and served on a whole wheat bun with the usual trimmings. Spanakopita ($5.95), a Greek phyllo pastry filled with spinach and feta cheese, comes with a small salad. Fresh tomato-basil pasta, made with egg linguini, is $6.95 ($8.25 at dinner). Caloric desserts fill a display case at the deli counter.

Other Choices

Thai Park (182 Sunset Ave., 771-3902), a short walk from the Edmonds ferry, offers 15 vegetarian choices in the $5 range, including three soups and nine entrées. Tum kah tofu is a hot and sour soup with tofu, mushrooms, lemon grass, coconut milk and vegetables. Basil tofu is a stir-fry with basil, onion, carrot, hot chile paste, green peppers, mushrooms and bamboo shoots. O-cha garden combines sautéed vegetables with a wine sauce. An unusual feature for a Thai restaurant is the vegetarian dinner combination ($10.25 per person), which includes a spring roll, hot and sour soup, two entrées and steamed rice. Open 11:30-2:30, 5-9 Tu-Th, 11:30-2:30, 5-10 F-Sat, 5-9 Sun. Credit cards accepted.

Lynnwood

Marco Polo Restaurant (17425 Highway 99, 742-5640), an elegant little eatery in a shopping center, serves Pakistani and Middle Eastern cuisine. Small oriental carpets hang on the wall above the tables, and a giant Pakistani mosque is painted on the back wall. Appetizers include hummus, baba ghanoush, pakoras and samosas ($3.25 each) as well as dal ($1.50/$2.25). Among entrees ($2.75 to $4.95) are sabz curry, vegetables cooked in a blend of tomato, onion and spices; cold eggplant bharta blended with yogurt, tomatoes, green peas and ginger, and saag paneer, cheese cooked with spinach and spices. Buttery naan bread ($1.25, $1.50 with garlic or onion) makes a nice addition to the meal. Open 4-10 Tu-Sat, 4-9 Sun. Credit cards accepted.

Talay Thai Restaurant (4520 200th Street S.W., 670-1340) serves eight vegetarian dishes for $5.50 each, including hot garden (vegetables and tofu sauteed with garlic and chilies), vegetable curry with coconut milk and ginger tofu with mushrooms. Open 11-9 M-Th, 11-10 F, 12-10 Sat., 4-9 Sun. Credit cards accepted.

Mountlake Terrace

Thai Terrace (21919 66th Avenue W., 774-4556), in the Melody Hill Village shopping center just west of Interstate 5 at the 220th Street exit, serves up 12 vegetarian dishes, soups and appetizers. To start, try the vegetarian spring rolls ($4.25) or hot and sour vegetable soup ($3.75), seasoned with chilies, lemon grass and lime leaves. Main course choices ($5.50) include such Thai standards as tofu and spinach topped with peanut sauce and sautéed vegetables with curry paste. Open 11-9 M-Th, 11-10 F-Sat., 4-10 Sun. Credit cards accepted.

Mukilteo

Chiangmai Thai Restaurant (12926 Mukilteo Speedway, 745-3968), just west of Highway 99 at the Park Pointe Plaza shopping center, offers 13 vegetarian dishes, ranging from hot and sour soup with tofu or bean thread ($5.95) to veggie cashew ($5.95) and vegetarian fried rice ($5.75). Open 11-10 M-F, 4-10 weekends. Credit cards accepted.

Everett

India Palace

1405 Hewitt Avenue
252-8543

Lunch, lunch buffet, dinner.
11-2:30, 5-10 M-Sat, 2-10 Sun.
Several vegetarian selections.
Credit cards accepted.

Everett health-food devotees are happy to have India Palace, since there's little else in this city for vegetarians. Located on the main east-west downtown street, India Palace serves quite passable food. The side walls are brick and the ceiling is high, giving the place a somewhat industrial feel. Floral patterns cover the booth seats and fake flowers are on each table. A few colorful Indian pictures line the walls.

Of the nine vegetarian entrées ($5.50 to $6), the vegetable curry is an excellent dish of cauliflower, peas, carrots, tomato and other vegetables. Channa masala also is very good: chickpeas sautéed with mild spices, tomato and onion. Saag paneer is a favorite dish of some: cubes of homemade cheese and spinach cooked in a spicy sauce. Appetizers include vegetable samosas (two for $1.95) and pakoras (six for $1.50). Vegetable biryani, a vegetable fried-rice dish using basmati rice, costs $4.50. Among the several tandoori breads are naan, onion kulcha, a leavened bread stuffed with onions, and aloo paratha, stuffed with spiced potatoes and peas.

The $5.95 all-you-can-eat lunch buffet allows you to sample a variety of these foods, including dal, two vegetarian entrées, salads, naan and chutneys.

Other Choices

Puget Consumers' Co-op (9121 Evergreen Way, 742-1240) is a huge health-food store with a small deli encompassing a handful of tables. You can order several salads for about $4.99 each, possibly including soba noodle salad with an Asian dressing, couscous and bean salad, arame and tabbouleh. You can also order vegan Essential Sandwiches here. Open 8-10 M-Sun. No credit cards.

Orchid Thai Cuisine (9506 19th Avenue S.E., 338-1064), just off Interstate 5 at Exit 189, includes a lounge with karaoke and live music, and dispenses five vegetarian dishes for $6 to $6.50: vegetable delight sautéed with bean thread noodles, sweet and sour vegetables, curried vegetables, peanut-chile sauce over a bed of cooked spinach and vegetarian fried rice. Open 11-9:30 Tu-Th, 11-10 F, 4-10 Sat, 4-9:30 Sun. Credit cards accepted.

Skagit and Island Counties

Vegetarian options are sparse on the rural mainland this far north of Seattle. But the Deli Next Door in Mount Vernon is an outstanding vegetarian cafeteria that should not be missed if you're traveling this way. It adjoins the Skagit Valley Co-op, a wonderful health-food store that ranks among the best in the Pacific Northwest. At least two other places in Mount Vernon offer vegetarian burgers.

La Conner, also on the mainland, borders the water just before you get to Island County. It's a great little town with lots of shops and the Calico Cupboard, which offers some tasty vegetarian fare.

Island County is made up of Whidbey Island -- the largest in the contiguous United States -- and Fidalgo Island to the north. On Whidbey Island, there are no strictly vegetarian eateries. But plenty of restaurants offer a couple or more meatless entrées, primarily in the appealing little town of Langley, whose main street of diverse and attractive shops in 19th-century buildings overlooks Saratoga Pass and Camano Island. Check out the Raven Cafe. Attached to an artists' co-op, this tiny eatery makes vegetarian soups and serves fruit and vegetable drinks (even with spirulina on request). Cafe Langley specializes in Greek vegetarian standards like hummus and spanakopita.

While touring the island, be sure to visit Deception Pass State Park, one of the prettiest places in Washington, with views of the San Juan Islands and Olympic Mountains. It offers a collection of beaches and forest walks. The Deception Pass bridge on Highway 20, connecting Whidbey Island with Fidalgo Island to the north, is spectacular, and tourists typically park and walk across for great views. Besides Deception Pass, the island claims several other fine state parks.

On Fidalgo Island, the industrial city of Anacortes is where throngs come in the summer to board ferries for the San Juan Islands. Its restaurants include the Calico Cupboard Old Town Cafe and Bakery (sister of the restaurant of the same name in La Conner), which dispenses wholesome breads, vegetarian and vegan soups and a garden burger.

Mount Vernon

The Deli Next Door

202 S. 1st Street
336-3886

Breakfast, lunch, dinner.
9-7 M-F, 9-6 Sat, 9-4 Sun.
Several vegetarian, vegan selections.
No credit cards.

Part of the wonderful Skagit Valley Co-op, the Deli Next Door is the best place for a pure vegetarian meal between Seattle and Bellingham. The place has the feel of a cafeteria, with a large, spacious dining room full of plants, square blue tables and wood chairs. Blackboards behind the deli tell you what's on the menu, as well as the daily specials. Help yourself to silverware; the soup is also serve-yourself. The deli uses filtered water and organic produce when possible. People come to the deli and the adjoining co-op from as far away as Camano and Whidbey islands. The co-op's aisles are filled with all the health foods and produce you can imagine, as well as books, cards and gift items.

Breakfast at the deli is served until 11. The small menu lists whole wheat waffles with real maple syrup ($2.95), egg frittata ($4.50) and plenty of fresh baked goods. At lunch and dinner, half of the 15 or 20 salads in the display case might be vegan, including tabbouleh, hummus and almond-garlic noodles, and many with grains, tofu or tempeh. Salads and sandwiches are mostly under $4. On the regular menu are a garden salad, a spinach salad with a honey-mustard dressing, parmesan cheese, sunflower seeds and sprouts. Other dressings include tangy-tamari, lemon-tahini, blue cheese and raspberry vinaigrette.

The garden burger is made of vegetables, grains, nuts, cheese and a bit of egg. The vegan garden sandwich includes tomatoes, sprouts, lettuce, mushrooms, cucumber, grated carrots and cabbage on whole wheat bread with homemade tahini sauce. The tofu salad sandwich is also vegan: the tofu is seasoned with herbs, mustard, eggless mayonnaise, scallions and finely diced vegetables. The Middle Eastern platter ($4.50) comes with hummus, dolmas, olives, cucumbers and tomato on a bed of lettuce, and whole wheat pita and lemon on the side. Deli sandwiches also are available, including dolphin-safe tuna and nitrate-free meats. Specials might include oriental tempeh barbecue, African ground-nut stew ($4.25) or other delicious ethnic dishes. Soups change daily, perhaps spinach lentil, curry lentil (with apples and raisins), sweet potato kale, miso with Japanese vegetables or pureed eggplant with sunflower butter. Every afternoon, the Deli makes a vegetarian pizza, sometimes with soy cheese. It sells many baked goods, including vegan cookies. The breads, though, are made with eggs and butter. Other desserts are rich as well, including cakes and cappuccino Nanaimo bars.

Other Choices

Cafe Europa (516 S. 1st Street, 336-3933) is run by the folks who own Torrey's Eggs Cetera on Capitol Hill in Seattle. Like that popular breakfast haunt, Cafe Europa serves a vegan Ecoburger ($4.50). A vegetarian sandwich and a daily soup (usually vegan) are also available at this upscale restaurant with brick walls and pictures of European scenes. Or try the vegetarian pizza made with soy cheese ($4.95 for one-quarter of the pie). Breakfasts on weekends include omelets, waffles and other standards; on weekday mornings, you can get coffee and muffins. Open 9-9 M-F, 8-3 S-S. Credit cards accepted.

The Blue Owl (1200 Cleveland Avenue, 336-2476), a few blocks south of downtown across from the post office, sells a garden burger, avocado garden salad with cream cheese and vegetable lasagna, each for $4.25 or $4.50. Open 9:30-5 M-Sat. Credit cards accepted.

The Hilltop Delicatessen and Store (102 Division Street, 336-5550) offers a vegan meatless burger and frequent vegetarian soup specials. Open 6-4 M-F.

La Conner

Calico Cupboard (720 S. First Street, 466-4451), a classy restaurant and bakery with a new sibling in Anacortes (see Page 127), provides a number of vegetarian choices: a vegetarian burger and veggie and cream cheese sandwich (each under $6), a cup or bowl of vegetarian soup and vegetarian lasagna. Breakfasts include pancakes, french toast and vegetarian omelets. The Calico Cupboard contains a large dining room and a separate bakery. Open 7:30-5 M-Th, 7:30-5:30 F-Sun. (Winter hours: 8-5 M-Sun.) No credit cards.

Langley

The Raven Cafe

197 Second Street
221-3211

Breakfast, lunch, Saturday dinner.
7-4 M-F, 8-4, 6-11 Sat (dinners about twice a month in winter), 9-1 Sun.
Several vegetarian options.
No credit cards.

Attached to the Artists' Cooperative of Whidbey Island (paintings from the gallery overflow into the small deli in back), The Raven Cafe is a restful place with wooden country tables and chairs indoors, and patio seating outside. New age music is likely to be playing over the speakers. Much of the food here is vegetarian; Sarah Eskenazi and Frank Gulacy wanted to create a good community hang-out with alternative food when they opened in 1992.

From the small juice bar, you can order apple, carrot or other seasonal juices; spirulina is optional. A display case contains lots of fresh-baked goods, many of them sugar-free. A chalkboard lists the specials, including quiches, three or four daily salads and two soups (both usually are vegetarian, and often one is vegan; choices might be broccoli-cheddar, curried lentil, black-bean, chili or minestrone). The garden burger ($4.75, with chips) is made of veggies, grains and cheese. A garden veggie sandwich with cream cheese is offered.

The Raven is open for dinner with live acoustic music every Saturday in the summer, and twice a month in the winter.

Other Choices

Garibyan Bros. Cafe Langley (113 First Street, 221-3090) dispenses pricey Greek specialties in a classy restaurant with wood beams and white walls sporting pretty prints of fish and fowl. Lunch appetizers ($4.95 to $6.95) include spanakopita, grape leaves stuffed with pine nuts, onions, rice and currants, quiches and a hummus and baba ghanoush plate with pita. The soup of the day occasionally is vegetarian, but may include chicken stock. Entrées ($4.95 to $5.25) are falafel, feta cheese pizza and an eggplant sandwich. The same appetizers (same prices, too) are available for dinner, along with a Greek salad ($7.95). Dinner entrées are Mediterranean vegetables ($10.95), a plate of sautéed eggplant, hummus, baba ghanoush, potato salad and the hot vegetable of the day, and pasta acropolis ($13.95), linguini tossed with olive oil, bell peppers, garlic, herbs, mushrooms, tomatoes and feta cheese. Open 11:30-2:30, 5-8 (until 8:30 F-Sat) daily. Closed Tuesdays in winter. No lunch on Sunday. Credit cards accepted.

The Dog House Backdoor Restaurant (230 First Street, 221-9996), at the back of a tavern that overlooks the water, offers vegetarians a handful of choices, such as a health-nut burger with blue-cheese dressing ($5), and a veggie sandwich ($4.50). But the ghivetch (vegetables cooked in broth and topped with melted cheese) -- proclaimed "vegetarian" on the menu during a 1993 visit -- included chicken broth, a cook said. Among munchies ($3 to $5.25) are tempura vegetables, nachos and sweet-potato fries. The Dog House is in the former Olympic Game Club building (1908), which is listed on the National Register of Historic Places. Open 11-9 M-Sat, 11:30-9 Sun. No credit cards.

JB's Ice Creamery (224 First Street, 221-3888), opened in 1982, has operated a juice bar since 1988. Here you can get standards like apple, grapefruit, carrot and orange for $1.50 to $2.25, and other fruit juices seasonally (lots of melon juices in the summer). Smoothies ($1.75) are available with fruit of choice, ice and banana (optional add-ons are ice cream, frozen yogurt, wheat germ and spirulina). Open 9-8 M-Sun, until 9:30 in summer.

Mike's Place (219 First Street, 221-6575) sells lots of meat, poultry and seafood dishes, but also offers a vegan burger for $4.25. You can get a veggie sandwich with avocado and swiss cheese or visit the all-you-can-eat salad bar ($4.95 lunch, $5.95 dinner). Open 8-8 M-Sun. Credit cards accepted.

Coupeville

Christopher's Creative Contemporary Cuisine (23 Front Street, 678-5480) is a fancy restaurant with a wine room, and offers largely meat and fish dishes of the Northwest. Also available on the monthly menu is a vegetarian dish; on one visit it was vegetable couscous baked with tahini ($10.95); another time it was baked eggplant with chunky fennel, bell peppers and tomato sauce ($10.25), while an appetizer was sautéed shiitake mushrooms with spicy black-bean sauce ($6.25). Open 11:30-2, 5-9 W-Sun. Credit cards accepted.

Anacortes

Calico Cupboard Old Town Cafe and Bakery

901 Commercial Avenue
293-7315

Breakfast, lunch.
7-4 M-Sat, 7-3 Sun.
Several vegetarian and vegan items.
No credit cards.

This second Calico Cupboard, which opened in 1992, is the companion of its namesake in mainland La Conner, a highly successful restaurant launched 10 years earlier by Linda Freed. It's a welcome addition to Anacortes, which long has lacked vegetarian options worthy of a town of 10,000 that is a gateway to the health-conscious San Juan Islands. The restaurant and bakery (part of the same large room) have a country feel, and large windows look onto Commercial Avenue and 9th Street. The bakery sells honey-sweetened whole-grain breads, muffins and pastries.

Breakfasts (in the $4 to $6 range) include standard egg, omelet and pancake choices, as well as things like potatoes rancheros and a honey-wheat waffle. Or try some of the muffins.

Lunch time brings many vegetarian options in the $4 to $7 range. The chili includes kidney beans, corn, chilies and tomatoes, and is topped with low-fat cheese and onions; vegans can get it without the cheese, since it's cooked with no butter. It is served with crackers and whole-grain bread made on the premises. One of the three daily soups is always vegetarian; often it's vegan. The garden veggie burger contains grains, vegetables, nuts and cheese. A hot tomato-broccoli sandwich with cream cheese, sun-dried tomatoes and red onion and an avocado and cheese sandwich are other options. Several salads are available, and make good companions to the vegetarian lasagna or cheesed vegetable pilaf. The special of the day usually is meatless, and might be spanakopita, Portuguese black beans and rice or vegetable rice bundles (phyllos stuffed with rice and vegetables).

Other Choices

Janot's Bistro (419 Commercial Avenue, 293-3355), in The Majestic hotel, is a classy restaurant that serves French food, as well as a vegetarian entrée for lunch and dinner. The menus change occasionally, but you might find a vegetarian oriental stir-fry with basmati rice ($6.50) for lunch or vegetarian hot pot ($12.50), a bean burrito topped with papaya salsa and served with basmati and wild rice, for dinner. A dinner salad might be hearts of romaine with apples and roquefort cheese in a walnut vinaigrette ($5.50). Open 11:30-2:30, 5:30-9:30 M-Sun, except closed Tuesdays in winter. Credit cards accepted.

Gere-a-Deli (502 Commercial Avenue, 293-7383) is a cavernous deli that serves a few vegetarian items, including a pocket of veggies pita or standard veggie sandwich ($4.75 each), or a spinach or garden salad. Open 7-4 M-F, 8-4 Sat. Credit cards accepted.

Bellingham

Bellingham, a city of nearly 50,000 people 90 miles north of Seattle and 50 miles south of Vancouver, B.C., is said by some to be the most scenic in western Washington. Beautiful views of Puget Sound dominate, and Mount Baker can be seen to the east.

With its large alternative community and 10,000 students at Western Washington University, Bellingham is a great place for vegetarians. Perhaps the best in town is Pepper Sisters, which serves exceptional Southwestern cuisine. Downtown, Casa Qué Pasa offers vegan Mexican dishes alongside standard beef burritos and chicken tacos. Also downtown, The Old Town Cafe is a fun place for a good vegan breakfast or lunch. The Old Fairhaven Village, a couple miles south of downtown, is an interesting group of shops and restaurants in historic buildings; several — the best being the Colophon Cafe — provide herbivores with satisfying meals. To the north of the city, several good restaurants can be found near and just south of the Bellis Fair Mall. Bangkok House Restaurant offers a lengthy vegetarian menu.

Pepper Sisters

1055 N. State Street
671-3414

Dinner.
4:30-9 Sun, Tu-Th; 4:30-9:30 F-Sat.
Half vegetarian.
Credit cards accepted.

Pepper Sisters, a 1988 addition to the Bellingham dining scene, has "winner" written all over it. Next door to the Community Food Co-op (*the* place where Bellingham gets its health foods) in a building where backpacks once were manufactured, it's one of the most lively restaurants in town. The atmosphere is buoyant with waitpeople bustling to serve the multitudes who come here, especially on a Saturday night. Pepper Sisters is colorful with a high ceiling and a long, narrow dining room. The wall on the right as you enter is brick; the others are painted in light, pale shades of pink, green and blue. On the right are booths; on the left, tables and an open kitchen where you can see the cooks at work. Even better than the atmosphere is the creativity of the chefs. They've come up with a menu and evening specials that dazzle.

A recent meal started with two appetizers from the specials board: perfectly spiced gazpacho (the cold Spanish soup made from a puree of tomatoes and other vegetables) that had just the right amount of garlic. The orange crisp jicama salad was superb: the jicama, a root vegetable similar to a potato, was crunchy, and was enhanced with small pieces of cabbage and red onion, and lots of coriander and tiny orange chunks to add zest. These appetizers were steals at $1.25 and $2.25, respectively. They were so good that they ought to become regulars here.

Half of the menu's 16 entrées are vegetarian (although all of the dishes include cheese, you can request almost any dish without it), and prices range from $4.75 to $7.75. Our meal continued with a vegetarian burrito in a whole wheat tortilla, filled with beans and topped with a fiery red-chile sauce (most dishes give the option of red chile, its milder green cousin, or ranchero sauce). On the side was the posole that comes with many of the dishes: a stew of hull-less, cooked dried corn in a sauce of tomato, onion, garlic, cumin and oregano. This vegetarian, who has come across more than a few interesting dishes in his journeys, has never tasted anything quite like it: the corn was chewy, and the tomato sauce exploded with flavor. Accompanying all meals is the Southwestern sopaipilla, a crisp, puffy pastry with honey butter on the side. Other entrées include green- or red-chile enchilada, roasted potato and garlic enchilada, blue corn rellenos and Southwest pizza made with a cornmeal crust and tomatillo sauce, and topped with roasted chilies, mushrooms, pine nuts, roma tomatoes and cheese.

The Legendary Colophon Cafe and Deli

1208 11th Street
647-0092

Lunch, dinner.
10-10 M-Sat, 10-6 Sun.
Several vegetarian and vegan choices.
Credit cards accepted.

Here's a great place to share hearty vegetarian food over conversation or while reading a good book. The Colophon Cafe stands out on two counts. First, it shares space with Village Books in the thriving Old Fairhaven neighborhood, making for an intellectually exciting environment. Second, the deli is about as vegetarian-savvy as they come.

The bookstore and cafe each are on two levels, and the two dining areas seem to blend into the bookstore. As you walk in from the street, a deli and small, simple dining area with local artworks on the walls greet you (check out the gigantic rack of coffee mugs on the wall behind the deli). Downstairs is a larger dining room, full of people and buzzing with conversation. Main-floor counter people communicate with the kitchen workers downstairs by shouting through a tube beside the upstairs cash register.

The deli serves a variety of soups, salads and sandwiches, as well as a lot of caloric desserts. The Colophon Cafe goes a long way to cater to people with special food needs. If you ask, staffers will show you a book listing all the ingredients in each dish they offer. They even have a monthly soup calendar that lists, by day of the month, the soups that will be available, and shows which ones have no meat or dairy. The Colophon dispenses five soups a day ($2.75 small, $3.65 large, with bread). Two are always vegan: Mexican corn and bean, and split pea. The special of the day may be vegetarian or vegan, perhaps lentil chili, vegan corn chili or Italian barley.

Salads and sandwiches are mostly under $5. Salads include a tossed green and a small salad with soup and bread. A veggie bagel with cream cheese, tomato, cucumber and sprouts or a bagel with hummus, cream cheese, peanut butter or jam round out a hearty lunch. Or try the veggie pita sandwich. You can substitute hummus for cream cheese in the garden of delights sandwich.

Desserts are standard: chocolate chunk cake, carrot cake, pies, mega-muffins and so forth.

Taste of India
3930 Meridian Street
647-1589

Lunch, lunch buffet, dinner.
11-2:30 M-Sun, 5-10 Sun-Th, 5-10:30 F-Sat.
Several vegetarian, vegan selections.
Credit cards accepted.

This popular Indian restaurant, opened in 1991, is nestled between Ross Dress for Less and Safeway in the Meridian Village shopping center, across from the Bellis Fair Mall (just off Exit 256 from Interstate 5). The food is terrific, though the decor is an awkward blend of American diner and ornate (some would say tacky) Indian accessories. Colorful Indian cloths with scenes from the Asian country hang on the walls, along with several gold plates. In the center of the restaurant, fake grape clusters hang clumsily from the ceiling.

Our party agreed that the $5.50 all-you-can-eat lunch buffet was outstanding. That price gets you three vegetarian entrées (including two vegan and one with dairy), potato fritters, salad, naan bread and chutneys. One buffet selection was aloo ghobi, curried cauliflower and potatoes in a delicious, very spicy sauce. Even more spicy was the channa masala, chickpeas cooked with ginger. The mint and coriander chutney is a perfect companion for the naan bread.

If you order à la carte, vegetable samosas or pakoras ($1.95 each) make excellent appetizers. Eight entrées (in the $5 to $7 range) include dal, bharta (a roasted eggplant dish) and navratan korma, vegetables cooked with cream, raisins, nuts and spices. The vegetarian dinner for two ($18.95) brings samosas, naan, dal, two vegetable dishes, yogurt raita and a dessert.

The Old Town Cafe
316 W. Holly Street
671-4431

Breakfast, lunch.
7-3 M-Sat, 8-2 Sun.
Several vegetarian, vegan options.
No credit cards.

A small but trendy eatery with wooden booths and tables at the edge of downtown Bellingham (you can learn about all the holistic health practices available in town on the large message board by the front door), The Old Town Cafe offers a mix of standard American fare and good vegetarian and vegan selections. The food is purchased from local cooperatives, and all paper, glass, plastic and metal are recycled.

Breakfast (most choices under $4.25) includes french toast with your choice of bread, omelets with whole wheat toast and homefries, and scrambled tofu (onions, tomatoes, mushrooms, sprouts or chili are extra) with toast and homefries. Or choose from a variety of fresh-baked goods for a buck or two.

The eggless whole-grain hotcakes are served, curiously enough, with two eggs on the side.

Lunch offers several salads (mostly under $3), including a small green one with homemade blue cheese, tofu or vinaigrette dressing; potato salad, or fresh fruit. The vegetarian chili and the soup of the day, which tends to the vegetarian, cost $3 each for a small bowl, $3.75 for a large (soups are not offered Sundays). Vegetarian sandwiches ($5.50 to $5.75) include a tofu burger, a marinated tofu sandwich and the funky special: grilled cheese, avocado, sprouts and tomato.

Bangkok House Restaurant

2500 Meridian Street
733-3322

Lunch, dinner.
11:30-2:30, 5-10 M-Th, 11:30-2:30, 5-11 F-Sat.
Several vegetarian choices.
Credit cards accepted.

Some 20 vegetarian entrées await diners at this Thai restaurant in north Bellingham. Most are in the $6 to $6.50 range. For starters, try one of the four exotic soups, such as tom yum mushrooms (four kinds of mushrooms with lemon grass and lime leaves). Main-dish possibilities include ginger tofu, vegetarian fried rice, see mee jay (egg noodles topped with mushrooms, bamboo shoots, napa cabbage and gravy), phad Thai and tofu with bean sprouts.

Casa Qué Pasa

1415 Railroad Avenue
738-8226

Lunch, dinner.
11-11 Sun-Th, 11-3 a.m. F-Sat.
Several vegetarian and vegan dishes.
No credit cards.

Perhaps the only Mexican restaurant in the Pacific Northwest to boast a menu with a section of specifically vegan entrées, Casa Qué Pasa was opened in downtown Bellingham in 1993 by Travis and Alana Holland. And they seem to be doing a lot of things right. There's the notebook on a table at the front of the restaurant where people can leave suggestions for improvements. At the back of their take-out menu, they talk about the importance of recycling and helping those in need. Prices are rock-bottom (nothing on the menu is more than $4.99, with plenty of dishes under $2). And with a frankness rarely seen in the food industry, their menu lets customers know exactly which meatless dishes come into contact with meat by-products (usually on the grill).

As for decor, Casa Qué Pasa is short on it. The floor is a reddish cement; a pinball machine stands in a corner. You order your meal at the back register, either from a take-out menu or from the Coca-Cola bulletin boards on the back wall. It's a brightly lit place with a high ceiling and windows looking onto Railroad Avenue, a popular shopping street.

Shortly after opening, its menu contained four vegan dishes: a special burrito, pinto-bean burrito, black-bean burrito and Spanish rice, beans and salsa. Meat-free (but not vegan) items include a black-bean tostada, bean-and-cheese chimichanga and quesadilla ("Cheese, but no meat surfaces," informs the menu). The owners are working on expanding the vegetarian selections, perhaps with marinated tofu and textured-vegetable-protein meat substitutes.

Southside Cafe

1303 12th Street
733-4511

Breakfast, lunch, dinner.
8-3 Sun., 6:30-3 M-Th, 6:30-11 p.m. Fri., Sat.
Several vegetarian selections.
Credit cards accepted.

This funky, high-ceilinged establishment with brick walls in the Old Fairhaven district serves earthy meals. Live classical guitar music is played on Friday nights. The cafe caters mostly to meat eaters and ovo-lacto vegetarians; vegans won't find much here to interest them.

For breakfast, the veggie scramble ($5.50, or $3.95 for a half-order) is a generous serving of eggs, peppers, tomatoes, potatoes and onions topped with cheddar cheese and sour cream, served with toast and salsa. Several omelets are offered (about $5 each), including a Mexican one made with mild chile peppers, onions and cheese topped with sour cream and salsa. Whole wheat or buttermilk pancakes and french toast also are available.

At lunch (choices under $5), you can get a walkabout sandwich, a hot pastry turnover filled with mushrooms and swiss cheese, or a broccoli and swiss cheese quiche. The black-bean chili is vegetarian, and comes with grated cheese and a corn muffin. The veggie delight sandwich is a typical cream cheese and avocado deal. The dinner menu (in the $5 to $6 range) offers a vegetarian stir-fry served with brown and wild rice, vegetarian enchiladas and pasta marinara, among others.

Dos Padres

1111 Harris Street
733-9900

Lunch, dinner, weekend breakfast.
11:30-10 Sun-Th, 11:30-11 F-Sat, breakfast 7:30-11:30 Sat, 7:30-noon Sun.
Several vegetarian selections.
Credit cards accepted.

Mexican restaurants that serve truly healthful food are a rarity in the Puget Sound area, especially outside Seattle. But Dos Padres, which opened in the Old Fairhaven district in 1973, now offers vegetarian dishes without lard. The attractive restaurant, with several decorated rooms and a skylight, even offers those with special diets — including vegetarians — a full page of suggestions.

(But not all is enlightened here: vegetarian soups of the day sometimes include fish stock, the menu says. And Dos Padres uses plenty of eggs and cheese in its vegetarian dishes.)

The garlic-vegetable sauté is probably the purest dish on the menu,(where vegetarian entrées are in the $7 to $10 range. The vegetable frittata is a medley of vegetables, spinach and cheese in eggs served with rice and tortillas. The burrito-guacamole dinner comes with rice and choice of soup or salad. The pasta salad à la San Francisco ($4.50) is tossed with vegetables.

Weekend breakfasts tend to be loaded with eggs and cheese, with such dishes as chiles rellenos and a black-bean omelet dominating. Vegans will have to be satisfied with oatmeal, toast and a cup of fruit ($3.25).

Other Choices

The Fairhaven (1114 Harris Street, 676-1520), in Old Fairhaven Village, is a steak and seafood establishment that serves a number of vegetarian dishes as well. For lunch (in the $5 to $7 range), vegetable quiche comes with homemade soup (often, a vegetarian choice is offered) or tossed salad. You also can try the vegetarian or avocado sandwiches, served on whole wheat, rye, sourdough or old-fashioned white bread. Or order one of two vegetarian omelets. Dinner offers wider variety (from $8 to $11): fettuccine with fresh tomatoes and basil, topped with parmesan cheese; vegetable Thai curry with fruit and vegetables; stir-fried vegetables with ginger and garlic, or vegetable quiche. Open 11:30-2:30, 5 until closing M-Sun. Credit cards accepted.

India Cafe (1 Bellis Fair Parkway, 738-2443), in the Bellis Fair Mall food court, serves vegetable samosas and pakoras for $1.95 each. A full vegetarian meal ($4.95) includes spinach and cheese or eggplant bharta, dal, cauliflower and potatoes in a spicy sauce, naan bread, vegetable biryani and salad or yogurt raita. Open mall hours. No credit cards.

Thai House Restaurant (3930 Meridian Village, 734-5111), across from the Bellis Fair Mall, dispenses three vegetarian dishes for $5.95 to $6.50, including phad Thai, garden delight (sautéed vegetables topped with peanut sauce) and kang pahk, vegetables cooked in red curry, coconut milk and basil. Open 11:30-2:30, 4:30-9:30 M-F, 4:30-9:30 S-S. Credit cards accepted.

Cafe Akroteri (1219 Cornwall Avenue, 676-5554), an attractive restaurant with white walls, blue tablecloths and lots of plants, serves Greek food (for $5.25 or less) in the downtown shopping district. For lunch, choose the vegetarian gyros with feta cheese, vegetable soup, a Greek salad or spanakopita. For dinner, you'll have to stick to the appetizer menu at this mostly carnivorous establishment. Open 11-9:30 M-Sat. Credit cards accepted.

The Echo House (1212 N. State Street, 676-1660) is an alternative restaurant that is appropriate mostly for teens and twentysomethings. Featured are blaring rock music, weird art and a potpourri of couches, easy chairs and tables scattered about a cement floor in the cavernous, smoke-filled dining area. The chef of The Echo House, which opened in 1993, is vegetarian, and much of the chalkboard menu follows suit. Included are a hummus plate, veggie and cheese sandwich, a daily vegetarian soup, garden salad and plenty of caffeinated drinks. Almost everything is under $4. Open 12-12 M-Sat. No credit cards.

San Juan Islands

Vegetarians usually don't have an easy time obtaining quality (or otherwise) meatless fare in rural areas. But the San Juan Islands — known for spectacular mountain island scenery and tranquility — are different. Here, you'll find that tofu and tempeh dishes are almost as much a part of the islands as lightly traveled country roads and quiet places. That, some residents say, is largely because many hippies call the islands home. While there are classy modern establishments that serve vegetarian fare, other eateries come right out of the 1960s or 1970s: small, humble cafes with low-budget furniture and a granola feel. The best islands for vegetarians are San Juan and Orcas. Both Friday Harbor on San Juan and Eastsound on Orcas have one good health-food deli each, and each island claims several restaurants that cater to vegetarians and vegans.

Friday Harbor

Way of Life

35 First Street S.
378-5433

Breakfast, lunch.
10-6 M-F, 10-5 Sat. (winter).
Strictly vegetarian, plenty of choices for vegans.
No credit cards.

Here is the purest vegetarian establishment in the San Juan Islands, a fine place to go for a good, solid, meat-free meal. Way of Life pairs a small whole-foods market — complete with bulk foods, vitamins and organic produce from the San Juan Islands arranged in boxes on a table in a tiny back room — with a laid-back vegetarian deli and juice bar. Wheatgrass junkies can get their fix here: $1.50 for one ounce, $3 for two. You can choose from carrot, celery, beet, cucumber, apple, orange, grapefruit, pineapple, pear or melon juices (prices range from $1.50 to $4.75). Or try a fruit smoothie, with or without yogurt ($4). Add amino acids, spirulina, bee pollen, flax seed oil or nutritional yeast to your drink for a little extra zing, and cash.

Breakfasts ($2.50 to $4), available all day, include granola with fresh fruit, fresh seasonal fruit salad and sprouted wheat bagel with cream cheese.

But the lunches ($2.75 to $5) are what people really rave about. Some of the dishes are prepared fresh at the tiny kitchen counter; others are made earlier and reheated in a microwave. The rice and beans du jour at our visit was a zesty mixture of pinto beans, a spicy sauce and brown rice. Dip the veggie California rolls — brown rice and vegetables wrapped with seaweed — in soy sauce for a tasty treat. The garden burger is just fine. The soup du jour costs $2.25. If you're really hungry, the soup, salad and bread make a hearty meal. You can order nachos with soy cheese, a hummus plate with pita bread and a green salad, rice and steamed veggies with a tasty lemon-tahini sauce or "Not Dogs!" ($2.50), tofu hot dogs with the works.

Springtree Cafe

310 Spring Street
378-4848

Breakfast, lunch, dinner.
8-11, 12-2:30, 5:30 to 9 or 10 M, W-Sat.;
Sunday brunch 8-2. Closed Tuesdays.
A few vegan choices.
Credit cards accepted.

James Boyle, owner and chef at this slick, contemporary establishment, gave up meat years ago when he was growing up in the meat- and dairy-industry-rich South. He went to culinary school, where he confesses to having reverted to his old diet for a time. But he became vegetarian again after finishing his studies. When he purchased the Springtree Cafe in 1992, he quickly added vegan items to the restaurant's repertoire. One day, he'd like to run a completely vegan establishment, but for a fancy restaurant in a resort town like this, that goal was not immediately viable economically. For now, vegetarians will have to settle for creative meatless dishes on a menu full of seafood and poultry. But that's not bad: there's an abundance of delicious food here. In season, 75 percent of the produce comes from an organic farm on nearby Waldren Island.

Springtree Cafe is a nearly half-mile walk up the main street from the ferry terminal. You'll find it underneath a majestic 100-year-old campardown elm tree. There's a patio in front for warm-weather dining; inside, the seats are plush and the tables are hardwood. Local artworks cover the light pink walls.

For breakfast ($4 to $6), try tofu rancheros with beans, salsa and sour cream, veggie hash browns with cheddar cheese, fruit salad with honey yogurt and toasted oats or french toast with real maple syrup and fruit. A fine vegan appetizer at lunch or dinner is polenta sautéed with spinach, mushrooms and marinara ($4.75). Also at lunch (entrées are $5 to $6.25), try the veggie burger, pasta primavera with fresh veggies in basil cream, or sesame tofu with veggies and basmati rice in a sauce made of cilantro, mint, garlic, tamari, coconut milk, tahini and mustard. Dinner includes stir-fried tofu in a Thai peanut sauce and the vegetarian special of the day (both $10), which might be Indian curry tofu, vegetarian shepherd's pie with tofu, fresh corn and other vegetables, sweet and sour tofu, or grilled eggplant roulades — spinach, mushrooms and peppers rolled up in eggplant. Boyle says he cooks a lot of vegan soups ($2.50) in the summer, perhaps lentil, black bean or potato chowder with coconut milk and soy milk. In the winter, he is more likely to prepare hearty cream soup with dairy.

Maloula's Middle Eastern Restaurant

5 Front Street
378-8485

Lunch, dinner.
11:30-3, 5:30-9 daily. Closed Tuesday in winter.
Several vegan choices.
Credit cards.

Named after Maloula, a cultural center in Syria that means "entrance," this upscale restaurant with a sweeping rooftop view of the harbor offers more interesting vegetarian fare than most Middle Eastern restaurants. Owner Adnan Nassarallah worked in the construction industry in Los Angeles for many years before coming to San Juan Island for a similar job. Several months later, he decided to open a restaurant and, in 1992, achieved his dream. His small establishment sits atop a new shopping center in the heart of Friday Harbor, and contains a patio with a water vista.

The Nassarallah family knows how to put together some great food. Most choices are available for both lunch and dinner. To start, try one of the appetizers ($2.50 to $3.50): the dolma, for example, are grape leaves stuffed with rice, parsley, tomatoes and green onion. Hummus, tabbouleh and baba ghanoush are available. An adventurous choice is artichoke bottoms, marinated in a house sauce and topped with peas, onions and carrots. The soup of the day ($1.50 or $2.75) might be lentil, hearty but not too spicy. At lunch you can order the falafel sandwich ($3.50), falafel patties with hummus, tahini and lettuce in a whole wheat tortilla. The combination plate ($5.25) includes hummus, tabbouleh and baba ghanoush, with pita bread. The moojedera ($6.25 for lunch, $8.50 for dinner) tops spinach and mushrooms, sautéed in olive oil and wine, over lentils and bulghur wheat that have been cooked with onions and garlic. That dish comes with choice of soup or salad. At dinner, the tofu kebab ($9.95) is a fascinating option: two 20-inch skewers with tofu, onions, mushrooms, green peppers and tomatoes at the end top a plate of rice and slivered almonds. We found the vegetables delicious, although the tofu would have been improved if it were marinated a little longer. A side dish of peas was pleasantly spiced and artfully presented in a lettuce leaf.

Other Choices

Roberto's (corner of First and A streets, 378-6333) is an Italian eatery with some pasta dishes ($9.50 to $13) for vegetarians. You can get spaghetti with marinara sauce; ravioli all' arancia (ricotta cheese and stuffed pasta pillows in an orange-cinnamon cream sauce) or pasta from hell (onions, red and green peppers, garlic and mushrooms in a hot pepper sauce). Open for dinner only, 5-9 Tu-Sun. Credit cards accepted.

Madelyn's (at the top of the ferry lanes, 378-4545), is a great place for a bagel, a banana-blackberry muffin, herbal tea or espresso. A bagel sandwich ($2.25) brings sprouts, tomato and cream cheese on a whole wheat bagel; with cucumbers and red onion, it costs $2.75. Madelyn's gets crowded when ferries come in. Open 7-4 M-Sat., 8-4 Sun.

Downrigger's (on Front Street, near ferry, 378-2700) is a rather nondescript waterfront American and seafood restaurant that happens to offer a few vegetarian choices. Order a hummus plate ($4.95) with Greek olives, red onions and pita bread, a hummus and garden vegetable sandwich on nine-grain bread ($5.95) or cashew stir-fry in a homemade teriyaki sauce ($6.95 at lunch, $10.95 at dinner). Open for lunch and dinner. Credit cards accepted.

Amigo's (40 Spring Street, 378-5908) serves Mexican food outdoors during the warm months, and closes for the season when it gets too cold to sit outside. You can get a bean and cheese burrito, cheese enchiladas, super nachos or a veggie bean salad. Prices range from $6 to $8. Amigo's uses no lard in vegetarian bean dishes. Open for lunch and dinner.

Orcas Island

Orcas Home Grown Market and Deli

North Beach Road, Eastsound
376-2009

8-10 M-Sun.
Mostly vegetarian and vegan.
No credit cards.

The deli here is a tiny counter at the back of the whole foods and organic produce market. You can get veggie juices or lunch here. The tempeh sandwich ($3.70) is delicious; locals say the veggie burger ($3.90) is equally tasty. Hummus and veggies cost $3.75. At one visit, the wild rice salad ($4.75 a pound) — organic brown and wild rice with snow peas, lightly steamed broccoli and carrots, celery, toasted pumpkin seeds and an herb-lemon dressing — was remembered long after the last bite. The daily special, a hearty chili and cornbread filled with peas, corn and other veggies, also was excellent.

Doe Bay Cafe

Star Route, in Olga
376-4755

Breakfast, dinner.
Summer: 8-11 a.m., 6-9 p.m., 7 days a week.
Winter: open only for dinner Friday, breakfast and dinner Saturday and breakfast Sunday.
Mostly vegetarian; several vegan choices.
No credit cards.

Part of the Doe Bay Village, a rural resort on the water especially for kayakers, hikers and other outdoors enthusiasts, the tiny and informal Doe Bay Cafe offers plenty of good, hearty vegetarian fare. The cafe's hours are irregular out of season, but there's also a special community kitchen for guests at the resort. The simple breakfast and dinner menus, copied as they are on standard typewriter paper, may not look like much, but they are savvy when it comes to vegetarianism.

The breakfast menu is in two parts, vegetarian and vegan specials, priced from $3 to $6.25. Ovo-lacto vegetarians will like the "no shoes special," two pancakes stuffed with homefries, cheese and salsa with two eggs on the side, or the sourdough french toast. Omelets include Mexican (black beans, salsa and guacamole), blue whale (mushrooms, jalapeno or cheddar cheese) and Orcas (sautéed spinach and mushrooms topped with salsa and sour cream). Vegans will be satisfied with the hot cereal with almonds and currants ($3, $3.75 with fruit), the pancakes ($4.75, $5.25 with fruit) or the granola ($3.75).

For dinner, start with the nachos ($4.95, $5.95 with guacamole). Entrées ($5 to $9) include tempeh curry, vegetarian lasagna, Thai bay vegetables and a baked potato topped with steamed veggies. Enhance your meal with a mixed green salad or a bowl of the soup of the day with bread ($2.75).

The dinner menu on Friday is special: it's pizza night. The basic pizza is $4.75 for a 10-inch pie; additional toppings, such as tempeh, roasted garlic, avocado or mushrooms, are 50 cents each. To avoid cheese, get the stir-fried veggies with tofu over brown rice ($7.95), topped with your choice of a spicy peanut, curry or sesame sauce. Save room for the homemade desserts.

Cafe Olga

At the Orcas Island Artworks in Olga
376-5098

Breakfast, lunch.
March-October: 10 to 6 daily.
November-December: 10 to 5 daily.
Some vegetarian choices.
Credit cards accepted.

Here's a tiny cafe with quality homemade food at the back of a cooperative gallery full of colorful arts and crafts produced by more than 70 Orcas Island artists. Upstairs is Nebula Books, a small new age bookstore. You can relax over a breakfast of cinnamon rolls or sour-cream coffee cake ($2.50 each), a bowl of granola served with a pitcher of milk ($3.50, $3.95 with sliced bananas) or eggs rancheros à la Olga ($5.75): eggs baked with cheese, a mild salsa sauce and green chilies, served with a corn tortilla and fruit. Lunch time offers a broader menu in the $7 range: the Sicilian artichoke pie is a crustless pastry layered with artichokes, tomatoes, black olives, herbs and cheese. Manicotti combines spinach, cheeses, walnuts and Cafe Olga's homemade tomato sauce in a pasta shell. The Greek salad tops a bed of lettuce and fresh spinach with feta cheese, Greek olives, marinated diced cucumbers and tomatoes. Look to the blackboard for more good vegetarian specials. At our visit, the choices were angel-hair pasta with peanut sauce and baked polenta with tomato and basil. Desserts vary, but three favorites are always available: french chocolate pie, blueberry cheesecake and blackberry pie ($3.25 each).

Victoria, B.C.

In a natural setting that is perhaps unsurpassed in the region, this Canadian city with a decided British influence has a vibrant vegetarian scene to match its exciting downtown. With stunning views of Mount Baker, the San Juan Islands and the Olympic Mountains, you might not think of food right away. But when you do, Victoria's surprisingly large and flourishing downtown offers two major vegetarian restaurants (including one with an all-vegan buffet), as well as many ethnic eateries. Contact the Vancouver Island Vegetarian Association for a helpful two-page guide to vegetarian dining in Victoria.

Victoria's best vegetarian choices: Green Cuisine, with its all-vegan buffet, and Re-Bar, which sports a giant fruit and vegetable juice menu.

Prices quoted here are in Canadian dollars, about 15 percent less than American.

8/19/93 lunch
√ Excellent buffet & desserts.

Green Cuisine

560 Johnson Street
(604) 385-1809

Lunch, dinner.
11-8 every day.
Strictly vegan.
Credit cards accepted.

It's hard to tell which is the highlight of this pure restaurant: the fine vegan buffet, or its location overlooking the lively courtyard in the middle of Market Square, a collection of shops and restaurants. Here you can dine while watching dancers or other performers outside entertain the throngs of people who come to this historic urban mall. The restaurant itself is small and friendly, with vegetarian literature on a rack by the front door (pick up a free copy of the Vancouver Island Vegetarian Association's quarterly newsletter).

You pay $5.95 a pound to choose from a buffet line of eight or ten entrées and a salad bar. During one lunch-time visit, choices included Boston baked beans, black beans, tofu ragu, wheat cutlets in a mushroom sauce, tabbouleh, wild rice pilaf, Indian samosas, lasagna (with cheese derived from tofu made in the kitchen), stroganoff and mashed yams. Green Cuisine also sells soups for $2.95 a cup, cornbread, organic coffee and desserts. The result is quite a filling and delicious meal.

8/19/93 supper @ 5:00
(before evening menu)

Re-Bar

50 Bastion Square
(604) 361-9223

Breakfast, lunch, dinner.
7:30-6 M-W, until 9 Th-F, 8:30-9 Sat, 11-3 Sun.
Mostly vegetarian.
Credit cards accepted.

Menu showed evening hours all week nights

The hallmarks of this trendy restaurant — reminiscent of Seattle's Gravity

Bar — are a huge selection of fruit and vegetable juices, a blackboard that offers several daily specials and an emphasis on healthful foods. The eggs are free-range, the water is filtered, and the fruits and vegetables are organic whenever possible. As you arrive at this downtown Victoria restaurant, you're struck by a stunning mosaic pattern of bananas, radishes and carrots on the floor of the entryway. The scene is eclectic, with vivid mismatched floral table cloths and a picture of Elvis on the wall.

Breakfast choices include such treats as whole-grain toast with Ginny's homemade jam, banana nut bread, Re-Bar granola ($4.25) with sliced bananas and milk, soy milk or yogurt and a series of egg dishes. One is eggs kurosawa ($6.50): scrambled eggs, tofu and green onions with sesame chile sauce served on brown rice, accompanied by toast and fruit.

For lunch (beginning at 11:30), try the miso soup ($4.95), made with tofu, soba noodles, hijiki seaweed, spinach and green onions; the Re-Bar salad ($6.75), which tops a mixture of red and green lettuce, fresh vegetables, chickpeas, feta cheese, sprouts and toasted nuts with choice of basil vinaigrette, honey-ginger or creamy lemon-dill dressing, or the Szechuan noodle salad ($7.25), a tasty concoction of buckwheat soba noodles, seaweed, grated carrot, red peppers and avocado, sprinkled with toasted cashews and mixed with a hot sesame chili dressing. The best-seller, though, is the almond burger ($6.50) — an almond and vegetable patty on a whole wheat kaiser roll with fresh salsa, tomato, red onion and sprouts. It comes with a side salad or salsa and corn chips.

Dinner choices ($8 to $10) vary daily, and are more interesting than the lunch menu. Look to the blackboard for the night's specials. On one autumn Friday evening, you could order pasta with a coconut, pineapple and citrus cream sauce with bananas, garnished with roasted peanuts, or pasta with a creamy pumpkin sauce including fontina cheese and a pumpkin seed garnish. Sweet bell peppers, stuffed with brie, feta cheese, sun-dried tomatoes and seasonal vegetables, are served on a bed of rice. On a Thursday night, red peppers were stuffed with spicy beans and veggies and covered with a pineapple-chile sauce. Desserts are said to be decadent.

If you can make it, don't miss the Sunday brunch, which might offer fancy dishes such as pancakes with pumpkin and sautéed apples ($6.50), baked eggplant and tomato turnovers with salsa and salad ($6.95), and omelets made of roasted garlic, onion and cambazola.

Other Choices

Special thanks to the Vancouver Island Vegetarian Association for the following information (all area codes 604):

Burrito Express (381-2333), a take-out-only joint in Market Square, serves vegetarian burritos and tortillas for about $4. Open 11:30-5 M-Sat, 12-4 Sun.

The Chinese Village (755 Finlayson Street, 384-8151) has an extensive vegetarian menu with dishes like sweet and sour mushrooms, chop suey with tofu and chow mein. The vegetarian dishes are cooked with vegetable oil (no chicken broth) and without MSG, and cost about $9. Open 12-10 M-Th, until 11 F-Sat, 4-8:30 Sun.

Da Tandoor Restaurant (1010 Fort Street, 384-6333) is a widely acclaimed and rather elegant East Indian establishment that serves such vegetable dishes ($7 to $10) as bharta (whole eggplants baked over an open flame, mashed and seasoned with herbs and sautéed with onions), vegetable jalfrazie (mixed vegetables cooked with fresh tomatoes, ground onion, ginger, garlic and spices) and malai kofta (mixed vegetables and fresh cheese balls served in butter). Open for dinner only, 5-10:30 M-Sun.

If you're looking for good vegetarian Japanese fare, **Futaba Japanese Restaurant** (1420 Quadra Street, 381-6141) fills the bill. Here you can try tofu sushi, pan-fried tofu with sesame sauce, tofu-stuffed nori (sweet seaweed) or miso soup. Entrées cost about $7. Open 11:30-2 and 5:30-10:30 M-F, 5:30-11:30 weekends.

For good vegetarian dining on weekends only, try **Gwen's Health Foods and Light Meals** (6002 West Saanich Road, 652-3132). At the lunch counter, order the soyburger, vegetarian soysage rolls, sandwiches, soups, vegetarian potpies, enchiladas, pies and other baked goodies. The soy ice cream (dairy-free) is said to be delicious. Prices are about $4. Open 9-5 weekends.

For Vietnamese food, head for downtown's **Le Petit Saigon** (1010 Langley Street, 386-1412). The menu includes a vegetarian section. Lunch and dinner.

Rising Star Whole Foods Bakery (1320 Broad Street, 386-2534) is another downtown haven for vegetarians. It sells soysage rolls, chickpea tortanos, tofu pizza, tofu burgers, sandwiches and falafels, along with baked desserts and breads. Cafeteria-style or take-out. About $4. Open 7:30-5 M-F, 9-4:30 Sat, also 8:30-2:30 Sun in summer.

Taj Mahal Dining Lounge (679 Herald Street, 383-4662) offers East Indian vegetable curries and biryanis in a downtown location. About $9. Open for lunch 11:30-2 M-F, 12-2 Sat; dinner from 5-9:30 nightly.

How to Avoid Problems when Dining Out

While Seattle ranks as one of the finest cities in the United States for vegetarian dining, many hazards still confront the unwary herbivore. Foods abound that seem like they should be vegan or vegetarian, but aren't. Does that Indian dish have butter in it? Is there fish sauce in that Thai entrée? Is that Chinese plate really vegetarian, or is it soaked in chicken stock?

Not all people who don't eat meat worry about such questions. Many vegetarians -- even vegans, who would never cook with butter or cheese at home -- think it's too challenging to be pure, and don't worry about the occasional chicken stock or shrimp paste that they may unknowingly encounter when dining out. For others, any animal product is off limits (even pasta made with eggs), and extra steps must be taken to ensure purity.

Some restaurants are safe. Purists who stick to the strictly vegetarian establishments shouldn't have any problems. The chefs and servers there usually are vegetarians themselves, and thus knowledgeable about your needs -- even if you are allergic to certain foods.

Yet it's still possible to order specifically a vegan tofu scrambler breakfast in a mostly vegetarian place and receive a side order of buttered toast. Worse, some restaurants seem to have a strange idea of what constitutes a vegetarian diet. Most Chinese restaurants cook "vegetarian" dishes in chicken stock. Fish sauce is as basic to Thai cuisine as tomatoes are to Italian. Everyone seems to think it's okay for vegetarians to eat oyster sauce. And a lot of people out there think vegetarians eat chicken and fish.

Sometimes, vegetarian dishes share pots and grills with meat, chicken or fish dishes.

The following strategies should help you avoid eating something that you'd rather not when dining out.

Most important: ask questions. Probe the staff to find out if there's any butter or chicken broth in the dish you want to order. Even then, you often have to go on faith that the server is telling you what's really what. Calling a restaurant ahead of time may be helpful. But communications can be a problem at ethnic restaurants; the waitstaff may not know enough English to understand your questions. In that case, there's not much you can do, except try it or leave.

Secondly, be assertive. You're paying good money for a good meal, and restaurants usually will go out of their way to accommodate you. If not, don't go back. Good restaurants, ever hopeful of winning repeat business, will take extra steps to meet your needs.

Fast-food and traditional restaurants sometimes offer food acceptable for vegetarians. Taco Time, a chain that specializes in Mexican fast food, for example, prepares good vegetarian bean burritos that can be made vegan. Red Robin Burger and Spirits Emporium makes a vegetarian burger. Some restaurants have salad bars. And many restaurants that don't contain a suitable vegetarian dish will offer a plate of steamed vegetables.

Here's a primer on what vegetarians should expect, in general, from some of the major cuisines.

Chinese

Chinese cuisine, given all of its tofu and vegetable dishes with steamed rice (alongside the traditional pork, beef and chicken listings), might seem ideally suited for vegetarians. Unfortunately, in most cases that is not true.

Chicken stock is the main culprit here. Chinese cooks routinely use it with soy sauce and other seasonings to flavor stir-fries and other dishes. You can ask for a dish without it. But, as one waitress at a Chinese restaurant in Lower Queen Anne put it, you should repeat "No chicken stock!" emphatically to make sure you get your message across. In some Chinese restaurants, especially those in the International District or in the suburbs and rural areas, you might ask for a vegetarian lunch special, only to find pieces of pork floating in a broth or resting in the vegetable fried rice.

A couple of Chinese restaurants in Seattle follow the tenets of Buddhism, providing fare that is purely vegetarian. These places offer meat analogs (popular among Chinese Buddhists), made of wheat gluten, that are surprisingly similar to chicken, pork or beef. Master vegetarian chefs in China are able to make dishes so authentic that the fake poultry appears to have skin (they also prepare more common vegetable dishes). Hsiang Ju Lin and Tsuifeng Lin, authors of *Chinese Gastronomy* (Hastings House), report that Chinese Buddhists developed vegetarian meals that resemble meat because the Chinese are an "all-embracing" people, and the Buddhists wanted to show their guests hospitality by giving them food that was like their own. It is interesting how different vegetarians react to the fake meat: some won't touch anything that reminds them of steak or chicken nuggets; others are happy to reminisce and satisfy old cravings.

Ethiopian

Ethiopians have a large appetite for meat dishes, and Ethiopian restaurants in this area reflect that. Most Ethiopian restaurants in Seattle offer a good amount of fare that is strictly vegan, however. That's because many Ethiopians are Christians and fast during Lent, giving up all animal products for several weeks. As a result, Ethiopian chefs have developed many delicious vegetable preparations.

Greek

Greek cuisine -- like Middle Eastern -- includes plenty of meat dishes, but also numerous vegetarian appetizers such as hummus, tzatziki and spanakopita. Salads also are prominent.

Indian/Pakistani

These nearly identical cuisines are quite compatible with vegetarianism. In India, Hinduism forbids hundreds of millions of followers from eating beef, so many wonderful, spicy and complex vegetarian dishes have been developed over the years -- some with cheese, but plenty without. Pakistani cuisine has retained many of those meatless favorites. Ovo-lacto vegetarians can eat happily at any Indian or Pakistani restaurant. But vegans have a concern: the use of butter or ghee (Indian clarified butter) in some restaurants. Dairy products are quite popular in India and Pakistan.

At home, Indian curries and vegetable dishes often are cooked in ghee. But many of the local Indian and Pakistani restaurants cook their dishes in vegetable oil instead. It depends on the chef and the dish, so be sure to ask.

Italian

Though most Italian restaurants have lots of meat dishes, they also sometimes have good vegetarian pasta dishes with pesto or tomato and cheese sauces. Vegans will have a more difficult time than ovo-lacto vegetarians, since pastas usually are made with eggs and come with cheese or cream. But antipasto salads often are good choices.

Japanese

In the suburbs and rural towns hereabouts, Japanese restaurants tend to be teriyaki stops: plenty of beef and chicken choices, and little else. In Seattle and some other urban areas, though, a Japanese establishment can be a fine place to get a vegetarian meal. Tofu dishes are common, either in appetizers or large noodle-filled soups. Avocado and cucumber rolls -- wrapped in seaweed and sticky white rice -- also are on many Japanese menus.

Mexican

Almost everyone loves Mexican food. Salsa even has replaced ketchup as America's favorite condiment. With so many great bean and cheese dishes, you'd think you could go into any Mexican restaurant for a fine vegetarian meal. But that is not the case.

Most Mexican restaurants still cook beans in lard (pork fat) to give them a robust flavor that Americans prefer. And even more restaurants cook their rice in chicken broth. This is especially true in the suburbs and rural areas. But increasingly, health-conscious folks are demanding that Mexican chefs cook beans in vegetable oil; several area Mexican restaurants have responded. If you're in a restaurant where beans are cooked in lard, you sometimes can ask the chef to cook a dish using whole beans from a can instead. Lard also is a common ingredient in flour tortillas.

Middle Eastern

Middle Eastern and Mediterranean restaurants -- although renowned for shish kebab, lamb, beef and chicken dishes -- are good places for vegetarians. Almost all offer hummus, baba ghanoush, tabbouleh, falafel and other meatless appetizers. Soups (frequently lentil) are often meatless. And interesting dishes such as grape leaves stuffed with rice, pine nuts, lemon juice and other tasty items are sometimes featured.

Thai

Thai cuisine is a mixed bag for purist vegetarians. On the one hand, Thai chefs are known for creating wonderfully flavored, exotic vegetable and tofu dishes. On the other, fish sauce and shrimp paste are basic to much of Thai cooking.

Some dishes -- such as Thai curries and phad Thai (the common rice noodle dish topped with peanuts, vegetables and eggs) -- are more likely than others to include fish paste. Swimming rama, for example, is a dish of cooked spinach topped with tofu and peanut sauce, and should be purely vegan.

But different Thai chefs use different cooking methods. Some routinely cook vegetarian dishes including fish sauce; others keep their vegetarian dishes pure by substituting other sauces. Many Thai cooks say they will leave fish sauce and shrimp paste out of vegetarian dishes when they know the customers are strict vegetarians.

Vietnamese

Like their Chinese counterparts, Vietnamese restaurants frequently use chicken stock in so-called vegetarian stir-fries, though they'll usually substitute vegetable oil if you insist. Another similarity: some Vietnamese restaurants follow the Buddhist vegetarian practice of cooking with meat analogs made from wheat gluten.

Vegetarian Resources

In addition to its great restaurants with abundant meatless offerings, the Puget Sound region claims many fine health-food stores and other resources. Following is a directory on natural-food markets, organizations that promote vegetarianism and food safety, and books and magazines.

Health-Food Stores

Besides beings places where you can stock up on food supplies for home cooking, many natural-food markets in the area sell ready-made sandwiches, prepared snacks and bulk foods like cashews or granola that can nourish a harried traveler.

Essential Sandwiches are the most common of the vegan roll-up chapati sandwiches now on the market. They come in many varieties, including gallo pinto, black beans and rice, Indonesian, northern Italian and Mediterranean. Hilltop Quickies, made in Tacoma and sold mostly there and in surrounding communities, include an assortment of tofu, tempeh and seitan sandwiches.

Many of the mainstream supermarkets are vying for the dollars of health-food fans. Almost any supermarket carries tofu. Some, like Larry's Markets, sell organically grown produce, too. Most Fred Meyer stores (which include supermarkets, clothing, electronics and hardware) have sections devoted to health foods.

Seattle

Puget Consumers' Co-op, five Seattle locations. These large, full-service health-food supermarkets carry bulk foods, organic produce, vitamins and the like. Extensive spring and fall classes on vegetarian cooking are offered. PCC's monthly newsletter is sent to 40,000 members. Some stores have delis. PCC also has stores in Kirkland and Everett. There's a mark-up on prices for non-members. Seattle stores:

Green Lake, 6522 Fremont Avenue N., 789-7144. Open 9-9 M-Sat, 10-7 Sun.

Ravenna, 6504 20th Avenue N.E., 525-1450. Open 9-9 M-Sun.

View Ridge, 6514 40th Avenue N.E., 526-7661. Deli. Open 8-10 M-Sun.

West Seattle, 2749 California Avenue S.W., 937-8481. Deli. Open 8-10 M-Sun.

Seward Park, 5041 Wilson Avenue S., 723-2720. Deli. Open 9-10 M-Sun.

Pike Place Natural Foods, Pike Place Public Market, 623-2231. A small store with some health foods and vitamins. Open 10-6 M-Sun.

Magnano Foods, Pike Place Public Market, 223-9582. Medium-sized health-food market with bulk foods, organic fruits, some vegetables. Open 9:30-5:30 M-Sat.

Central Co-op Grocery, 1835 12th Avenue S., Capitol Hill, 329-1545. Large full-service store with organic produce, bulk foods, vitamins. Monthly newsletter. Open 9-9 M-Sun.

Rainbow Grocery, 409 15th Avenue E., Capitol Hill, 329-8440. Medium-sized health-food market with organic produce, bulk foods, vitamins. Open 9-8 M-Sun.

Mari-Don HealthWay Natural Foods, 1900 N. 45th Street, Wallingford, 632-7040. Medium-sized store with lots of groceries, vitamins, small juice bar. Open 9-6 M-Sat.

Mother Nature's Natural Foods, 516 1st Avenue N., Lower Queen Anne, 284-4422. Bulk foods, vitamins, cookbooks, mostly vegetarian take-out deli. Open 9:30-6 M-Sat.

Pilgrim's Nutrition, 5607 20th Avenue N.W., Ballard, 782-6377. Medium-sized store with vitamins, groceries. Open 10-6 M-Sat.

CCUP Health Foods on Green Lake, 7910 E. Green Lake Drive N., 526-8755. Small store with some groceries and vitamins. CCUP stands for Community Co-op for Universal Peace. Open 11-7 M-Sat, 1-5 Sun. May stay open later in summer.

Pilgrim's Nutrition, 4217 University Way N.E., 634-3430. Medium-sized store with vitamins, groceries. Open 10-7 M-F, 10-6 Sat, 12-6 Sun.

The Eastside

Nature's Pantry, 10200 N.E. 10th Street, Bellevue, 454-0170. Large, full-service health-food market with organic produce, bulk foods. Mostly self-serve deli. Open 9-7 M-F, 9:30-6 Sat, 12-5 Sun.

Evergreen Health Pantry, 1645 140th Avenue N.E., Bellevue, 746-4776. Small store, specializes in vitamins, some health foods. Open 9:30-7 M-F, 9:30-6 Sat, 12-5 Sun.

Puget Consumer's Co-op, 10718 N.E. 68th Street, Kirkland, 828-4621. Large supermarket with organic produce, aisles of bulk foods and health-food products, vitamins, deli. Open 8-10 M-Sun.

Harvestime Nutrition, 8052 161st Avenue N.E., Redmond, 883-0171. Bulk foods, health-food products, nutrition books, vitamins. Open 10-6 M-Sat.

Planet Earth Natural Foods Co., 6810 N.E. 153rd Place, Bothell, 488-3553. Large selection of mostly organic produce, grocery products, bulk foods, vitamins and herbs. Open 6-9 M-Sun.

Woodinville Health Foods, 14225 Woodinville-Duvall Road, 481-1826. Vitamins, tanning, some food items. Open 8-9 M-F, 8-6 Sat, 12-6.

The Good Little Food Store, 55 W. Sunset Way, Issaquah, 391-1584. Full-service, with organic produce and large selection of health-food store basics; lunch deli. Open 9-7 M-F, 10-6 Sat, 11-4 Sun.

Front Street Specialty and Nutrition, 141 Front Street N., Issaquah, 391-5392. Small store specializing in vitamins; also sells some food including bagged grains and beans. Open 10-6 M-F, 10:30-5:30 Sat.

Nature's Pantry of Mercer Island, 7611 S.E. 27th Street, 232-7900. A smaller store than its Bellevue companion, with health foods and vitamins. Open 10-6:30 M-F, 10-6 Sat.

South King County

Minkler's Green Earth Nutrition, 125 Airport Way S., Renton, 226-7757. Large selection of health foods, bulk items, vitamins. Open 9:45-6:30 M-F, 9:45-6 Sat.

Sunrise Nutrition, 3007 N.E. Sunset Boulevard, Renton Highlands, 226-4715. Health foods, frozen foods, vitamins. Open 10-7 M-F, 10-5 Sat.

Burien Special Foods, 148 S.W. 152nd Street, 243-6111. Specializes in vitamins and herbs; some groceries and bulk foods. Open 10-6 M-Sat.

Nature's Market, 26011 104th Ave., Kent, 854-5395. Sizable selection of organic produce, health-food products, vitamins, books. Small juice bar. Very modern and clean. Open 10-8 M, Th, F; 10-6 T, W, Sat; 12:30-5 Sun.

Auburn Health Foods, 106 E. Main Street, Auburn, 939-1323. Medium-sized store with groceries, vitamins. Open 9-7 M-F, 10-6 Sat.

Rainier Natural Foods, Auburn-Enumclaw Road, Auburn, 833-4369. Bread bakery. Open 9-6 Sun-Th, 9-3 F. Closed Saturday.

Marlene's Market & Deli, 31839 Gateway Center Boulevard S., Federal Way, 839-0933. Named top medium health-food store in the nation by a trade magazine in 1993, Marlene's offers a large selection of organic produce, health-food products and supplements. The mostly vegetarian deli contains a juice bar. Attached is an espresso shop. Open 9-9 M-Th, 9-10 F, 9-7 Sat, 11:30-6 Sun.

Viable Products Co., 2335 S.W. 336th Street, Federal Way, 838-7576. Specializes in vitamins, but also has good selection of health foods, as well as a juice/espresso bar and homemade salads and sandwiches in back. Open 5 a.m.-8 p.m. M-F, 9-8 Sat, 9-6 Sun.

Minglement, 20316 Vashon Highway S.W., Vashon Island, 463-9672. Bulk foods, health-food products, some organic produce. Open 10-6 M-F, 10-7 Sat, 10-5 Sun.

Pierce and Thurston Counties

Westgate Nutrition Center, 5738 N. 26th Street, Tacoma, 759-1990. In Westgate South shopping plaza. Vitamins, skin products, shampoo, bags of beans, peas, lentils, oats, grains, etc. Bags of spices. Good selection of cookbooks. Small selection of organic produce. Open 9-7 M-F, 10-5 S-S.

The Wholefoods Market, 6810 27th Street W., Tacoma, 565-0188. Small store with a selection of organic produce, vitamins and health foods. Open 9:30-6 M-F, 9:30-5:30 Sat.

Graham's Health Stop Inc., 22007 Meridian East, Graham, 847-9124. A small store with vitamins, cosmetics, some groceries. Open 9-6:30 M-F, 9-5 Sat.

Lakewood Natural Foods, 5808 100th Street S.W., Lakewood, 584-3929. Huge selection of health-food products, lots of organic produce. Mostly vegan lunch deli with take-out in the evenings. Open 9-9 M-Sat.

Olympia Food Co-op, 921 N. Rogers Street, Olympia, 754-7666. Large full-service market; co-op has 8,000 members. Ten percent mark-up on prices for non-members. Organic produce, bulk foods, vitamins, etc. Open 9-8 M-Sun.

Red Apple Natural Foods, 400 Cooper Point Road N.W., Olympia, 357-8779. Specializes in vitamins; some health-food items. Mostly vegetarian deli. Open 9-7 M-F, 9-6 Sat, 12-5 Sun.

J-Vees Health Foods, 3720 Pacific Avenue S.E., Olympia, 491-1930, and 3405 Capitol Boulevard, Tumwater, 943-8255. Both stores carry many health-food items, bulk foods and vitamins. The Olympia branch has a luncheon restaurant. Both stores are open 9:30-6 M-Sat, until 6:30 F.

Olympic Peninsula

The Country-Aire, 117 E. 1st Street, Port Angeles, 452-7175. A large full-service health-food store with some organic produce, lots of refrigerator space for frozen items, bulk foods. Massage oils, books, incense, candles, cosmetics, toiletries, eco-friendly products, etc. Open 9:30-5:30 M-F, 10-5:30 Sat. (12-4 Sun in summer).

Natureway, 116 E. Front Street, Port Angeles, 457-4502. Mostly vitamins, a few food items. Open 10-5:30 M-F, 10-5 Sat.

Sunny Farms Country Store, 1546 Highway 101 West, Sequim, 683-8003 Gigantic selection of fresh produce and most of the health-food-store basics. Butcher's shop in the back. Open 8-7 M-Sun, open until 8 in summer).

Waterfront Naturals, 810 Water Street, Port Townsend, 385-3290. Good juice bar; small selection of foods, including some herbs and spices in jars. Open 9:30 - 5:30, 10-5 Sat, (11-4 Sun in summer)

Natural Gourmet, Harold's Square, Bainbridge Island, 842-2759. Health-food standards and vitamins, mostly vegetarian deli. Open 9:30-6 M-F, 10-5:30 Sat.

Healthways, 337 N. Callow Avenue, Bremerton, 373-4747. A small selection of health foods; lots of vitamins. Open 10-6 M-F, 10-5 Sat.

Natural Health, South Kitsap Mall, 1700 Highway 160, Port Orchard, 876-1134. Large selection of bulk foods, health-food products, vitamins. Juice bar in back. Open 10-8 M-F, 10-6 Sat, 12-5 Sun.

Here's To Your Health, Bethel Junction Shopping Center, 3311 Bethel Road S.E., Port Orchard, 876-1549. Frozen foods, small selection of health food, vitamins, cookbooks. Open 10-6 M-Th, 10-7 F, 10-4 Sat.

Nature's Best Natural Foods, 131 W. Railroad Street, Shelton, 426-9197. Small selection of health foods. Open 10-5:30 M-F, until 6 Wed.

Heartland Nutrition and Country Keepsakes, Olympic Village Shopping Center, Gig Harbor. Organic produce, vitamins, natural foods. Open 10-6 M-Sat.

The Wholefoods Market, 3122 Harbor View Drive, Gig Harbor, 851-8120. Teas, vitamins, milk, bread, books and herbs. Organic produce. Open 9:30-6 M-F, 9:30-5:30 Sat.

Snohomish County

Puget Consumers' Co-op, 9121 Evergreen Way, Everett, 742-1240. Large grocery store with all the health-food basics, like organic produce, bulk foods and vitamins. Deli. Open 8-10 M-Sun.

Manna Mills, 21705 66th Avenue W., Mountlake Terrace, 775-3479. Large selection of health foods, bulk items. Open 9:30-8 M-F, 10-5 S-S.

Natureway, 23632 Highway 99, Edmonds, 774-7777. Health foods, vitamins. Open 10-7 M-Sat, 12-6 Sun.

Island and Skagit Counties

Skagit Valley Food Co-op, 202 S. 1st Street, Mount Vernon, 336-9777. Giant selection of organic produce, health-food products, bulk foods, vitamins, books, gift items. Attached to Deli Next Door, a large, mostly vegetarian eatery. Open 9-7 M-F, 9-6 Sat, 9-4 Sun.

Star Store Basics, part of Langley's Market & Merchantile, 201 First Street, Langley, 321-2425. Unusual mix of health foods and hardware sold here. Bulk foods. Open 10-5 M-Sun. Langley's Market, across the street, sells refrigerated health foods like tofu and tempeh, and occasional organic produce.

Pioneer Natural Foods, 1248 W. Pioneer Way, Oak Harbor, 679-2646. Medium-sized store, sells almost everything except produce. A veggie sandwich with cream cheese is available to go. Open 9:30-5:30 M-F, 9:30-5 Sat.

Anacortes Health and Nutrition, corner of 7th Street and O Avenue, Anacortes, 293-8849. Medium-sized store with vitamins, some health foods. Open 10-5:30 M-Sat.

Bellingham

Good Earth Nutrition, in Meridian Village shopping center (across from Bellis Fair Mall), 733-2211. Specializes in vitamins; some food products. Open 9:30-9 M-F, 9:30-6 Sat, 12-5 Sun.

Good Earth Nutrition, 107 W. Magnolia, 733-3480. Specializes in vitamins; some food products. Open 10:30-5:30 M-Sat.

Community Food Co-op, 1059 N. State Street, 734-8158. Full-service grocery store with organic produce, bulk foods, health foods, vitamins. Open 9-8 M-Sat, 11-6 Sun.

San Juan Islands

Way of Life, 35 First Street S., Friday Harbor, 378-5433. Health-food market with organic produce from the islands and a vegetarian deli. Open 10-6 M-F, 10-5 Sat in winter; 9:30-6 M-F, 10-5 Sat, 11-4 Sun in summer.

Orcas Home Grown Market and Deli, North Beach Road, Eastsound, 376-2009. Large selection of organic produce, bulk foods, health-food products. Mostly vegetarian deli. Open 8-10 M-Sun.

Blossom Natural Foods, Lopez Plaza, Lopez, 468-2204. Small store with groceries and vitamins. Open 10-5:30 Tu-Sat (until 6 in summer, and on some Sundays in summer).

Victoria

Good Nature Market, 109-3995 Quadra Street, Saanich Center, 727-9888. Vitamins, organic produce, bulk and specialty foods.

Colwood House of Nutrition, G-310 Goldstream Avenue, 478-3244. Groceries, vitamins. Open seven days.

Seed of Life Natural Foods, 1316 Government Street, 382-4343. Beans, nuts, bulk foods, vitamins.

Natural Fare Natural Foods, G-1516 Fairfield Road, 592-3136. Organic produce, bulk foods, groceries, vitamins.

Viteway Natural Foods, 1019 Blanshard Street, 384-5677. Groceries, bulk foods, vitamins.

Non-profit Organizations

For people who are making the transition to a more healthful diet, **EarthSave Seattle** is *the* place to be. It's the Seattle chapter of the EarthSave Foundation, created by *Diet for a New America* author John Robbins to educate people about the connection between food choices, the environment and personal health. On the second Thursday of every month, EarthSave Seattle sponsors a vegetarian potluck dinner and program (in The Unity Church of Truth at 200 8th Avenue N., beginning at 6:30 p.m.), usually attended by 100 to 250 people. Guest speakers cover a variety of topics, from vegetarian backpacking and how to raise vegetarian children to juicing and genetically altered foods.

The Seattle chapter is quite active throughout the metropolitan area. It offers monthly showings of the Diet for a New America video and classes on transitioning to a plant-based diet. Volunteers staff informational booths at street fairs and other community events. A school results team has developed curriculum on healthful and environmentally sensitive eating that it shares with students, teachers and parents at public and private schools.The chapter also issues a quarterly newsletter.

The EarthSave Seattle information hotline is 781-6602; the group's address is P.O. Box 9422, Seattle 98109.

In 1993, satellite groups formed on Seattle's Eastside (781-6602), and in Tacoma (925-7035) and Olympia (352-6716). Those groups also offer monthly potlucks and volunteer opportunities.

The Vancouver Island Vegetarian Association (VIVA) holds frequent potlucks, picnics and events in Victoria, B.C. It produces a quarterly newsletter and offers a listing of Victoria's vegetarian dining choices. Contacts are Keith and Mignon Lundmark, 529 Stornoway Drive, Victoria, BC, V9C 3G8. (604) 478-8477.

The Provender Alliance, established in 1977 as part of the Natural Foods Businesses and Associates in the Northwest, provides a vehicle for producers, sellers and consumers of natural foods to influence the grocery industry, lawmakers and the general consumer on food safety and environmentally sensitive agricultural practices. The alliance holds a yearly conference and publishes a quarterly journal. P.O. Box 10305, Eugene, OR 97440. (503) 683-1653.

Consumers United for Food Safety, organized in 1984, lobbies lawmakers and educates the public on issues such as food irradiation. P.O. Box 22928, Seattle 98122. 747-2659.

The Progressive Animal Welfare Society (PAWS) meets on the first Thursday of each month at Bastyr College, 144 N.E. 54th Street in Seattle. PAWS strongly supports vegetarianism. 15305 44th Avenue W., Box 1037, Lynnwood 98046. 742-4142.

The Washington Biotechnology Action Council (WashBac) serves as an information clearinghouse and lobbying presence on the issues of biotechnology. A committee on genetically altered foods opposes the use of new technologies to insert the genes of plants, animals and humans into all sorts of foods. One particular concern for vegetarians is whether a tomato that includes genes of a horse, for example, is still a vegetarian food. The committee can be reached by writing WashBac, Committee on Genetically Altered Foods, 2418 Western Avenue, Seattle 98121.

The Northwest Animal Rights Network (NARN) takes an aggressive approach on animal-rights issues, holding frequent protests. 1704 E. Galer Street, Seattle 98112. 323-7301.

The Vegan Network is a non-membership Seattle-based group run by Cary Kesselring and Debra Ferrell. While the network doesn't have ongoing activities, it does engage in periodic projects such as publishing a vegan cookbook. 319 Nickerson Street, Suite 102, Seattle 98109. 784-2764.

Books and Magazines

Whether you want to learn more about the reasons for eating vegetarian or to obtain recipes to use at home, there are many resources available at area bookstores and libraries. Here are some of the best:

John Robbins' *Diet for a New America* (Stillpoint Publishing, 1987) is a must-read for anyone who wants to better understand the relationship between diet, health, animal welfare and the environment. His 1992 sequel, *May All Be Fed* (William Morrow and Company) includes many interesting vegan recipes.

Vegan Nutrition (Gentle World), by Michael Klaper, provides a solid understanding of the health benefits of a vegetarian diet.

The American Vegetarian Cookbook from the Fit for Life Kitchen by Marilyn Diamond includes numerous delicious recipes for vegan foods.

Vegetarian Times (P.O. Box 446, M. Morris, IL, 61054-9894), the largest of the national vegetarian magazines, comes out monthly. It can be found at most newsstands. Two excellent quarterly magazines are also available: Vegetarian Gourmet, which includes many recipes, and Vegetarian Journal, which contains recipes, tips and information about new products. *Vegetarian Gourmet* (P.O. Box 7641, Riverton, NJ, 08077-7641) is available at some newsstands, while *Vegetarian Journal*, published by the Vegetarian Resource Group in Baltimore (P.O. Box 1463, Baltimore, MD, 21203), is found at only a few.

Glossary

A glossary of common (and not so common) vegetarian foods and ingredients mentioned in this guide.

Baba ghanoush -- a Middle Eastern mixture of eggplant, tahini, lemon juice, garlic and olive oil.

Chutney -- a spicy condiment to Indian food, usually consisting of fruit, sugar, vinegar and spices.

Couscous -- a grain made of semolina, which can be substituted for rice.

Eggplant bharta -- an Indian dish of spicy sautéed eggplant.

Falafel -- a Middle Eastern patty made of garbanzo beans and spices, often eaten in a pita topped with tahini.

Ful mudames -- a Mediterranean dish of fava beans cooked with garlic, cumin, cilantro and olive oil.

Ghee -- clarified butter used frequently in Indian cooking.

Ginger -- a spicy root often used in Asian cooking. Small pieces put through a juicer can add nice zest to a fruit or vegetable drink.

Hummus -- a Middle Eastern appetizer made of mashed chickpeas, garlic, lemon and olive oil.

Miso -- a soybean paste used to make broth, especially in Japanese cooking. Can also be used as an ingredient in sauces.

Moussaka -- a Greek eggplant dish baked with garlic, tomato, spices and pine nuts, and topped with cheese. Usually includes meat, but some restaurants offer vegetarian versions.

Naan -- an Indian white-flour unleavened bread cooked in a tandoor oven.

Pakora -- Indian batter-dipped and deep-fried vegetables.

Paratha -- a whole wheat Indian bread fried on a griddle.

Raita -- an Indian yogurt salad, usually made with cucumber.

Samosa -- fried Indian pastry appetizers filled with vegetables.

Seitan -- often used as a meat substitute, seitan is made out of wheat gluten.

Spanakopita -- a Greek pastry filled with spinach and cheese.

Spirulina -- highly nutritious microscopic freshwater plant sometimes added to vegetable juices.

Tahini -- a Middle Eastern sesame paste.

Tempeh -- made of fermented whole soybeans, tempeh is a relative of tofu, but has a better, nuttier flavor and has a chewy texture like that of meat. Frequently used in stir-fries or sandwiches.

Tempura -- Japanese batter-dipped, deep-fried vegetables or fish.

Tzatziki -- a Middle Eastern yogurt-cucumber dip.

Tofu -- a common stir-fry substitute for meat in Asian and American meals, made from curdled soy milk.

Wheatgrass -- a highly nutritious but somewhat unpleasant tasting grass made from the wheatberry. Commonly used for juice, in small one- or two-ounce shots.

Index by Name

Index

Index by Style of Cuisine

Mostly or strictly vegan

Mostly or strictly vegetarian

Afghan

Asian

Chinese

Ethiopian

European

Georgian

Greek

Indian/Pakistani

Indonesian

Italian

Japanese

Juice Bars

Korean

Malaysian

Mediterranean/Middle Eastern

Mexican

North American

Philippino

Russian

Southwestern

Taverns

Thai

Vietnamese